ORDINAL METHODS
FOR
BEHAVIORAL
DATA ANALYSIS

ORDINAL METHODS
FOR
BEHAVIORAL
DATA ANALYSIS

Norman Cliff

Professor Emeritus,
University of Southern California

LEA   **LAWRENCE ERLBAUM ASSOCIATES, PUBLISHERS**
1996   Mahwah, New Jersey

Lawrence Erlbaum Associates, Inc., Publishers
10 Industrial Avenue
Mahwah, New Jersey 07430

Cover design by Jessica LaPlaca

Library of Congress Cataloging-in-Publication Data

Cliff, Norman, 1930–
   Ordinal methods for behavioral data analysis / Norman Cliff.
      p.   cm.
   Includes bibliographical references and indexes.
   ISBN 0-8058-1333-0 (alk. paper)
   1. Psychology—Mathematical models. 2. Social sciences—
Statistical methods. 3. Analysis of variance. 4. Regression
analysis. I. Title.
   BF39.C53 1996
   300′.15195—dc20   96-22689
                                                                CIP

Printed in the United States of America
10 9 8 7 6 5 4 3 2 1

To Rosemary

Contents

Preface

For at least two generations, statistical methods in the behavioral sciences have been dominated by normal-based linear models, analysis of variance and regression, and their relatives. I have taught and written on those methods for many years, and still have a great respect for them, but I have become increasingly concerned that often they are not the best possible ones for our purposes. They overestimate the quality of our data; they answer questions that are not really the ones we want to ask; they are overly sensitive to the failure of assumptions that are frequently unrealistic.

This volume is an attempt to make our data analysis methods in the behavioral sciences more realistic and more valid. It came about partly as a consequence of a perceived discrepancy between the nature of the data we often have in the behavioral sciences and the properties that it should have if we are to legitimately apply the linear models statistics that we typically employ. It is hard to give more than ordinal justification for many of our variables, across almost the whole spectrum of our field, yet regression and analysis of variance methods rely on models that sum differences on them. Although it is true that statistical analysis, relying simply on the properties of numbers as numbers, can always be employed and conclusions can be drawn, those conclusions apply only to the data as given. Yet our variables are usually used as empirical manifestations of theoretical constructs, and there is usually considerable arbitrariness about the specific form of the variable we are using: a monotonic, or many monotonic, transformations of it would be equally legitimate as definition of the construct. If a different form of the variable is used, and the same linear models analysis is carried out, then the conclusions from the analysis will certainly be different quantitatively, and they may well be different qualitatively. If the object of the analysis is to allow us to come to substantive conclusions about the constructs, surely we do not want those conclusions to be conditional on the particular form of the variable that we happened to use. It is this potential effect of transformation on conclusions that makes linear models analyses of variables that have only ordinal justification so questionable. A key part of good research design is being able to answer as many as possible of the "What if . . ." questions that a peer who is skeptical of the results could ask. With ordinal analyses the research is immune to the "What if the data were transformed?" form of this question, whereas the traditional methods are not. Thus, if the variables are only ordinal, it seems obviously preferable to analyze them ordinally. That way, the conclusions will stand, no matter what transformation of the variable is used.

It also is apparent that, if you listen to the question that an investigator is attempting to answer with an analysis, the question itself is often ordinal. "Do people in this group tend to score higher than people in that?" "Is the order on this variable similar to the order on that?" These, and many variations and elaborations on them, are often the questions that the investigator states when describing the information that is of most fundamental interest. Yet traditional forms of statistical analysis answer such questions only indirectly, and then often only with the aid of very strong assumptions. If the questions we are trying to answer are ordinal, it seems preferable to use ordinal methods to answer them. That way, the answer will be as close as possible to the question being asked, which is again a desirable property of scientific research.

Probably the most commonly cited motive for using ordinal analyses is their assumed relative robustness in the face of distributional characteristics of the data. Paradoxically, the most commonly used forms of ordinal analyses are far from immune to influences of this kind. The types of analyses that are used here are less so, but even they are sometimes susceptible to distributional effects that can distort somewhat the probabilities associated with inferences from them. Overall, these ordinal methods are more robust than traditional normal-based ones, but such dominance is not absolute.

The reader may have noted that the term "nonparametric" has not been used so far. This is because I feel that the key aspect of using ordinal methods is to use them *parametrically*. Ordinal statistics are used here as numerical descriptions of the important and invariant aspects of the data, not as mere hypothesis-testing devices. As such, they have population counterparts, that is, there are corresponding ordinal parameters of the populations from which we have sampled, and, as is traditional in statistics, it is these parameters that we are trying to infer. The fact that we are treating the ordinal statistics in this parametric way means that we are able to use the appropriate theory of the sampling behavior of these ordinal statistics to make inferences about them. In particular, we estimate their standard errors from the sample data rather than by arbitrary assumptions that are unrealistic in most research contexts. Thus, statistical estimation is treated as at least as important as hypothesis testing.

The book is by no means a handbook of ordinal methods in the sense of presenting a wide compilation of available ordinal methods. Rather, it is highly selective. It focuses on Kendall's tau as a measure of correlation and its counterpart for comparing populations, delta, with a secondary discussion of Spearman's rho. This choice results from two beliefs. First, these two can be adapted to answer a wide variety of research questions. In fact, a major motive for the book is trying to suggest just how wide this variety is. Second, their statistical sampling properties are quite well understood, being derivable via rather elementary methods. As a consequence, the methods described here can be treated in quite a unitary way, much as normal-based linear models can, rather than providing a compendium of seemingly isolated methods, each of which must be learned separately.

The book is intended to be readable by all behavioral scientists who have had a sound yearlong graduate statistics course that has acquainted them with fundamental statistical principles. It is written assuming that the reader has some acquaintance with analysis of variance and regression. Although not intended as a text, lacking exercises, it has detailed worked examples of the main methods, and might well be used as a text in a second statistics course or as a supplement to a more traditional one.

It is moderately, but not heavily, mathematical. I feel that this is preferable to a more completely verbal presentation, in spite of what I know to be the preferences of many in its intended audience, because, let us face it, statistics is a mathematical subject. Something is lost when one tries to make it purely verbal. However, the level of the mathematics is low; there is no calculus. This is partly because I know that most or all of our data is discrete, not continuous, and I want to be sure that the mathematical conclusions apply directly to discrete data, but it may also make the going easier for many readers. There are also lots of words, so the reader who skips or skims the formulas will still get a great deal out of the book, I hope.

The elements of the book are not claimed to be original. All of its major bases are well established in the statistical literature, often going back decades. Its most direct precursor is M. G. Kendall's *Rank correlation methods*, first published in 1948, and going essentially unchanged through four editions through 1970 before being substantially revised in collaboration with J. D. Gibbons in 1991. The original book contains the basic descriptive and inferential aspects of Kendall's tau, along with much else, and I refer primarily to it rather than the latest revision. The methods that have been developed for inferences about delta, through its sample version the *d* statistic, which are actually just forms of tau where one variable is a dichotomy, follow exactly the same path that Daniels and Kendall first traveled in 1947. So does my own 1991 extension of delta to the repeated measures case and the derivation of covariances between ordinal statistics, first with Ventura Charlin for tau and then for the various forms of delta in my 1991 paper. The modern statistical literature seems to me not to give Daniels and Kendall's work due precedence.

What is, I think, unique about my book is the ways in which it shows how this small armory can be used to answer many of the questions that researchers want to answer with their data. This, too, has some antecedent in G. A. Ferguson's little 1965 book, *Nonparametric trend analysis*, but I think I have gone quite a bit beyond that, as well as putting the methods on a sounder basis, both descriptive and inferential, and providing a more unified framework.

This volume owes a great deal to many other individuals. I was first introduced to tau by Professor John A. Keats of the University of Newcastle, Australia, when we were fellow students at Princeton. He and I have had numerous fruitful interchanges on these topics over the years. A great debt is owed to graduate students with whom I have had the pleasure of working. To some extent this book indirectly has origins in a project on ordinal measurement on which several of them worked in the 1970s, but the most direct contributions from members of that group to the topics covered here were by Professor Thomas J. Reynolds of the University of Texas at Dallas with whom I have had many interesting discussions, particularly on ordinal regression. Dr. Ventura Charlin was also an important collaborator on that topic as well as on the covariances of taus. Most recently I have greatly benefited by collaborations and discussions with three current students, Du Feng, Jeffrey Long, and John Caruso. Their individual and collective work on the sampling behavior of ordinal statistics has clarified many issues on that topic as well as developing new methods.

Several colleagues in the Psychology Department at the University of Southern California have also been helpful. Professors Stephen A. Madigan and John Horn have made thoughtful suggestions and provided encouragement that the ideas here might not be entirely wrongheaded. My office neighbor for a number of years, Professor Rand R. Wilcox, has also been the source of many suggestions and fruitful discussions. He shares many of my concerns about the efficacy of the currently popular methods while taking his own route to their improvement.

Mr. Caruso also gave a careful reading to an earlier version of the manuscript, greatly reducing the errors that might otherwise have occurred. I am also indebted to Professor Shmuel Sawilowsky of Wayne State University for a very thoughtful review of a version of the manuscript as well as for a review of the paper on the *d* statistic that appeared in the *Psychological*

Bulletin in 1991. The book and the papers that underlie it also owe a great deal to several anonymous reviewers, particularly one from the *British Journal of Mathematical and Statistical Psychology* who helped greatly with the presentation in that journal of ordinal multiple regression.

Some of the basic work for this book was done as a Visiting Fellow at Macquarie University in North Ryde, New South Wales, Australia, where there were numerous discussions with Professor Roderick P. McDonald, now of the University of Illinois. The book has benefited greatly from all these people, as well as others not named, including the editorial staff at Lawrence Erlbaum Associates; its remaining shortcomings are my responsibility. I am also indebted to the University of Southern California for free access to its excellent computing facilities.

—Norman Cliff

1

Why Ordinal Methods?

ORDINAL METHODS MAKE SENSE

Statistical and psychometric methods that make use of only the ordinal information provided by the data enjoyed a brief flurry of popularity during the middle of the current century, but their use has decreased substantially since then, at least on a proportionate basis. In the present chapter, as well as at other points in this book, it is argued that this decline has been counterproductive from the point of view of maximizing the overall effectiveness of empirical research and application.

The reasons for this assertion are grouped into three categories. First, it will be argued that much of the data in behavioral research has only ordinal justification. This makes ordinal methods preferable because of the possibility that conclusions from a metric analysis of ordinal data could be changed, even reversed, under ordinal transformation of the data, whereas ordinally based conclusions will not. Second, it is argued that in a substantial fraction of applications the questions that are to be answered by the data are themselves ordinal. This makes ordinal methods preferable because they answer the ordinal research question more directly than does a metric analysis of the same data. The third category of motive, which is perhaps the one that has traditionally been most often cited, is that ordinal methods have greater statistical robustness. This is true both in the inferential sense of providing generalizations from the data that are more likely to be valid than are traditional methods, in the face of the distributional peculiarities that are so common (robustness), and in the more descriptive sense of being less influenced by a small fraction of the observed data (resistance).

OUR DATA ARE ORDINAL

Levels of Scales

An important contribution by psychologists to scientific metatheory, or the philosophy of science, has been in the differentiation of levels of quantification. Although it has roots in the work of others, the formulation by S. S. Stevens that culminated in his chapter on measurement in his book on experimental psychology (Stevens, 1951) provides the complete formulation that forms the basis for most of our current thinking. There, he distinguished four levels of measurement, the familiar nominal, ordinal, interval, and ratio scales.

In these original definitions, the characteristics that differentiated the different types of scales were the transformations that were "admissible" for each—that is, how the scales could be changed without the loss of important information. In the case of ratio scales, epitomized by the familiar physical scales of length and mass, the only admissible changing transformation is multiplication by a positive constant, such as feet to meters or inches, pounds to kilograms, and the like. If x is one version of the variable and y another, then the only admissible relation is multiplication by some conversion constant a such that $x = ay$. Such transformations are sometimes called *linear* transformations. The zero point of the scale is determined by a rational empirical process.

The interval scale is similar to the ratio scale except that the origin, or zero point, is arbitrary. Given values of a variable on one version of the scale, it is permissible to convert them to another equivalent version by multiplying by one constant and adding a second: $x = ay + k$ for any positive value of a and any value of k. Such transformations are often called *affine* transformations. The typical example given is the everyday temperature used in weather reports, degrees Fahrenheit or Celsius. Converting one to the other requires two constants: F = 1.8C + 32. The point about the ratio and interval scales is that the choice of which version to use is arbitrary or a matter of convenience, and any other version within the constraints would serve as well, once one got used to it.

Ordinal scales permit much more freedom in the transformation. An ordinal scale can be transformed to a different but equally legitimate version in any way as long as the transformation preserves the order and the distinctions among values. The class of transformations fitting this constraint is called *strictly monotonic*. Logarithmic, square root, exponential, and a whole host of other mathematical functions are examples of monotonic transformations, but an unending variety of others is possible, including completely unsystematic or wiggly ones, as long as the order of values is preserved. In the current literature on measurement theory, which has become highly technical mathematically, the ratio, interval, and ordinal scales are called one-point, two-point, and many-point scale categories (Narens, 1981) respectively, because of the number of values that need to be fixed in order to define a given version of a scale.

The final category of scales is the nominal. A nominal variable consists of unordered categories, or distinct single entities, and each can be given a name. The name can be a number, but the number has no numerical interpretation. Therefore, any transformation that preserves identification is possible. Such transformations are called one-to-one transformations. Social security numbers are an example of a nominal scale. The numbers could be reassigned without loss of information, albeit to the disruptive confusion of numerous financial records.

Scale types are usually arranged in a hierarchy (an ordinal scale of scales) in terms of the transformations they allow, with ratio scales at the top. The reason is that the transformations are a nested set: every linear transformation is affine; every affine is monotonic; every strictly monotonic is one-to-one, but the subject and predicate in each of the clauses cannot be reversed without finding exceptions. The topic of defining scale types has an extensive literature. See Cliff (1993b) for an introductory discussion, Michel (1990) for a more extensive intermediate one, and Krantz, Luce, Suppes, and Tversky (1971) for a full technical treatment.

What Determines the Level of a Scale?

The preceding paragraphs have given the Stevensian definitions, which say that scale type is defined in terms of whether certain transformations are legitimate and others are not, without going into how it was decided whether a transformation was legitimate. The next step in the intellectual evolution of scale types was the inquiry into how the kind of transformation could be limited. Before turning to that, one can comment on the superficiality of the analogies to physical variables that are often used in examples of interval and ratio scales. Length and time are frequently cited as examples of ratio scales, yet even by the standards of 19th-century physics this would be questionable. "Length," in itself, is not the relevant variable in even classical physics. The variable is *distance*, the difference in coordinates of two points, measured in a straight line. The coordinate system has an arbitrary origin (Greenwich, England, the corner of my desk, or the center of the sun) and an arbitrary unit (kilometers, inches, or parsecs). Even in the case of a lever, the "length" of a lever is merely a surrogate for the distance through which a center of mass moves. So there is assumed to be a coordinate system, space, which has no definable zero point, and it is *differences* with respect to space that are the variable, distance. Similarly, it is not "time" itself that enters into relations, but *elapsed time*, the difference in the time coordinates. Time itself had no zero point, any more than space did. The clever thing that physicists did was to take these interval scale variables, the space and time coordinates, and use the intervals on them as the variables. The *intervals* on interval scales behave like ratio scales. Trying to find the origin for space and time is one goal of the modern field of cosmology, which tries to find out when/where space/time begins, but so far seems not to be absolutely sure.

Temperature is a false example of an interval scale because it has been known for more than a century that there was a zero point for this scale, resulting in the Kelvin (K or Absolute) scale of temperature, which allows only linear transformation. The traditional Fahrenheit and Celsius versions are retained in weather reports and cooking directions because the numbers in them are cognitively more comfortable for everyday use, as well as more familiar. (The Fahrenheit scale was devised with weather reporting specifically in mind; 0°F is about as cold as it usually gets in the winter in many temperate parts of the world, and 100°F is about as high as it gets in the summer.) Thus, not only do the frequently cited examples of ratio scales turn out to be the intervals on interval scales, but the prime example of an interval scale is easily converted to a ratio scale.

The important thing, though, is not to quibble about the examples but to accept the fact that different kinds of scales exist and consider what it is that makes one scale an interval scale and another some other kind. What makes a transformation legitimate or illegitimate? Looked at one way, a transformation is legitimate if it does not disturb, or lead to contradictory, empirical relations. A more demanding view is to take the opposite tack and require positive reinforcement in the form of empirical relationships that support a scale's status in the hierarchy of types before it can be awarded that status. It is this latter view that seems to provide the soundest basis for research and application.

The scale distinction that is most salient to the behavioral sciences is that between ordinal and interval scales. The reasons for this salience include, first, that many statistical procedures assume interval-scale status for the variables. Second, the distinction between interval and ratio scales is rarely important in behavioral science because plausible claimants to the latter status are rare. Finally, there are frequent situations where there is scientific or practical desirability in comparing differences that are at different points on a scale; thus, it would be nice to have interval scales. Since ordinal methods are the focus of this book, and a good deal of the motivation for using them lies in uneasiness about the interval-scale status of many variables, we concentrate on this distinction.

What Makes a Variable an Interval Scale?

The major development in the theory of measurement subsequent to Stevens' (1951) enumeration of the scale types and their ties to classes of transformations was the elucidation of what the basis was for deciding that a scale merited a certain classification. The landmark paper here was Luce and Tukey (1964), where "conjoint measurement" was introduced. This, and related subsequent work, such as the three-volume *Foundations of Measurement* (Krantz et al., 1971; Luce, Krantz, Suppes, & Tversky, 1990; Suppes, Krantz, Luce, & Tversky, 1989), is couched in a mathematical framework that many find to be austere and difficult, so its diffusion into the main stream of psychology has been slow (Cliff, 1992), but its content is fundamental to serious thinking about measurement.

At a highly simplified level, the distinction that allows an ordinal variable to achieve interval-scale status is fairly direct. There must be an empirically nontrivial way of demonstrating the equality of differences at different points on the variable. Probably the most striking formulation of conditions under which this would be possible is the original one (Luce & Tukey, 1964), called conjoint measurement. Its first requirement is three variables observed simultaneously (conjointly), at least one of which provides an order. The paradigm most familiar to behavioral scientists that embodies this idea is a fully crossed factorial design, the factors providing two of the variables, and a dependent variable, which is the third. The latter provides an order for the cells of the table. Then a mild-looking constraint on the order of the cells on the dependent variable is necessary for there to be an interval scale of all three. This constraint can be formulated as a single axiom, but it is easier to understand in parts. The first part is that, within any row of the table, the order of the values of the independent variable in the columns is the same in all rows, and similarly for the columns. This amounts in analysis of variance terminology to saying that there is no crossing interaction.

The other part of the constraint is that there must be an additional consistency on the orders. To formulate this, we have to consider each three-by-three subtable, which is a combination of three levels of the row variable, say R_0, R_1, and R_2, and three of the columns, C_0, C_1, and C_2. We are already assuming consistency of row and column orders, as in the previous paragraph, so $R_iC_0 \leq R_iC_1 \leq R_iC_2$ and $R_0C_j \leq R_1C_j \leq R_2C_j$ for any row i and column j. Suppose (i) $R_0C_1 \leq R_1C_0$, which is a symbolic way of saying that the step from R_0 to R_1 had at least as big an effect as the step from C_0 to C_1. Suppose also that (ii) $R_1C_2 \leq R_2C_1$, implying that the step from R_1 to R_2 was at least as large as the step from C_1 to C_2. (If both of these changes are not in the same relative size, then this 3×3 does not tell us anything.) The requirement that supports interval status for the variables states that, whenever these two ordering conditions are met, it should also be true that (iii) $R_0C_2 \leq R_2C_0$. This rather formal statement has a commonsense interpretation. The interpretation is that (i) showed that the first step on R was at least as big as the first step on C, and (ii) showed that the second step on R was at least as big as the second step on C. This means that, if things are behaving nicely, the two steps on R should be at least as big as the two steps on C, as summarized in (iii). If this is always true, for all the 3×3 tables, then the idea of *additivity of differences* is supported; if not, it is not. It is this additivity of differences that makes an interval scale. It is important to realize here that all the ordering comparisons must be empirically independent.

These properties, consistent ordering of columns within every row, and vice versa, and the consistency of combined differences that was described in the previous paragraph are not enough to define the interval scales, although they support that status. What is also needed is the ability to make fine distinctions on the variables: For any two levels on a variable, we must always be able to find one that lies between them. When all of these conditions are satisfied, interval status for all three variables is established.

The foregoing description is only one of a number of ways of formulating the characteristics necessary for defining an interval scale, but the general property that the ways share is that of showing that differences are additive. As a minimum, what is needed is a way of comparing differences at different points on a variable. This is why three variables are necessary. The compensatory aspect of the system, showing that changes in one variable have an effect equivalent to changes on the other, with respect to a third variable, is what provides confirmation that the three can be expressed as interval scales.

Defining Scales by Fitting Models

A few years before the development of abstract measurement theory, a different approach to defining interval scales was introduced. This is what might be called the model-fitting method. The earliest explicit suggestion of this sort, although the roots of the idea go back perhaps to Gulliksen (1946), was by Anderson (1962), but the idea did not gain impetus until the publication of Shepard's two landmark papers (Shepard, 1962). The idea here was that one could propose that a certain kind of data should fit a particular algebraic model, the algebraic model being one that required interval-level variables. What these writers suggested was that, even though the main variable seemed to be defined only ordinally, the process of fitting the model could be used to find a monotonically transformed version of that variable that best fit the algebraic model. Once that was done, the transformed version of the variable was an interval scale because, if it were transformed away from the best-fitting version, the model would no longer fit as well.

The scale status of a variable does require more than this single demonstration. After all, it is always possible to find a transformation of the scale that fits the model better than the original one did. Additional support for the transformed version is needed. For example, it should fit the data *very* well; it should simplify interpretations; it should *generalize* to other data. If much activity verifying these sorts of properties had gone on over the last 30 years, it could be that behavioral science would be in possession of a repertoire of variables with assured interval-scale status. Clearly this has not happened, any more than there has been an important amount of activity designed to show that certain kinds of data satisfy the axiomatic requirements of abstract measurement theory (Cliff, 1992). The upshot is that we are now left with few if any psychologically defined variables that have well-assured interval-scale status. I have speculated (Cliff, 1992) on why we in the quantitative research community have avoided efforts in this direction.

Are Variables in Behavioral Research Interval Scales?

Very few behavioral variables provide the sort of information required to support interval-scale status. Research that even attempts to provide evidence for this status is extremely rare. A few partial exceptions exist (e.g., Anderson, 1981; Cliff, 1972; Townsend, 1992) but for the most part our variables are too poorly defined, and their interrelations are too inconsistent, to support interval-scale status. Even the physical variables, such as time, length, and electrical resistance, that are used in behavioral research are of doubtful status in that regard. There are two reasons for this. One is that the choice of one form of the physical variable over another form of it is often arbitrary. Rate of response could be substituted for time to respond. Some other indicator of size, such as area or volume, can be used in place of length. Conductance can replace resistance. The use of one form of the variable over another rarely has empirical justification; which one is used is matter of tradition or convenience.

In many other applications, the physical variable—age in a developmental study is a good example—is a convenient manifest index of an underlying or latent psychological variable. The relation between the latent and manifest variable is unknown. It is plausible to assume monotonicity, perhaps with some error, but linearity is hard to justify. Thus, as *behavioral* variables, the comforting interval or ratio status of physical variables is hard to justify.

Insensitivity of Conclusions to Transformation

The argument is sometimes made (Abelson & Tukey, 1963; Labovitz, 1967; Velleman & Wilkinson, 1993) that it matters little if scale transformations are possible; the conclusions are unlikely to change because scale transformations have only a small effect. That may sometimes be the case, but examples can be provided where standard, parametric statistical measures can be substantially, even profoundly, affected by scale transformation. It is true that the transformations usually have to be extreme in order to produce those effects, but still they are possible.

An example is in the common independent groups t test. This, or some related quantity such as the F ratio in a one-way ANOVA or for a between-subjects main effect in a factorial ANOVA, is the statistic on which conclusions are based in many studies. The usual feeling is that it is rather insensitive to monotonic scale transformation, yet such effects can be substantial. For example, one kind of monotonic transformation is simply adding a large constant to the k highest score values or subtracting a large constant from the k lowest ones. Let t^* stand for the value of the unpooled-variance version of the t ratio for a mean difference after scale transformation. Suppose the k highest scores are from the same group; then t^* can always be made to approach

$$t^* \approx \left(\frac{k(n-1)}{n-k} \right)^{1/2} \tag{1.1}$$

by making the constant arbitrarily large. With 10 scores in one group, and the three highest scores are from that group, $t^* = 1.96$ can then always be achieved by transforming the scale so that those three scores are moved a large distance above the others. Another example of a similar effect is to take the single highest score and move it a large distance up. Then $t^* \approx 1.0$, in favor of its group, no matter what t's original value was—large positive, large negative, or anywhere between. If the lowest score is from the same group, then t^* can be made equal to -1.0 by the same process! The same reasoning shows a more general effect. The sign of t^* can be made both positive and negative, depending on how the scale is transformed, *unless the two cumulative distributions do not cross*. Even if t's sign cannot be changed, there is ordinarily much freedom in the value t^* can be made to have.

Similar effects can occur with correlations. Kimeldorf and Sampson (1978) have an algorithm that evaluates the changes that can be made in Pearson r when the scale is transformed. The program is not completely general because it collapses the scale to a relatively small number (<10) of categories, and it seems likely that the greatest effects will occur when the extreme values are moved, but even here the effects can be substantial. Reasoning such as that which led to (1.1) can be applied to r as well as to t, and the effects seem to be sometimes comparable, but they are hard to characterize as simply.

Sensitivity of Conclusions to Scale Transformation

A case has been made here that many, probably nearly all, behavioral variables have only ordinal-level justifications, but the real issue is whether the conclusions the investigator makes are affected by this in any appreciable way with any frequency. One approach is to insist that the observed scale is not to be transformed (cf. Labovitz, 1967), and so the conclusions cannot be changed. This seems like a rather narrow view from the point of view of scientific validity. There is frequently a certain arbitrariness in the specific variable used, whether it be psychometrically defined, the outcome of a model-fitting process, or an overt physical variable because there are alternative, equally valid forms of the variable that could be used instead, or because the observed variable is a surrogate for ("a measure of" or "an operational definition of") a latent variable that is assumed to underlie it. A much more generally defensible strategy is to prefer that the conclusions should hold no matter what forms of the variables are used.

Against the fact that the effects of transformation can be large, it could be argued that radical transformation is required for that to happen, and such transformation may be indefensible or unlikely to represent the "true" nature of the variables. There is no way to defeat such an argument objectively except to disagree with its premises. Even if it is accepted, however, it can be argued that mild transformations can have mild effects, and such effects can often have considerable influence on the conclusions that are drawn from a study. Many effects or noneffects are in fact near the border of statistical significance, in one direction or the other. Moderate transformations can easily push a result across the critical boundary in one direction or the other. Although many would deplore an overemphasis on statistical significance to the exclusion of estimation of size of effects as the primary basis for deciding what is "real" or important, it is a fact that this is what forms the basis of the conclusions of a large proportion of studies. Therefore, statistical procedures whose significance levels are invariant under transformations of scale have considerable justification.

Davison and Sharma (1988) prove several theorems regarding the possible effects of transformation upon statistical inferences. Their conclusions seem, at first reading, to provide justification for continued use of traditional methods, but a careful examination of the theorems, and particularly of the premises that are used, shows that the conclusions apply under a very limited set of circumstances. They do not cover the broad set of possibilities that experience and scientific common sense tell us should be our concern.

Similar arguments can be made in favor of ordinal psychometrics. Deriving orders from data rather than purported interval-level variables has considerable justification. Overinterpretation of score differences is a habit which it is easy to fall into, yet virtually all psychometrically defined scores have only ordinal justification for the kinds of reasons that were presented earlier. Staying within the bounds of interpretation that are justified by the data has the virtue of honesty as well as probably providing practical advantages by reducing the frequency of errors of interpretation.

OUR QUESTIONS ARE ORDINAL

Ordinal Questions

Ask a typical researcher in the behavioral sciences what he or she wants to find out in his or her research. Most of the time, the answer is a variation on one of a few prototypes. One prototype is "I want to find out if people in this group tend to score higher on this variable than people in this other group." A related one is "Are scores higher after this treatment than they were before it?" One that is a bit more complex is "Is positive change more likely after this treatment than after that one?" Another is "Do these people score higher than these on the posttest, holding pretest scores constant?" These are all questions about the *location* of distributions. The characteristic they all have is their *ordinal* nature. We tend in our thinking about many research issues to formulate them in this ordinal way.

A different set of questions refers to correlational matters. When asked to interpret a correlation coefficient, there is a strong tendency for a researcher to answer that it reflects the extent to which the scores are in the same order on both variables. Correspondingly, the question being answered by a correlation coefficient is very often of the form, "Do people who score relatively high on this variable also score relatively high on that one?" Sometimes there is a prediction context: "Given their scores on these predictor variables, which person will score higher on this criterion?" Again, the research questions tend to have their initial formulation in an ordinal framework.

Measurement questions are also stated ordinally. "How reliable is the order on this test?" "What is the percentile rank of this score?" "How close is the observed order to the true-score order?" "What is the preference order for these products?" "To what extent can these people be ordered with respect to attitude using these items?" These are the kinds of questions that psychometric research is designed to answer. At least, these are the ways in which the questions tend to be formulated in their most basic, closest-to-the-heart, form.

It is true that there are a number of questions that do not fit this ordinal rubric. There are highly parametric questions that we try to answer with our data. Sometimes these questions are tested with well-quantified variables. Occasionally the answers have the ringing clarity that makes a researcher's heart sing along with the ringing. It would be nice if there were more such studies. This book is for the other, more common ones.

Parametric Answers to Ordinal Questions?

Once the ordinal question has been formulated, we have been taught to translate it into a parametric form such as $\mu_1 \neq \mu_2$ or $\rho > 0$, and then to translate these again, this time into null hypothesis form, $\mu_1 = \mu_2$ or $\rho = 0$.

The parameters are then estimated with data; the null hypothesis is tested; some conclusions about the parameters, sometimes quantitative but often qualitative, are drawn. These conclusions are then often restated as answers to the original ordinal questions (cf. McGraw & Wong, 1992).

This process represents a pretty long chain with which to connect the research question to its answer. The chain of connection requires considerable support in the way of assumptions about the nature of the data, assumptions that might or might not be valid. The problem is particularly serious when we want a quantified answer—that is, something that we intend to interpret as an expression of the degree to which the question asked is true. What are the chances that a person in this group scores higher than one in that? To what extent are people in the same order on both variables? Translating the parametric data into a quantified answer to such ordinal questions becomes fraught with uncertainty.

Common ways of quantifying the answers include estimates of effect size, $(\mu_1 - \mu_2)/\sigma$; proportion of variance accounted for, η^2, ω^2, or ρ^2; and Pearson correlation, ρ. Sophisticated members of the research community have recommended these measures repeatedly for decades (e.g., Cohen & Cohen, 1975; Hays, 1963), pointing out their advantages over simply assessing significance levels, yet researchers have been slow to adopt them. One can ask about the reasons for this reluctance.

The reasons are undoubtedly multiple, but one of them may be that, as researchers, we perceive a mismatch between these measures of effect size and our data, particularly as answers to our ordinal research questions. We know that effect size directly reflects probability of score difference only under very special assumptions about homogeneity of variance and normality of distribution. We know that variances are highly influenced by the presence or absence of outliers. We know that interpretations of correlations depend on assumptions of linearity and homoskedasticity. These are all grounds for not basing our interpretations of results upon these quantities. Furthermore, the process by which the traditional statistics can be translated into quantified answers to our ordinally stated questions are complex (McGraw & Wong, 1992) and the specifics of how to do so are not widely known, and rest on questionable assumptions about distributions. Therefore, if numbers that quantified the answers to our ordinal questions were more available, we might be more willing to use such quantifications than we are the parametric versions.

Researchers who employ categorical methods such as contingency table analysis in its simple or more complex forms should also find the methods useful. Often, categorical variables such as questionnaire responses are ordered in a fairly clear way, yet most forms of categorical analysis do not take account of the order. The researcher may make ordinal interpretations of relations that are revealed, but they are often not directly supported by the data analysis. The ordinal methods that will be described here provide clear and direct ways of making use of the ordinal character of the data, both descriptively and inferentially.

One motive for this book is to show that there are some ways of getting quantified answers to our ordinal questions and to show how to get those answers. Some of the methods will be familiar, some will not. The variety of ways they can be used will be familiar to only a few.

ROBUSTNESS, RESISTANCE, AND POWER

Classical Inference

The procedures by which one can reach conclusions that have a certain empirically ascertained degree of firmness from fallible data have to rank as one of the major achievements of late 19th- and early 20th-century Western thought. The basic aspects of the theory of inference are worth reviewing so that a context can be provided for points that are made later in this section and later in this book.

Although the general approach has several variants, differing in preferences for strategies, they all share a common basis—that "out there" there are, at least potentially, populations that have distributions on an empirical variable or set of variables. These distributions are characterized by parameters. We use η to refer to a generic parameter. When samples are taken from the populations, characteristics of the samples—statistics—are used to estimate the parameters of the populations. We let v stand for a generic statistic. Usually, the sample statistic employed to estimate a parameter is the sample counterpart: sample means to estimate population means; sample correlations to estimate population correlations, and so on. This need not be the case, because one can use the sample median to estimate the population mean, the sample Spearman rank correlation to estimate the population Pearson coefficient, and so on, but usually there is a direct correspondence between the nature of the population parameter and that of the estimator.

The central concept in the inferential process is the sampling distribution, which defines the probability, or probability density in the case of continuous quantities, that the statistic will take on any given value. The characteristics of these distributions are important determiners of inferential practice. The mean of the sampling distribution, which is the expected value (see Hays, 1963, for a review of expected values) of the statistic, expressed as $E(v)$ or μ_v, should be close to the true value of the parameter being estimated. The extent to which this is not the case is referred to as the "bias" of the statistic, bias = $\eta - E(v)$ if v is used to estimate η. The standard deviation of the sampling distribution, σ_v, is referred to as the "standard error" of the statistic, which is the basic measure of how close the statistic is likely to come to its expected value. The square of the standard error is referred to as the sampling variance of, or simply variance of, the statistic: $\sigma_v^2 = E(v - \mu_v)^2$. If two statistics are used to estimate the same parameter, the relative size of their respective standard errors is the "relative efficiency" of the one in the denominator. Standard errors of well-behaved statistics decrease with increasing sample size. A statistic whose standard error and bias, if any, decrease with increasing sample size is referred to as "consistent."

The sampling distributions of statistics are deduced strictly from the nature of the population distributions, but certain characteristics of the sampling distributions can often be inferred in a way that does not require that knowledge. For example, if the population distribution is normal with mean μ and variance σ^2, one of the things learned in elementary statistics is that the sampling distribution of the mean, m, is also normal with mean μ and variance σ^2/n, where n is the number of independently sampled units. (We adopt the convention that $N(\eta, \lambda)$ means that a variable is normally distributed with mean η and variance λ.) However, in a wide variety of situations it is possible to mathematically determine what characteristics of the population determine the mean and variance of a statistic without specifying the population. For example, if certain peculiar and empirically unlikely cases are ignored, the properties of the normal distribution that $E(m) = \mu$ and $E(m - \mu)^2 = \sigma^2/n$ hold in any other distribution as well. Similarly, $E(s^2) = \sigma^2$, where $s^2 = \sum(x - m)^2/(n - 1)$, for any reasonable distribution, and $E(s^2 - \sigma^2)^2 = [(n - 1)\mu_4 - (n - 3)\sigma^4]/n(n - 1)$, where μ_4 is the fourth moment around the mean: $E(x - \mu)^4$.

Many statistics display the property called "asymptotic normality." This means that, as the sample size gets larger and larger, its sampling distribution comes more and more to resemble the normal distribution. It is nice to make use of this property because many times the exact form of the sampling distribution is unknown, or even unknowable, yet it is possible to prove asymptotic normality. The fact that the sampling distribution of a proportion displays this property was important to the early history of statistics. Almost all of the order-based statistics discussed in any detail in this book display this property.

Virtually any statistic that involves summing and dividing by n (or something close to it) has asymptotic normality. Most of the time in modern statistics it seems that this property is deduced by way of rather abstract mathematics, but in the case of the mean itself rather elementary methods can be used to show why the distribution of the mean tends toward normality with increasing sample size. Suppose X is a random variable whose distribution has some mean μ_X, variance σ_X^2, third moment $E(x - \mu_x)^3 = \mu_3$, and fourth moment μ_4. The degree of "skewness" of a distribution is better expressed by standardizing the variable, letting $\mu_3^*(x) = E[(x - \mu_x)/\sigma_x]^3$. Similarly, let $\mu_4^*(x) = E[(x - \mu_x)/\sigma_x]^4$. The normal distribution, being symmetric, has $\mu_3^* = 0$. A normal distribution has $\mu_4^* = 3$, so distributions are described relative to this figure. Those with $\mu_4^* > 3$ are leptokurtic or long-tailed; those with $\mu_4^* < 3$ are platykurtic. Thus, for any distribution, the closer μ_3^* is to zero, and the closer μ_4^* is to 3, the more it resembles the normal.

By simply following the rules of taking expectations, it is possible to show that $\mu_3^*(m_x) = \mu_3^*(x)/\sqrt{n}$. That is, the relative skewness of the mean is the relative skewness of the variable, reduced by the square root of the sample size. The effect on the kurtosis is even more rapid: $\mu_4^*(m_x) - 3 = [\mu_4^*(x) - 3]/n$. That is, the relative kurtosis of the mean is only one-nth the relative kurtosis of the original distribution. Thus, the samping distribution of the mean becomes normal quite rapidly with increasing sample size even when the population is not normal.

The sample variance s^2 also displays asymptotic normality because it, too, is a kind of average, this time the average of a sum of squared deviations from the mean. The squaring slows down the approach to normality, but still it takes place.

The drawback to assuming asymptotic normality for the sampling distribution of a statistic is that one does not know how fast the approach is. This is for two reasons. One is that the nonnormality of the population is not known. After all, in an extreme case where $\mu_3^*(x) = 50$, even with $n = 100$ $\mu_3^*(m_x) = 5.0$, when $\mu_3^* = 3$ is considered highly skewed; it is possible that $\mu_3^* = 50$ is the kind of data one is dealing with. Second, the behavior of the statistic in question is usually not as well understood as the behavior of the mean under nonnormality is. Thus, using the asymptotic normality property has to be partly based on faith that the property will hold adequately in samples of the size one has. Experience shows that, with some statistics, the Pearson r being one, the asymptote is reached so slowly, even in normal populations, that simple inferential methods (Olkin & Finn, 1995) are not adequate (cf. Long & Cliff, 1995).

Hypthesis Testing and Confidence Intervals

The two main inferential tools of the classical, as distinguished from the Bayesian and the fiducial, approach to inference are the test of a hypothesis about a parameter and the confidence interval for a parameter. ("Parameter" can stand for a difference or any other linear combination of two or more parameters or for the ratio of two parameters, etc.) These tools make use of the characteristics of the sampling distributions of the statistics used to make the inferences.

In hypothesis testing, a null-hypothesis value η_0 is established for the parameter η on some grounds. Most commonly in modern usage, η_0 is a straw-person, established as the converse of what the investigator expects, or at least hopes for. For example, if she or he expects two variables to be correlated—that is, that $\rho \neq 0$, which is often called the *research* or alternative hypothesis, H_a—then the null hypothesis, often denoted H_0, is the opposite: $H_0: \rho = 0$.

A sample of size n is available and assumed to be a random sample from a population where the true correlation has some value ρ, and the sample correlation r is calculated. If the two variables have a bivariate-normal distribution, the characteristics of the sampling distribution of r are known from statistical theory. The investigator chooses an α level, the probability of rejecting H_0 when it is true, the value of α reflecting his or her degree of willingness to make this Type I error. Knowledge of the sampling distribution for r enables the investigator to set up two limiting values for r, r_L and r_U, such that the sample r will fall outside those limits just $100\alpha\%$ of the time. Then the investigator compares the sample r to these limits. If it is outside them, H_0 is rejected, and the investigator concludes that the correlation is not zero. If it is inside them, H_0 is accepted; the correlation is "not significant" at the given α level. Strictly speaking, the Neyman–Pearson, or decision-theory, inferential rules say that she or he then concludes that $\rho = 0$. In practice, of course, researchers do not operate in this mode but follow a less stringent interpretation of the process (Takayanagi & Cliff, 1993).

In this context, there are four possible outcomes of the hypothesis-testing process, depending on whether H_0 is true and whether r is judged significant. (1) H_0 can be true, and it is accepted because r fell inside the limits. (2) H_0 is false, ρ has some value other than 0, and it is rejected because r fell outside the limits. These two are correct decisions. However, there are two other possibilities: (3) H_0 is true but r falls outside the limits, so H_0 is rejected. This is a Type I error. Finally, the result can be that (4) H_0 is false, $\rho \neq 0$, but r falls within the limits, so H_0 is accepted. This is a Type II error. Thus, there are two possible outcomes that are correct, rejecting when H_0 is false and accepting when H_0 is true, and two that are incorrect, making the wrong decision under each of the two possible true states with respect to ρ.

The probability of a Type I error is the α level that has been used. The probability of a Type II error, usually designated β, is unknown because it depends on the actual value of ρ in the population, but again statistical theory can be used to deduce what β would be with this sample size and chosen α, assuming any particular value of ρ. What is called the *power* of the test is $1 - \beta$, the probability of correctly rejecting when H_0 is false. If the goal of the research is to show that $\rho \neq 0$, then the more power the better. The two most important ways to have good power are to have a sample that is adequate in size for the level of ρ one is concerned about and defining the variables in such a way as to make the relation between the variables a substantial one—that is, make H_0 "as false as possible," if the reader will forgive the poor logical status of that expression.

It is not necessary to test the hypothesis about ρ using r. It can be done, for example, by instead computing the Spearman rank correlation r_S because statistical theory provides the sampling distribution of r_S (Kendall, 1970) under the bivariate normality assumption in the null case. If the same α level is used as with r, leading to the designation of upper and lower limits for r_S, and H_0 is rejected if r_S falls outside them, the probability of Type I error will of course be the same as in testing r, but it turns out that Type II errors will be slightly more likely. Thus, using r_S instead of r to test a hypothesis about ρ results in a slightly less powerful procedure when the variables are normal.

In many applications of hypothesis testing, some aspects of the process as it has been described here become obscured because the quantity that leads to the decision about the parameter is not the value of the statistic itself but some quantity derived from it such as a t or F statistic. It is this test statistic that has the critical values that lead to acceptance or rejection, rather than the value of the estimate itself. Nonetheless, the same concepts are involved, whether a hypothesis is tested directly using the statistic itself or more indirectly by means of a test statistic.

Although estimating a parameter with a statistic gives us a "best guess" as to its value, and hypothesis testing may allow us to dismiss the possibility that it has some null value, we know that the true value is not exactly the obtained estimate; even if the null hypothesis is accepted, we know that this does not prove that the null value is the true value. Therefore, it is useful to have a range of values for the parameter that are plausible, thus by implication ruling out other values as being implausible.

The confidence interval (c.i.) serves this function in statistical inference. The c.i. for η is a range of values for η, constructed on the basis of sample data, such that the probability that η is within that range is $1 - \alpha$. There is a logical duality between c.i. and testing hypotheses such that when the hypothesis $\eta = \eta_0$ is accepted, η_0 will be found to be within the c.i. for η, and it will be outside it if H_0 is rejected. One of the nice things about the classical inference theory that is based on assuming normality for distributions is that it makes the construction of c.i. relatively simple. Some of this simplicity is lost when normality does not hold, for reasons that will be mentioned in later contexts.

Robustness of Inferences

An important aspect of this sketch of classical inference is that it was necessary to make assumptions about the nature of the population distributions involved in order to derive the sampling distributions and, through them, the critical values for the statistic. Some sort of assumptions about the population, or sometimes more directly about the characteristics of the sampling distribution, must be made. If distributional assumptions are not valid, but the same critical values are used, then the Type-I-error probability will not be what was assumed but could be greater or less. This actual probability is referred to as the "size" of the test to distinguish it from the assumed α level.

The concepts of power and robustness apply to c.i. in a way that parallels their application to hypothesis testing. One statistical procedure is more powerful than another if values of η that are outside the c.i. formed using the first are inside that of the second. This corresponds directly to the fact that hypotheses that would be rejected using the first would be accepted using the second. That is, narrower c.i. are analogous to, and directly related to, greater power. Robustness applies to c.i. in the sense that a $1 - \alpha$ c.i. formed under one set of assumptions actually should contain η that proportion of the time even when the assumptions are not true. The proportion of times that the c.i. does contain the parameter is called the "coverage probability." Coverage is the generalization of size to the non-null case, but it is expressed in the complementary way; ideally, coverage is $1 - \alpha$, where α is chosen by the investigator.

If the assumptions are false, then the true size or coverage could be greater or less than α. If the differences from the assumed α are small, then the inference process is described as "robust" with respect to the assumption violation. More generally, a statistic or test is described as robust to the extent to which it is little influenced by variations in characteristics of the data, such as normality/nonnormality, that are not directly related to the inference to be made. Where there is reason to expect that assumptions are false, robust statistics are preferable to nonrobust ones.

The calculations of the power of statistics and the relative power of different statistics must also be done on the basis of assumptions about the characteristics of the data. When the parent distributions have characteristics different from those assumed, the absolute and relative powers can consequently be different. Since we often have reason to believe that our data do not conform to classical assumptions, working with statistics that have good power under a broad range of situations is preferable to using ones that have optimum power under a narrow range of special ones.

The foregoing aspects of the inferential process summarize the desirable properties of an inferential statistic. The size should equal the assumed α when H_0 is true. Power should be as high as possible when H_0 is false. Coverage should be $1 - \alpha$ under all circumstances. The c.i. should be as narrow as possible. A "perfect" statistic would have all these characteristics, and none of them can be singled out as the sole basis for evaluation. Good behavior when H_0 is true should not be at the expense of poor behavior when it is false. Power and narrowness of c.i. should not be sacrificed in order to ensure that size is never more than α; good power should not be at the expense of poor coverage.

The traditional, normal, and homogeneous-variance statistics have these desirable properties *when the assumptions are met.* Experience shows (Micceri, 1989) that they are rarely met in behavioral data. Therefore, alternative procedures may be preferable. However, the alternative procedures, such as the ones described in this book, may introduce their own assumptions. Therefore, it is important that those assumptions be made explicit and examined, and the consequences of their violation assessed. This is probably the most neglected aspect of the study of ordinal statistical methods, their protagonists, including me (Cliff, 1993a), tending to assume that such issues can safely be ignored.

Illustration of Inference

A familiar application of hypothesis testing is provided by the mean. Suppose the U.S. Census reports the mean years of education of the U.S. population as 14.2 years with a standard deviation of 3.5 years. A researcher is interested in a general question of whether the education of a certain subgroup of the population, such as people of Cornish ancestry, is the same as the general population. Data on this subpopulation is not available from the census, but the researcher is somehow able to get a random sample of such people. She could investigate one aspect of her research interest by testing the hypothesis that the mean of the subpopulation, μ_c, is the same as the mean of the whole population. This can be stated formally as H_0: $\mu_c = 14.2$. Intuitively, it seems reasonable to test the hypothesis by comparing the sample mean, m_c, to 14.2, and this is what we typically do.

The formal testing of this hypothesis depends on the sampling distribution of m_c. The general principles we have described guarantee that the mean of this distribution is μ_c and that its standard deviation is $\sigma_c/\sqrt{n}$. If the sampling distribution were normal (the basis for assuming that this is reasonable is examined later), then, assuming we set α, our intended probability of making a Type I error, equal to .05, a table of the normal curve shows that 95% of the time m_c will fall between $-1.96\sigma_c/\sqrt{n}$ and $1.96\sigma_c/\sqrt{n}$. We have to decide what to use for σ_c, and this necessity introduces an important issue, one that is very elementary but that requires examination repeatedly when deciding what form of statistical analysis would be appropriate. The alternatives here are that we can *assume* that $\sigma_c = \sigma$, which is 3.5, or we can attempt to estimate σ_c from the sample. The former approach is sometimes given justification on the grounds that what we are really assuming under the null hypothesis is that the Cornish distribution is no different from that of the general population in any respect. The mean has been selected for examination because location is of primary interest, but we are assuming now that the distributions are identical in other respects, even if the means are different. The dangers in such an approach will be seen in a moment.

Now our test of H_0 is quite straightforward. Suppose $n = 49$; then, if the sample mean m_C falls in the acceptance region, which is between $\mu - z_{\alpha/2}\sigma/n^{1/2} = 14.2 - 1.96 \times 3.5/7$ and $14.2 + 1.96 \times 3.5/7$, or 13.22 to 15.18, H_0 will be accepted. If it falls outside those limits, H_0 is rejected. Not only is it rejected, and this is another important but often ignored point, but we conclude that μ_C is greater than 14.2 or that it is less than 14.2, depending on the direction of the deviation.

Suppose that our assumption that $\sigma_C = \sigma$ is wrong; Cornish are unusually variable in their education; so suppose that instead $\sigma_C = 7.0$. The same rules that state m_C falls between $\mu_C + 1.96\sigma_C/\sqrt{n}$ and $\mu_C + 1.96\sigma_C/\sqrt{n}$ 95% of the time must hold, but now this interval is really twice as wide as the one we are assuming. This has four possible consequences when we actually come to our conclusion, depending on what the outcome of the calculations is, on what the true mean is, and on the luck of the draw. Suppose first that the null hypothesis is true, $\mu_C = \mu$. Two things can happen. The sample mean can fall within our boundaries, and we correctly accept H_0, or it will fall outside and we incorrectly reject. Because the true variance is larger than the assumed one, the probability that we reject when H_0 is true is .327 instead of the intended .05. The "size" of the test, the true probability of rejecting H_0, is more than six times as large as was intended.

Now suppose instead that the null hypothesis is false. The probability that m_C falls outside the limits is larger than if the true standard deviation were 3.5. This looks good, because we want to reject the null hypothesis when it is false, avoiding Type II errors, but the desirability of this outcome again depends on which of two possibilities occur. Suppose $\mu_C = 14.5$, a bit higher than μ. Then the probability that m_C falls above 15.18 is .252, and we correctly conclude that $\mu_C > \mu$, but the other thing that can happen is that m_C is less than 13.22. If this happens, then surely we will conclude that $\mu_C < \mu$. If our assumption about the Cornish variance had been true, this would happen a negligible proportion of the time when $\mu_C = 14.5$, less than 2%. Unfortunately, given that the true variance is larger, we will make an incorrect decision about the direction of the difference nearly 10% of the time: 10% of the time we will reject $\mu_C = 14.2$ at the .05 level and conclude that $\mu_C < 14.2$, when in fact $\mu_C > 14.2$, all because we were willing to assume that the only possible difference between the two populations was in their means.

Kaiser (1960) called attention to the danger of mistaking the true direction of a relationship, calling this the "Type III error." That name has since been applied to other errors, sometimes whimsically, but the point is an important one. Most of the time, a Type III error will have more serious consequences than either of the traditional two. One can suggest that avoiding such errors is the real basis for using a null hypothesis of zero difference or correlation because the probability of rejecting the null hypothesis in a certain direction is even lower than if the actual difference or correlation has the opposite sign. This is, of course, providing some assumption failure such as the one used above has not taken place.

One can wonder what the consequences are of $\sigma_C < \sigma$. A little thought reveals that the answer again depends on μ_C. If $\mu_C = \mu$, then the chance of getting outside the acceptance region is even less than α; the Type I error rate is less than α. If H_0 is false, the main consequence is loss of power; m_C has too little chance of getting outside the acceptance region in the correct direction, although there is even less chance of a Type III error.

Of course, few researchers would have used the population variance in this situation. Almost all of us would estimate σ_C^2 from the data, necessitating the use of Student's t distribution to set the acceptance boundaries, which widens them a bit, on the average, but not much unless the sample is very small. The example was chosen to emphasize the principle that the distribution of two groups, or conditions, is unlikely to differ only in means, or any other measure of location. Far more plausible, almost all the time, is the expectation that whatever is causing two groups to differ in location will also cause them to differ in almost any other characteristic of their respective distributions (O'Brien, 1988). This contention is sometimes dismissed as irrelevant because "If the groups are different, they are different, and that is what I am trying to find out." Such reasoning would be fine if the only conclusion were going to be whether the Cornish have the same *distribution* as the general population, but the researcher's conclusion is rarely going to be the vague one that the distributions differ or do not differ, but will instead be a much more specific one that the means differ and that they differ in a particular direction.

The example illustrates the principle that other characteristics of the distribution affect not just the probability of concluding that the distributions differ but even the probability that one will make the correct conclusion about the direction in which they differ when they do. This makes the issue of robustness of statistical inferences in the presence of assumption violations a highly salient one because it shows that assumptions we make about one aspect of the data influence the validity of conclusions we make about other aspects.

Confidence Intervals

A test of a hypothesis about a parameter takes the form of assuming the null hypothesis about η is true and on that basis constructing an interval outside of which v will fall $100\alpha\%$ of the time. The confidence interval reverses the process of hypothesis testing, in a sense, although the two have a very close logical relation. Given an obtained value for v and σ_v and some other information about the sampling distribution of v, it constructs an interval around v such that η will fall outside the interval $100\alpha\%$ of the time, assumptions being correct. It is called a $1 - \alpha$ confidence interval because $1 - \alpha$ represents the "confidence" we have that η is in the interval that has been constructed for it. This confidence is in the sense that, of all the c.i. that are constructed, $100(1 - \alpha)\%$ of the time η will be in the interval and $100\alpha\%$ of the time it will not. A c.i. is answering the question, "What values for the parameter cannot be ruled out with this degree of confidence, on the basis of our data?"

One of the surprising aspects of the history of the application of inferential statistics in behavioral science is the reluctance of researchers to adopt the use of confidence intervals. (A few researchers are beginning to supply "error bands" in graphs showing means or similar statistics, which amounts to the same thing as presenting c.i. numerically.) It seems desirable, in the abstract, to be able to report not only the value of a parameter estimate and whether it was significantly different from zero but also the range of alternative values for it that are plausible. Omitting c.i. is particularly puzzling when the presentation of a c.i. makes redundant the reporting of a hypothesis test. It is tempting to speculate on the social influences and cognitive pressures that have led to this preference, but this is not the place to attempt that in any detail. However, one possibility that can be mentioned is that very often the units of a dependent variable are arbitrary, so reporting that a mean difference was 3.2 with a .99 c.i. of 0.5 to 5.9 does not convey any very direct information to the reader. It is true that in some areas the units can be meaningful, for example, if the difference were 3.2 seconds, and sometimes the statistic is unitless, as with a correlation coefficient, where it might seem reasonable to report that $r = .5$ and the .95 c.i. is .10 to .80 for ρ. The fact that c.i. often cannot be given in meaningful units would mean that researchers would have to have two approaches to reporting results: c.i. in situations where units are meaningful or for unitless parameters but only hypothesis testing in others. Experience shows that there are strong social and cognitive currents that work toward having only one procedure that applies in all contexts rather than two that must be applied discriminately. This principle may help explain the lack of popularity of c.i.

Since ordinal methods inherently lack interpretable units, it might be thought that the emphasis in their inferential use would be on hypothesis testing, and this is certainly the case traditionally, but the opposite will tend to be argued here; c.i. will be formulated along with tests of hypothesis as often as possible. The reason is that a unifying theme of the methods presented here is on estimating ordinal parameters, parameters that have quantitative interpretations of the kind that have been suggested in earlier sections. Although the parameters are unitless, they have a ready interpretation of the "proportion of times that . . ." sort. This interpretative context may help communicate the breadth of applicability that the methods are felt to have.

Relative Power, Efficiency, and Robustness
of Ordinal Methods

Theoretical sources on ordinal methods (Hettmansperger, 1984; Hodges & Lehman, 1956; Randles & Wolfe, 1979) provide formal evaluations of the efficacy of ordinal methods compared to classical ones. The most common number used to express this is the asymptotic relative efficiency (A.R.E.) of a statistic compared to a classical counterpart. This can be understood intuitively as the ratio of their standard errors, appropriately scaled, with an indefinitely large sample. The basic figure is reported under conditions most favorable to the classical statistic—that is, its assumptions of normality, and so on, are true; but the A.R.E. can also be reported under other assumptions.

A typical finding (Hettmansperger, 1984; Hodges & Lehman, 1956; Randles & Wolfe, 1979) from these theoretical analyses is that the ordinal statistics have A.R.E. of .90 when the classical assumptions are true. That is, the c.i. based on the ordinal statistic is about 10% wider than that of the classical statistic, assuming that the two can be made comparable. What this means in terms of hypothesis rejection is more complicated to formulate because the relative size of Type II error probabilities will depend on just what the true parameter value is, but the implication is that they will in general be slightly larger for the ordinal method. On the other hand, circumstances under which the A.R.E. is greater than 1.00 can often be identified, and Monte Carlo studies can find that an ordinal method can have greater power than the corresponding classical one (e.g., Fligner & Policello, 1981). The operative, perhaps oversimplified, conclusion seems to be that ordinal methods may sacrifice efficiency or power, but if so, not much, and may often gain it. Therefore, concerns about power and efficiency are at most very mild motives for avoiding ordinal methods.

Another point on the efficiency issue is that these discussions are virtually universally couched in terms of the classical inference being the main object of concern. I argue that the ordinal parameters may themselves be more relevant than their classical counterparts. If so, the question of efficiency or power should be turned around. How good are classical methods at estimating or testing hypotheses about Kendall's τ or the ordinal measure of location difference δ. As far as I know, there are no investigations of this kind, but the point should not be overlooked. When the appropriate calculations are made to convert classical statistics in order to estimate τ or δ, they may or may not be as efficient or powerful as the directly estimated versions t or d.

The robustness issue is generally felt to favor ordinal methods, but this conclusion needs to be examined with some care because there may be circumstances where the opposite is true (Feng & Cliff, 1995; Feng, 1996).

With robustness, the focus has been on performing Monte Carlo studies[1] in which assumptions underlying classical statistics are violated in varying degrees, including not at all. Given that assumptions must be made in order to make inferences using any statistic, including ordinal ones, the validity of those assumptions must be examined, and the extent to which violation of them will affect the inferential process must be considered. We attempt this in several contexts.

One purpose for reviewing the basic aspects of the inference process was to provide a background for this consideration, centering around the properties of the sampling distributions of ordinal statistics. Inferences are made appropriately; that is, Type I and II error rates are controlled in the intended way, insofar as the true sampling distribution of the statistic has the same form as that which is assumed. This means that there should be minimal bias in the statistic as an estimator; the estimate of its standard error should be efficient and itself unbiased; the assumed shape of the sampling distribution (e.g., normal) should accurately reflect the actual shape. Insofar as these principles are not followed, our attempts at inference will be misleading. In many ways, and under many, but not all, circumstances, ordinal statistics offer advantages over the traditional ones.

Alternatives With Presumed Robust Properties

The inferential methods that will be recommended here will center around estimating an ordinal parameter, primarily tau or its location-comparison analogue delta, and its standard error from the sample, rather than by assumption. Then a confidence interval will be constructed for the parameter using the standard error, sometimes with an adjustment to the c.i. that has been found to improve its coverage. This c.i. also provides a test of the hypothesis that τ or δ is zero.

These procedures have been tested extensively through Monte Carlo studies and evaluated by all three criteria: coverage probability of the c.i.

---

[1]A Monte Carlo study attempts to find out the behavior of a statistic by artificial experimentation in cases where mathematical analysis is deemed to be too difficult. Typically, one or more population distributions for one or more random variables, each with specified characteristics or parameters, is assumed. Random samples of specified sizes are drawn from each distribution, typically using computer-generated random numbers, and the values of the variables are recorded. The statistics of interest are calculated for each sample and themselves tabulated into a distribution. That distribution is examined to see its properties. For example, to study the robustness of the t test for independent groups in the presence of heterogeneous variances, two normal distributions with the same means but different variances could be formulated. Pairs of random samples of certain sizes are generated repeatedly, say, 10,000 times, and the t statistic is calculated in each pair. The percentage of samples in which the obtained t exceeds the tabled value for some α can be found. If all is well with the t test, then this percentage will be very close to α.

for a wide variety of parameter values, Type I error probability in the null cases, and power in the non-null. They have been found to behave well, although not always ideally, under a wide variety of distributional assumptions. The specifics of their performance will be discussed in the appropriate chapters that follow.

These procedures, estimating a parameter and using a sample-based estimate of its standard error to construct c.i. and test hypotheses, is an old one in statistics. In recent decades, there has been a movement toward "robust" inferential procedures as ways of improving the performance of traditional methods or close analogues of them, and it may be useful to sketch the reasons for preferring the present methods as inferential tools.

One class of such methods are "resampling" methods, which fall into two types: randomization methods and bootstrap procedures. They have the attractive property of not requiring assumptions about distributional forms, but they do so in two different ways.

The randomization methods form the bases not only of parametric inferences such as mean differences and Pearson correlations but also of the inferential procedures for ordinal statistics that are most commonly encountered outside this book. I prefer the ones described later because I feel that the randomization methods have an applicability that is too limited. Location comparisons, such as mean differences or the Wilcoxon-Mann-Whitney U (Conover, 1981) test, are valid under a wide variety of assumptions about the distributions of the variables, but they are all assuming that the distributions are *identical*, whereas a more realistic concern is that the distributions may differ in more than one characteristic rather than only in location. If that is so, for example if they differ in spread or skewness, then the Type I error probability can be quite different from the nominal alpha level, which is precisely problem that the user may be trying to avoid by using the randomization method.

In the related case of using independence to test for the existence of correlation, the conclusions can be similarly suspect because the variables can be nonindependent in a way that is not reflected by the coefficient being tested, such as there being a curvilinear correlation. In that case, the sampling distribution of the statistic does not have the form that is assumed by the test. Also, with the increased emphasis on estimating effect sizes, it is not clear how one employs the randomization or independence-testing in non-null cases such as to form c.i. Thus, I feel that randomization methods are only applicable under a narrow range of circumstances, whereas my goal is to describe methods that I think have very wide application.

The other main kind of resampling method is the bootstrap (Efron, 1982). In it, the sample is treated as a population, and samples are repeatedly drawn, with replacement, from this pseudopopulation. The value of the statistic that is of interest, such as a mean, mean difference, or correlation, is calculated in each of these bootstrap samples, and they are tabulated into a frequency distribution. Percentiles of that distribution are then used as a basis for inferences about the parameter that is of interest.

While enthusiasm for these methods has been great, experience suggests that they are not as efficacious as had been hoped. Wilcox (1991) shows, for example, that there are common situations where bootstrap inferences about Pearson r do not have the properties one would like, and Westfall and Young (1993) give reason to doubt their applicability in the case of location comparisons. Thus, the hope that the computer could substitute for thought may not be any more applicable here than it has proved to be elsewhere.

Another possibility for those seeking robustness in their statistical inferences, epitomized by Wilcox (1996), emphasizes methods that use some form of differential data-weighting. There are many variations on these methods, but a simplified description is that the more deviant values receive less weight in determining the estimator than the more central ones. It is true that these methods can behave more stably than their traditional counterparts, particularly when there are outliers in the population, but I feel they do so at some descriptive cost. This can be thought of as changing the population distribution that has been sampled. A trimmed mean or variance is estimating the mean or variance of a distribution where the density or probability of the more extreme values has been reduced, not that of the original distribution; that can even be the point of the process.

This may not be a serious difference in the case of, say, the mean, when the distribution is symmetric; the mean of the new distribution is the same as that of the original one. The consequences are more significant when the distribution is asymmetric. Then, the new distribution is more symmetric than the original; the longer tail is shortened more than the shorter one. This moves the mean of the distribution is shifted toward the mode, making the result a biased estimate of the mean of the original population.

It can be argued that such effects are desirable. Not only will a trimmed mean have a smaller standard error when the original distribution is leptokurtic, but it is likely to be closer to the "important part" of the original distribution. On the other hand, it can be argued that all the observations are equally important, so they should have equal weight in providing estimates of their central tendency. There are enough influences that tend to keep the most deviant observations out of our data without introducing such principles into our statistical analysis. In addition, the best-behaved variations on these methods can be extremely complex (Wilcox, 1996).

The ordinal methods that are recommended in this book are based on a "one observation, one vote" principle. Not only do all members of the sample have equal influence on the statistic, but all members of the population thus have equal probability of influence. Furthermore, the procedures on which they are based usually avoid by their very nature the possibility of overinfluence by extreme values.

Considering the alternatives of resampling methods and "robustified" estimation procedures, the ordinal methods stand up very well as inferential as well as descriptive tools. As will be described in later chapters, they have been evaluated with a wide variety of populations, and their performance has been good as judged by all three criteria: size in null cases, power in non-null ones, and coverage under all circumstances.

CONCLUSION

Motives for Ordinal Statistics

This book is based on the premise that statistical analysis is a facet of the scientific enterprise, and as such its procedures should conform to basic principles of scientific practice. A scientist wants to find out what is "out there" in the real world on the basis of what is "in here" in the data. The conclusions from the data should reflect the real world as accurately as possible. A feature of scientific practice that is crucially important to maximizing this correspondence is that the conclusions are subject to critique by skeptical and knowledgeable colleagues who attempt to offer alternative explanations of or conclusions from the data. The skill of the scientist in large part lies in his or her ability to perform the research in such a way as to minimize the number and plausibility of these alternative explanations.

The contention here is that ordinal statistics can increase the scientific value of much of our research in this regard, and certain ordinal methods and approaches are emphasized over others because I feel that they are the most likely to enhance that scientific value. The three classes of reasons for ordinal methods that were cited at the outset fall under this rubric. First, if we make an ordinal conclusion, it should be based on ordinal characteristics of the data. For example, the skeptical colleague could say, "Just because you found that the mean of As is higher than the mean of Bs does not necessarily imply that As generally score higher than Bs, which was your conclusion." If we have a direct statistical description of the extent to which As do score higher than Bs, then we can dismiss that contention.

Similarly, if our analysis has been a parametric one that assumes interval scales, then the critic could say, "A different, but equally defensible, version of that variable might have led to different conclusions," or that the relation on the latent variables might be different from that on their monotonically related observed versions. Such criticisms cannot apply when the analysis is ordinal.

There are like considerations with respect to the inferential uncertainties. An inferential conclusion is always with respect to some parameter of the distributions, typically means or other measures of location or some measure of correlation. To a greater or less degree, these conclusions about location or correlation are conditional on assumptions about other characteristics of the distributions: variances and higher moments, cross-moments in the case of correlations. Thus, a critic could assert that the statistical significance of a finding about location or correlation has been substantially distorted by incorrect assumptions about these variances or higher moments. A finding significant at a given level would not have been significant if appropriate side assumptions had been made, or a finding that is not significant would have been. Therefore, methods that seem to be less sensitive to these uncertainties are preferable to those that are more.

Ordinal statistical methods of the kinds described here have advantages over parametric ones of all three kinds in a wide spectrum of research contexts, although admittedly not all. Thus, their employment would often result in research that is more nearly in the ideal scientific mold.

Quantification of Results

An additional principle of science is that quantified conclusions are preferable to qualitative ones. The world is complex. If our scientific goal is to have the conclusions correspond as closely to the external world as possible, then quantification of conclusions can provide a closer match than simple qualitative ones: "the locations differ" or "correlation exists." This consideration manifests itself in all three of the motives discussed. We want our quantification of conclusions to be relatively immune to criticisms, and the details of our quantified conclusions are likely to stand up better if they are ordinally based.

This also means that the emphasis here is on ordinal statistical methods that are amenable to such quantification. Thus, the statistics employed have direct quantitative meanings and do not merely serve as vehicles for the detection of qualitative results, which is usually the emphasis when texts describe ordinal methods. This means that our whole approach is to assume that ordinal measures exist as characteristics of populations and that their sample versions are estimates of those population characteristics. Therefore, the principles of sampling distribution theory apply to them: When we test hypotheses, we try to do so in ways that reflect the aspects of the population distributions that are mathematically known to affect the sampling behavior of the estimates in a broad range of situations, rather than assuming some special properties—such as independence, randomization, or identical distributions—that a reasonably skeptical person would doubt are applicable.

This approach has a positive advantage as well. It allows the construction of confidence intervals for the population parameter. This is a further step toward quantification of the results over just reporting the sample value and whether it was significantly different from zero because it provides the range of plausible values for the parameter. Where this is broad, it shows that the parameter's value is not very well known, and where it is narrow it shows that the population value is closely estimated. That is, it shows, in a sense, how much true quantification there is in the conclusions.

The scarcity of programs to perform ordinal analyses has been mentioned here as one of the reasons for their lack of use, particularly in the ways that are recommended in this book. As a step in remedying this lack, simple programs for doing many of he analyses have been written by co-workers and me. At the time of writing, they are available via the Internet using the following commands from an Internet terminal:

```
ftp usc.edu
password:anonymous
cd\pub
cd\ordinal
```

The list of program files is fairly self-explanatory.

The range of statistics covered in this book is not broad. It is not a handbook in the sense of Siegel and Castellan (1989) or Conover (1980). However, I hope that the reader finds that this rather narrow coverage of basic statistical techniques can have surprisingly broad application, providing substitutes not only for the most common procedures such as t tests and correlations but for many of their extensions as well.

Limitations

These ordinal methods are not optimum in all situations. Some researchers have the good fortune to work with variables that are so precisely defined and controlled that statistical analysis of the usual kind mainly serves to demonstrate how irrelevant it is. Some data is explained by elegant mathematical models[2] whose fit is so close that quarreling is quibbling. Some variables are so precisely measured and have demonstrated such close relations in the past that their status as measurement scales is without question. These ordinal methods are not needed in research that fits those criteria. However, it is safe to say that a large segment of attempts at behavioral, and even biological, science do not meet those criteria. The methods here can be applied in a variety of those situations, although some ingenuity may be required.

---

[2]It should be clear that "models" fit to covariance matrices or to cross-tabulated frequencies are not likely to meet the criteria presented here. Indeed, the virtual certainty of the failure of such models to fit by statistical criteria often can be interpreted as reflecting the fact that the variables used in them do not have the characteristics that such a model would require if indeed it was a valid description of the behavior of the variables. Those who apply such models seem often to display a virtual disregard for the principle of science that has been applied here. Ruling out alternative explanations of the data is seemingly a very remote concern to them.

2

Ordinal Correlation

WHAT DO WE MEAN BY ORDINAL CORRELATION?

When trying to give an intuitive explanation of correlation, one frequently resorts to formulations such as, "It is a measure of the extent to which two sets of scores are in the same order." Of course, in the case of Pearson correlation, that is not exactly what a correlation represents. A more accurate verbal description would be that it is a measure of the similarity of standard scores on the two variables, similarity being measured as the average product of standard scores. However, even that description suffers from the usual discrepancy between a verbal description and the numerical operations that go into a formula. One of the advantages of ordinal approaches to correlation is that they provide a closer match between the intuitive verbal description of correlation as similarity of order and the numerical operations that go into the quantification of degree of relation, which is what we are trying to do with a correlation coefficient.

There are two approaches to measuring correlation ordinally: Kendall's tau (τ) and Spearman's rho (ρ_S). The former is based on counting the number of times that pairs of things are in the same versus opposite order on both variables, and the latter converts the scores to ranks and computes a Pearson correlation between the ranks. In some ways, τ seems ordinal in a "purer" sense because ρ_S converts the data to ranks and then does arithmetic on the ranks, but in a pragmatic sense ρ_S seems often to work well. Most of the methods described in this book are based on τ because of its closer conformity to the idea of ordinal analysis and because its theoretical properties are much simpler to investigate, but some attention will be devoted to ρ_S.

KENDALL'S TAU

Definition of Tau

Tau is a literal translation of the verbal statement that correlation represents the proportion of times a pair of subjects will be in the same versus opposite order on both variables:

$$\tau = \Pr[(x_i > x_h) \text{ and } (y_i > y_h)] - \Pr[(x_i > x_h) \text{ and } (y_i < y_h)]. \qquad (2.1)$$

That is, if x_i is higher than x_h, τ is the proportion of times that the corresponding Y scores, y_i and y_h, are in the same order minus the probability that they are in the opposite order. When there are only a finite number of elements in a population, the probabilities can be translated into counts: the number of pairs in the same order on both variables minus the number in the opposite order, the difference being divided by the number of pairs.

There are ways of reinforcing this definition in terms of the amount of discordance between two orders. Suppose the scores on X are 1 2 3 4. If the scores on Y are 5 6 7 8—same order—then this represents complete agreement, and a sensible coefficient will equal 1.00, and τ does have this value here. This can be illustrated concretely by looking at all the possible pairs, as in the following table, where all 12 possible pairs are listed, and a + means that the first member of the pair has a score higher than the second on that variable, and a − means the opposite:

i,h	1,2	1,3	1,4	2,3	2,4	3,4	2,1	3,1	4,1	3,2	4,2	4,3
$x_i > x_h$	−	−	−	−	−	−	+	+	+	+	+	+
$y_i > y_h$	−	−	−	−	−	−	+	+	+	+	+	+
conc.	+	+	+	+	+	+	+	+	+	+	+	+

The last line of the table, "concordance," uses a + to indicate that the two signs for the X and Y comparisons are the same, and would use a − if they were opposite. It is clear that, when a pair is selected at random in this example, the direction of difference will always be the same on both variables, so by the definition τ should equal 1.0. If, on the other hand, the scores on Y were 8 7 6 5—opposite order to X—all the minus signs in the Y line of the table would change to +, and all the + to −, and the "conc." line changes to all −. Complete disagreement should result in $\tau = -1.0$, and it does here because every pair we sample will be in the opposite order on both variables and have negative concordance.

Two other things are illustrated by the table. One is that there are $4 \times 3 = n(n-1)$ pairs. The second thing is the complete redundancy of the right and left halves of the table; whenever $x_i > x_h$, $x_h < x_i$, and the same is true for Y, so that whenever signs are in agreement for i versus h, they are in agreement for h versus i; when they disagree for i versus h, they will disagree for h versus i. This means that for most purposes it is only necessary to consider half the table. Also, in many contexts it is convenient to think of the scores on one variable being in the natural order, as X is here, so that the entries for it are always +. Even though data usually does not come that way, it is often simpler to present things as if it were true, and there is no harm in doing so because one can always start by ordering the xs.

Tau and the Number of Interchanges

A concrete way of interpreting the amount of disorder in two variables is to count the number of steps that would have to be taken to bring them into the same order. Consider our 8 7 6 5 versus 1 2 3 4. We want to turn the 8 7 6 5 into 5 6 7 8 by *interchanging adjacent elements* one step at a time and counting the number of steps it takes. If it takes a lot of steps, compared to the maximum number possible, the similarity of the orders is low or even negative; if few, then it is positive. We can accomplish our goal here by first interchanging 8 and 7, giving *7 8* 6 5; then 8 and 6: 7 *6 8* 5; then 8 and 5: 7 6 *5 8*. Now we can work on 7: 6 *6 7 5 8*; 6 *5 7* 8. One final exchange brings them into the same order as X: 5 6 7 8. Going back and counting steps, we find that it took six interchanges. This is an example of the general principle that the maximum number of interchanges of adjacent elements necessary to bring two orders into agreement is $n(n - 1)/2$, in this case $4 \times 3/2 = 6$.

Complete ordinal agreement, $\tau = 1.0$, means that the number of interchanges necessary is zero. Complete ordinal disagreement, $\tau = -1.0$, means that the number of interchanges necessary is the maximum, $n(n - 1)/2$. If we let S equal the number of interchanges, in general

$$\tau = \frac{[n(n - 1)/4] - S}{\frac{1}{2}n(n - 1)} \tag{2.2}$$

These meanings of τ can be illustrated with an intermediate example. Suppose that the scores on on a third variable Z are 7 5 8 6. Then the table of relations, now using only the right half, is

i,h	2,1	3,1	4,1	3,2	4,2	4,3
$x_i > x_h$	+	+	+	+	+	+
$z_i > z_h$	−	+	−	+	+	−
conc.	−	+	−	+	+	−

Note that, since all the entries in the x row are +, the conc. row is always the same as the Z row. Counting plus and minus signs, we find $(3 - 3)/6$, so

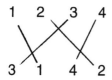

FIG. 2.1. Illustration of computing tau via S by counting intersecting lines.

$\tau = 0$. Similarly, three interchanges are necessary to bring the scores into ascending order. One way to do this is *5 7 8 6*, followed by 5 7 *6 8*, followed by 5 *6 7* 8.

A simple, scratchpad method for finding S when there are only a few scores, without listing all the pairs, is to start by assigning ranks to x and to Z. In this example, these would be 1 2 3 4 and 3 1 4 2. Now, write one set of ranks under the other and draw lines connecting the corresponding digits, 1 to 1, 2 to 2, and so on, as in Fig. 2.1. Then count the number of times one line intersects another. The number of line intersections is S! This method only works well with up to 10 or so observations because it becomes hard to see how many intersections there are when there are many lines to draw.

Dominance Variables and Tau

A numerical way of defining τ is in terms of the signs of differences. This is a process that will be used repeatedly in this book. Let

$$d_{ihx} = \text{sign}(x_i - x_h), \tag{2.3}$$

where $\text{sign}(\cdot) = 1$ if the difference is positive, $\text{sign}(\cdot) = -1$ if it is negative, and $\text{sign}(\cdot) = 0$ if it is zero. This is called a "dominance" variable; it assigns a value of 1, -1, or 0 to every pair of observations on x. The corresponding thing can be done with Y. Then, for a finite set of scores,

$$\tau_{xy} = \frac{\sum_{\text{pairs}} d_{ihx} d_{ihy}}{\#(\text{pairs})}, \tag{2.4}$$

where $\#(\cdot)$ means "the number of." An equivalent alternative to (2.4) is

$$\tau_{xy} = E(d_{ihx} d_{ihy}). \tag{2.5}$$

In theoretical discussions, the expected value form (2.5) is generally the more convenient form to use (and is necessary when the number of pairs is potentially infinite), whereas sometimes the more literal multiplication process of (2.4) is more representative, particularly when dealing with sample data.

   The description of τ in terms of dominance variables sometimes leaves the impresssion that the value it takes is not affected by the degree to which a score is misplaced in one order, relative to its place in the other, but only by whether or not it is misplaced. A little thought leads to the conclusion that that is not really the case. If a Y score's rank is much different from its rank on X, then it will be a member of many pairs whose difference has opposite sign on the two variables. If its rank is not much different, then there will be only a few such pairs. In the same sense, from the interchange perspective, it would take numerous interchanges to get the highly discrepant value into the same position on both variables, whereas, with a small difference in ranks, only a few will be necessary. Thus, tau reflects degree of discrepancy in the ranks of scores, not just presence or absence of discrepancy.

   Another useful definition is a score for the concordance of a pair:

$$t_{ihxy} = d_{ihx}d_{ihy}. \tag{2.6}$$

This variable indicates whether the pair i,h is in the same $(t_{ihxy} = 1)$ or the opposite $(t_{ihxy} = -1)$ order on the variables or is tied on one or both $(t_{ihxy} = 0)$. For some purposes, it is useful to arrange the d_{ih} and t_{ih} into square matrices. For example, Table 2.1 shows d_{ihx}, and d_{ihz} and then t_{ihxz}. The t_{ih} matrices are always symmetric, and the d_{ih} are always skew-symmetric, $d_{ih} = -d_{hi}$, and both have zero diagonals. One way to imagine constructing the t_{ih} is to overlay one d_{ih} on the other; the t_{ih} are the products of the corresponding elements.

Treatment of Ties

The presence of ties on one or both variables can be dealt with in a number of ways, depending on what interpretation or purpose is dominant in the analysis. Some of these variations can be formulated by adaptations of the probability definition (2.1), but others cannot.

TABLE 2.1
Illustration of d_{ih} and t_{ih} Matrices

i \ h	\multicolumn{5}{c}{d_{ihx}}					\multicolumn{5}{c}{d_{ihy}}					\multicolumn{5}{c}{t_{ihxy}}				
	1	2	3	4	5	1	2	3	4	5	1	2	3	4	5
1	0	−1	−1	−1	−1	0	1	−1	−1	−1	0	−1	1	1	1
2	1	0	−1	−1	−1	−1	0	−1	−1	−1	−1	0	1	1	1
3	1	1	0	−1	−1	1	1	0	1	−1	1	1	0	−1	1
4	1	1	1	0	−1	1	1	−1	0	−1	1	1	−1	0	1
5	1	1	1	1	0	1	1	1	1	0	1	1	1	1	0

$$t_{xy} = (16-4)/20 = .60$$

The simplest approach, and the one followed most often here, is to retain the simple probability definition (2.1) and its counterparts defined in terms of dominances, (2.4) and (2.5), whether there are ties or not. This version is called τ_a (Kendall, 1970). In a concrete sense, and in samples, it still simply represents the probability of being in the same order on both variables minus the probability of being opposite. When a pair is tied on one or both variables, it meets neither condition. Thus when there are ties τ_a cannot attain the $-1,1$ limits, but can only reach the proportion of pairs not tied on either variable.

A second form is usually called Somers' d (Somers, 1968), but we have too many other uses for that letter, and it is desirable to retain notation that recognizes that these are all forms of tau, so here it will be called τ_d. It is particularly relevant in the context of predicting order relations on a dependent variable Y from order relations on a predictor X. Pairs that are tied on Y are removed from consideration. The probability definition is the same as τ_a except that it is made conditional on not being tied on Y:

$$\tau_{dyx} = \Pr[(x_i > x_h \text{ and } y_i > y_h) \,|\, y_i \neq y_h]$$
$$- \Pr[(x_i > x_h \text{ and } y_i < y_h) \,|\, y_i \neq y_h]. \tag{2.7}$$

In the definition of tau using dominance variables, (2.4), the numerator stays the same, but since τ_d focuses on agreement in Y, eliminating the pairs that are tied on Y can be accomplished by using $\Sigma\Sigma d_{ihy}^2$ in the denominator, so τ_{dyx} can be expressed as

$$\tau_{dyx} = \frac{\Sigma\Sigma d_{ihx} d_{ihy}}{\Sigma\Sigma d_{ihy}^2}. \tag{2.8}$$

Both sums, as usual, run over all pairs.

What τ_d is saying is, "Among the pairs that are not tied on Y, how often are there differences in the same, as opposed to opposite, direction on X and Y?" That is, how often can the direction of difference on Y, when there is one, be predicted from the direction of difference on X? There is, of course, a τ_{dxy} as well, where now the conditionality refers to being not tied on X. While both have the same numerator, the two are not equal unless the number of ties is the same on both.

A more extreme approach to ties is to eliminate consideration of pairs that are tied on either variable. This is done in the coefficient called, in the context of categorical variables "the Goodman–Kruskal γ" (Goodman & Kruskal, 1954, 1959), but it was originally introduced by Yule (1900) and designated Q. Since it is a special form of τ, we refer to it as τ_Q. It can be expressed in the probability sense as

$$\tau_Q = \Pr[(x_i > x_h \text{ and } y_i > y_h) \mid (x_i \neq x_h \text{ and } y_i \neq y_h)]$$
$$- \Pr[(x_i > x_h \text{ and } y_i < y_h) \mid (x_i \neq x_h \text{ and } y_i \neq y_h)]. \qquad (2.9)$$

In dominance variables, it is

$$\tau_Q = \frac{\Sigma d_{ihx} d_{ihy}}{\Sigma d_{ihx}^2 d_{ihy}^2}. \qquad (2.10)$$

This coefficient is often applied to dichotomous variables, where there are, of course, a large number of ties. For two such variables, for example, dichotomous test or questionnaire items X and Y, it is often convenient to think of the data as being organized into a 2×2 table, as follows, where a, b, c, d represent the frequencies of combinations of scores on the two items.

	Item Y		
Item X	*Right*	*Wrong*	*Total*
Right	a	b	$a + b$
Wrong	c	d	$c + d$
Total	$a + c$	$b + d$	n

The scores on each variable can be defined as either "right" or "wrong." Then, a person with a score of "right" on an item dominates every person who gets a score of "wrong" on it. In the table, a represents the number of persons who are "right" on both items; b is the number scoring "right" on X and "wrong" on Y; c is the reverse; and d is "wrong" on both. The totals giving each response are given in the marginals on the right and at the bottom.

The value of τ_Q is readily computed from the table. The proportion of pairs in the same order on both variables is ad because a person who is right on both items compared to a person wrong on both are in the same relation on both items. There are a persons of the first kind and d of the second, so ad is the number of pairs that are ordered the same on both items. Similar reasoning leads to bc as the number of pairs ordered oppositely by the two items because everyone in the b cell dominates everyone in c on X, whereas the reverse happens on Y. The number of pairs that are ordered by both items is $ad + bc$, so $\tau_Q = (ad - bc)/(ad + bc)$. These simplifications occur when both variables are dichotomous, although τ_Q has generality beyond that situation.

For dichotomies, τ_{dxy} and τ_{dyx} will have the same numerators as τ_Q but different denominators. In dichotomous items, the number of untied pairs on X is $(a + b)(c + d)$, whereas the number not tied on Y is $(a + c)(b + d)$, so, in predicting Y from X, $\tau_{dyx} = (ad - bc)/(a + c)(b + d)$, whereas, predicting

X from Y, $\tau_{dxy} = (ad - bc)/(a + b)(c + d)$. On the items, we can think of ad as the number of concordant (or consistent or consonant or confirmatory) pairs and bc as the number of inconsistent (discordant or dissonant or contradictory) ones. If the items are presumed to measure the same latent variable, such as an ability or an attitude, then it may be useful to think of the person–person relations that are provided by each item, considered in relation to each other item, as falling into one of these two categories, consistent or inconsistent. However, there is a third category for each item, namely the number pairs that are ordered by that item but not by the other. We can call these relations *unique* to that item. In dichotomies, the count of unique relations is available from the 2×2 table as well: For X it is $ac + bd$, and for Y it is $ab + cd$. Thus, the $(a + b)(c + d)$ dominance relations provided by X can be partitioned into ad that are consistent with Y, bc that are inconsistent with Y, and $ac + bd$ that are unique to X. Y has the same ad consistent relations and bc inconsistent, but $ab + cd$ that are unique to it.

The variants on τ described so far can be restated in another family of formulas. Following a system like one suggested by Freeman (1986) and a similar one by Gonzalez and Nelson (1996), let $c = \#$ consistent pairs, $i = \#$ inconsistent pairs, $u_x = \#$ pairs tied on Y but not x, $u_y = \#$ pairs tied on x but not Y, and $v = \#$ pairs tied on both. Then $c + i + u_x + u_y + v = \frac{1}{2}n(n - 1)$, the total number of pairs. The numerator of any form of tau is $c - i$, and the denominator of τ_a is the sum of all five terms. The denominator of τ_{dyx} is $c + i + u_y$, and for τ_{dxy} it is $c + i + u_x$. In the case of τ_Q, it is $c + i$.

A form of tau with a different treatment of ties is called τ_b. It is based on an attempted analogy to the Pearson correlation:

$$\tau_b = \frac{\Sigma d_{ihx} d_{ihy}}{\sqrt{\Sigma d_{ihx}^2 d_{ihy}^2}} . \tag{2.11}$$

That is, it is a correlation coefficient computed between dominance scores and so has the "cosine of angle between vectors" interpretation, which is a property of Pearson correlation, but here the vectors are the vectors of dominance scores. τ_b has the same numerator as the other versions, but in dichotomies its denominator is $[(a + b)(c + d)(a + c)(b + d)]^{1/2}$ but, more generally, $[(c + i + u_x)(c + i + u_y)]^{1/2}$.

However, τ_b loses any interpretation in terms of the proportion or probability of consistent relations shared by the others that have been discussed. To me, this is a poor trade-off for its cosine of angle between vectors of dominances property. Using τ_b suggests a desire to make numerical interpretations that are of dubious validity, particularly in the multivariate contexts where it is often applied. For example, it tends to support such notions as computing partial taus. These are potentially misleading, as discussed later.

The fact that the numerators of all these forms of tau are the same and their denominators consist of various combinations of the five terms means that τ_Q is always the largest of the coefficients, followed by one of the τ_d, then τ_b because its denominator is the geometric mean of the two denominators for the τ_d, then the other τ_d, and τ_a is always the smallest.

Still another version of tau is called τ_c (Stuart, 1953). It was designed for application to cross-tabulations of ordered categorical variables. In that situation, the limits that τ_a can attain are constrained when the number of categories on the two variables is unequal. τ_c tries to remove that constraint, but it does so in only a limited way. It is therefore not recommended for use (Freeman, 1986), and it is not discussed further here.

There are, then, a number of ways of adjusting τ in the presence of ties. Most of them, τ_a, τ_d, and τ_Q, permit a "proportion of pairs in the same direction" interpretation, with the latter two adjusting the basepool from which the proportion is drawn. τ_b is an attempt to extend the analogy between tau and product–moment correlations, an analogy that I feel is is most often a misplaced one.

Illustration

The differences among the forms of τ can be illustrated with a short example. Table 2.2 shows the scores of five cases on two variables, followed by the dominance scores for the 10 pairs. Three scores are tied on X, and there are two sets of two ties on Y. The numerator of τ is the same for all forms, but the denominator is $n(n-1)/2 = 10$ for τ_a, $8 = 10 - 2$ for τ_{dYX} (Y from X), $7 = 10 - 3$ for τ_{dXY} (X from Y), $6 = 10 - 4$ for τ_Q (one pair is tied on both x and Y), and $7.48 = \sqrt{7 \times 8}$ for τ_b.

Which of the forms of τ one chooses to use is a matter of what one prefers to convey. If one wishes to describe the proportion of *all* pairs that are ordered the same way by both variables, τ_a is appropriate. If one wishes to

TABLE 2.2
Illustration of Adjustments of τ for Ties

	i	1	2	3	4	5					
	X	4	6	6	6	9					
	Y	4	3	3	4	6					
i,h	1,2	1,3	1,4	1,5	2,3	2,4	2,5	3,4	3,5	4,5	Σd^2
d_{ihx}	1	1	1	1	0	0	1	0	1	1	7
d_{ihy}	-1	-1	0	1	0	1	1	1	1	1	8
t_{ih}	-1	-1	0	1	0	0	1	0	1	1	6

$\tau_a = 2/10 = .20$; $\tau_{dyx} = 2/8 = .25$; $\tau_{dxy} = .29$; $\tau_q = 2/6 = .33$; $\tau_b = 2/(7 \times 8)^{1/2} = .27$.

limit the consideration to those pairs that are ordered rather than tied on one of the variables, then τ_d, based on that variable, is the choice. If a measure of agreement in ordinal information is preferred, then τ_Q seems like the best choice because it is saying, "Insofar as there are ordinal relations on both variables, this is how well they agree." If one is fond of the "cosine of the angle" interpretation, then she or he would use τ_b.

Of all the possibilities, τ_a is most often used in this book. One reason is that it is the simplest; no conditionalizing clause is required in its probabilistic description. Experience with conditional probabilities of any kind indicates that our minds are not well-adapted to conditional statements. A related reason is that it is also by far the easiest to work with in developing inferential methods. So, from this point on an unsubscripted τ refers to τ_a.

τ and ρ

Most of the experience with correlations that a researcher has is with Pearson coefficients, so it may be useful to compare τ and ρ in various ways. One of the many formulas for the sample correlation coefficient is the one based on standard scores:

$$r_{xy} = \frac{\sum z_{ix} z_{iy}}{n-1}, \tag{2.12}$$

where $z_{ix} = (x_i - m_x)/s_x$; that is, the deviation of the score from the sample mean is divided by the sample standard deviation—in other words, the deviation from the mean expressed in standard deviation units. A seeming peculiarity of τ is that it is based on pairs of scores rather than the scores themselves, but another way to express r_{xy} is in terms of pairs of scores also:

$$r_{xy} = \frac{\sum\limits_{i<h}\sum (z_{ix} - z_{hx})(z_{iy} - z_{hy})}{n(n-1)}. \tag{2.13}$$

That is, r is half the average product of z-score differences.[1] No one uses this formula because it leads to $(n-1)/2$ times as many multiplications as (2.12), but it has conceptual uses, as in the present case. We can think of ρ as representing the average product of differences in z scores, whereas τ represents the average product of signs of differences. It is as if the directions

---

[1]The factor of one-half is hidden in the formula by the fact that the sum is over half the pairs in the numerator, but $n(n-1)$ is used in the denominator.

of difference, represented by the dominance scores, were being weighted in ρ by the amounts of the differences. We make use of the idea behind (2.13) in the later chapter on predicting dominances.

There is no way to "get a feel for" taus without seeing a lot of them in data, but a general idea of what to expect of an unfamiliar coefficient may be useful. Although there is no direct mathematical relation between r and the sample counterpart of τ, t, the two tend to be similar in magnitude, with t usually a bit closer to zero. If one were dealing with a bivariate normal population in which the Pearson correlation was ρ, it turns out that (Daniels & Kendall, 1947; Kendall, 1970)

$$\tau = \frac{2}{\pi} \sin^{-1} \rho. \qquad (2.14)$$

That is, τ is the angle, in radians, whose sine is ρ, multiplied by the factor $2/\pi$. This relation is illustrated in Fig. 2.2. In practice, (2.14) means that τ tends to be about two-thirds of ρ over the range of moderate values that are usually found in data, remembering that $\tau = 1$ when $\rho = 1$ so that the two coefficients have to get closer at the extremes. With sample data, this relation provides a reasonable guide on what to expect *when the data distributions are roughly normal*. The possibility of outliers or long tails or marked skewing or very flat distributions makes this generalization a very

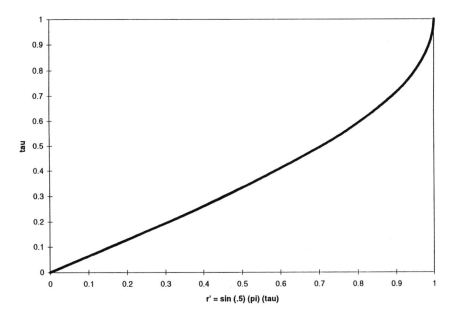

FIG. 2.2. Relation between τ and Pearson ρ in normal populations.

tentative one, and the two coefficients can sometimes be quite different, need not have the same sign, and tau can even be the larger of the two. The only purpose of the foregoing rough generalization is to give an idea of what to expect.

If a person has developed a familiarity with the typical size of correlations in a research domain and then looks at some corresponding taus, the perceptual principle called "adaptation level" tends to make the person feel that the taus are low. For example, $r = .6$ may correspond to $t = .4$. Since correlations are often disappointingly low anyway, a coefficient that tends to make them look even lower may not be very attractive. It may help one's attitude toward tau to think of it, since it is based on a proportion of congruent relations, as more directly analogous to r^2, a proportion of variance, than it is to r. Thus, the t of .4 is better compared to the r^2 of .36.

PARTIAL TAU?

Partial Correlation

One occasionally encounters applications of or references to a "partial tau," so it may be well to describe what is meant, even though this coefficient is not recommended here because it turns out that this superficially attractive concept has a more questionable basis, and a different interpretation, than is often implied. It shares few of the properties of the partial Pearson correlation on which it is modeled and whose formula resembles its own.

The formula for the partial Pearson correlation between Y and Z, partialing out X, is

$$\rho_{YZ \cdot X} = \frac{\rho_{YZ} - \rho_{XY}\rho_{XZ}}{[(1 - \rho_{XY}^2)(1 - \rho_{XZ}^2)]^{1/2}} . \tag{2.15}$$

(In samples, the formula has the same form, with rs substituted for ρs.) The role of X is sometimes referred to as being a "control" variable, but in purely correlational data this is an exaggeration of its role.

This formula has two meanings, one general and one specific. The general one is that it is the correlation between residual Ys and residual Zs. That is, Y and Z are each regressed on X, and their deviations from their respective linear regression lines are found. Then the correlation between these two sets of residuals is calculated; that correlation is $\rho_{YZ \cdot X}$. The general interpretation of partial correlation is thus that it is the correlation between deviations from regression on the control variable, not necessarily that it is the correlation between Y and Z controlling for X in the stronger sense of holding X constant.

Partial correlation does have the stronger interpretation of correlation, holding X constant, under some circumstances. The clearest one is where the three variables have a trivariate normal distribution. Under that circumstance, the partial correlation formula gives the value of ρ_{YZ} that would be obtained at *any fixed value* of X. Thus, it is indeed the correlation between Y and Z, controlling for X in the strong sense of holding it constant. This narrower, stronger interpretation holds literally under normality, a property that is very rarely present, even approximately, for behavioral variables.

Other circumstances where partial correlation has this strong interpretation are imaginable, but extremely unlikely to be encountered in practice. It is possible to calculate the correlation between Y and Z for a given constant value of X. (If X is finely graded, it might be necessary to deal with a short interval on X.) This would literally be a "correlation between Y and Z, holding X constant." Then the values of such correlations could be averaged across different Xs, presumably weighted by the probability of each X value or interval on X to give a summary number. It is very unlikely that that number will equal the one that results from the standard formula. (It was inaccurate for me to suggest this interpretation in Cliff, 1987.) However, if the correlation between Y and Z really is constant, regardless of the value of X, then the two correlations, one computed by the formula and one computed by averaging the r_{YZ} that occur at different values of X, will be pretty close. However, for most data, not only will there be a range of different $r_{YZ \cdot X}$, depending on the value of X, but their average will deviate from that computed by (2.15). Thus, $\rho_{YZ \cdot X}$ has two kinds of interpretations: (1) a generally applicable one that it is the correlation between deviations from the regressions of Y on X and Z on X, and (2) the one that is more rarely applicable, that it is the correlation between Y and Z at any constant value of X.

Formulation of Partial Tau

Kendall (1970) proposed a partial tau on the basis of an analogy between a correlations between residuals from regression and a correlation between t_{ih}s, the ternary variables that can be considered the elements that make up a tau. That is, given the ordinal relations t_{ihXY} and t_{ihXZ} of two variables Y and Z with a third (control) variable X, what is the (Pearson) correlation of t_{ihXY} with t_{ihXZ}? This coefficient is what has been called partial tau. After some algebra, the formula for partial tau turns out to look like a partial Pearson:

$$\tau_{YZ \cdot X} = \frac{\tau_{YZ} - \tau_{XY}\tau_{XZ}}{[(1 - \tau_{XY}^2)(1 - \tau_{XZ}^2)]^{1/2}} \cdot \tag{2.16}$$

The resemblance is an algebraic accident; in my view, it is an unfortunate one because it has led to mistaken interpretations and applications of partial tau. However, as far as I know, this has not resulted in any serious injury—physical injury, at least. The reasons (2.16) works out this way lie in the nature of Pearson correlation and how we get t_{ih}. One of the formulas into which the Pearson correlation can be translated is the ratio of the covariance to the product of the standard deviations. The covariance between variables U and V is $E(UV) - E(U)E(V)$, but in partial tau it is t_{ihXY} and t_{ihXZ} that are in the roles of U and V. $E[(t_{ihXY})(t_{ihXZ})] = E[(d_{ihX}d_{ihY})(d_{ihX}d_{ihZ})]$, but the latter expression can be rearranged into $E(d_{ihX}^2 d_{ihY} d_{ihZ})$, which in turn is $E(d_{ihY}d_{ihZ})$, or τ_{YZ}, because $d_{ihY}^2 = 1.0$. Also, $E(t_{ihXY}) = \tau_{XY}$, and $E(t_{ihXZ}) = \tau_{XZ}$. Putting these relations together, we can see that the covariance between t_{ihXY} and t_{ihXZ} is $\tau_{YZ} - \tau_{XY}\tau_{XZ}$. By similar reasoning, it can be shown that the variances of t_{ihXZ} and t_{ihXY}, viewed as random variables, are $1 - \tau_{XZ}^2$ and $1 - \tau_{XY}^2$, respectively, so we arrive at the previous expression for partial tau. It is a Pearson correlation between t_{ihXZ} and t_{ihXY}. Note its hybrid nature: a Pearson correlation between t_{ih}s. Although there is also a sense in which $\tau_{YZ\cdot X}$ relates to the probability that dominances on Y and Z agree, given that $d_{ihX} = 1$, this sense is a complex one.

It seems rather strange to make use of a Pearson correlation between t_{ih}s, but there is one facet to it that supports its use. This is an interpretation that is in the spirit of considering tau as a correlation between dominance vectors, which is prominent in the the the τ_b version of tau. It may be recalled that τ_b is the version of tau for use in the case of ties that treats tau as a Pearson correlation between dominance variables. Kendall's partial tau can be considered a correlation between residualized dominance vectors. If d_{ihY} is regressed on d_{ihX} in the sense of treating the two dominance variables as ordinary variables, the "regression coefficient" for "predicting" d_{ihY} from d_{ihX} is τ_{XY}, and similarly for predicting d_{ihZ} from d_{ihX}. Then, as is the case with partial Pearson correlation, $\tau_{YZ\cdot X}$ is the correlation between these residuals. The problem again, though, is that it is the *Pearson* correlation between the residuals. Also, the residuals are of the ternary dominance variables and so will no longer be equal to 1, −1, or 0. Thus, partial tau is a tau in only a limited sense. This issue arises again in the context of some versions of multiple tau that are discussed in chapter 4.

Deficiencies of Partial Tau

As the reader may have gathered, I find partial tau unsatisfactory. There are a number of reasons for this. First is the fact that it cannot be simply interpreted as any sort of a probability of being in ordinal agreement, which is one of the strengths of tau itself. More than that, there is its hybrid nature as a Pearson correlation between t_{ih}s or as a Pearson correlation between quantitative deviations from least-squares regressions involving d_{ih}s. Thus, it is at best a tau correlation in the τ_b sense of a cosine of the angle between (residual) dominance vectors.

For related reasons, there is difficulty in generalizing partial tau beyond a single control variable. In this case, it seems one can no longer even think of it as a correlation between t_{ih}s; only the interpretation as a correlation between residual dominances remains, and here the dominance residuals are those resulting from a discredited (Somers, 1974; Wilson, 1971) kind of "multiple regression" that predicts dominance variables from dominance variables on the controls.

Perhaps an even more disappointing aspect of partial tau is its failure to correspond to "conditional tau." By conditional tau is meant a tau that results when one does literally hold the control variable constant and computes the tau between the two others at each level of the control variable. For example, consider trivariately normal variables X, Y, and Z. It will be recalled that in this situation it is literally true that $\rho_{YZ \cdot X}$ is the correlation between Y and Z at any constant value of X. Because trivariate normality implies conditional bivariate normality for Y and Z at any value of X, the relation in (2.14) implies that τ_{YZ} at that constant value of X will be $(2/\pi)\sin^{-1}\rho_{YZ \cdot X}$. On the other hand, the definition of partial tau implies that it can be found by substituting the inverse sine functions of the ρs into (2.16) in the normal case. If this is done, the two computations do not agree. For example, suppose $\rho_{XY} = .80$, $\rho_{XZ} = .60$, and $\rho_{YZ} = .48$. This means that $\rho_{YZ \cdot X} = 0$; that is, Y and Z are independent at any fixed value of X. Therefore, at that fixed value of X, τ_{YZ} will be zero also. However, substituting the $\sin^{-1}$ transformations of the ρs into (2.16) gives a partial tau of .104, which is misleading because the variables are independent at any constant value of X. That is, the conditional tau is zero, but the computed partial tau is not. The difference lies, of course, in what is being "partialed out," d_{ihX} in the case of partial tau and X itself in the case of partial ρ.

Similar anomalies occur when partial tau is applied to categorical data. If a partial tau is computed by the formula, and taus between Y and Z within constant values of X are also computed, the results do not agree. The partial taus computed by the formula are consistently too high. It seems like more than a simple matter of taste to avoid partial tau because of these deficiencies in interpretation, in spite of any mathematical elegance it might have. The seeming elegance is in ways that have little to do with the data that the coefficient is trying to characterize.

If these comments on partial tau seem unduly querulous or acerbic, this may have resulted from being caught myself by a failure to understand this distinction. In one of my attempts to develop a theory of test measurement based on ordinal concepts (Cliff, 1989; see Cliff & Donoghue, 1992, for more successful results in this direction), in effect I assumed that conditional independence and partial tau of zero were interchangeable. This led to erroneous estimates of taus between total score on a multi-item test and the underlying trait (Donoghue & Cliff, 1991), which was a considerable disappointment. The conclusion from this discussion is rather succinct: Partial tau is an index that is inappropriate for any purpose that I have been able to imagine.

Conditional Tau

Conditional tau, $\tau_{YZ|X}$, is a coefficient that has more potential utility than partial tau, $\tau_{YZ \cdot X}$. It is the value of τ_{YZ} for a fixed value of X. It simply refers to computing an average of taus within values of X. (When X is quasi-continuous, with many possible values, it will be necessary for practical reasons to use short intervals on it rather than constant values.) Typically, one would find different $\tau_{YZ|X}$ for different values of X, and it is natural to want a summary figure to represent the correlation. This can be found by averaging the $\tau_{YZ|X}$ across the different values of X. A weighted, rather than a simple, average can be appropriate. The most obvious principle is to weight the different $\tau_{YZ|X}$ by the probability of each x_i. This would represent the average conditional tau in the population.

A different weighting system is to weight according to the relative number of dominance relations at each value of X, $[P(x_i)][1 - P(x_i)]$, and still others may be appropriate when ties are numerous, as in categorical data. For example, if Y is a dependent variable and Z is a predictive or explanatory one, then conditional τ_d might be of the most interest. In that case, one might want to weight them according to the proportion of dominance relations on Y that were represented on each. Or one might want to look at conditional τ_Q and think of weighting in terms of the the number of dominance relations on both variables at each level of X. The choice of which conditional tau to use, and how to combine them into an overall estimate, should depend on the investigator asking, "What is it I am trying to find out? and then, "Which number will most directly answer that question?"

Often, one wants to control more than one variable in order to find $\tau_{YZ|X1,X2,\ldots}$. But the practicality is that the probabilities associated with combinations of values $x_1, x_2, \ldots$ become small once there is more than one x, and the relative frequencies in samples are likely to become even more so, so the idea of conditional tau may seem limiting because it can be applied to more than one control variable only with some difficulty. My attitude toward that limitation may seem shockingly radical: I think it is not a bad thing. Imagining that more than one variable can be "held constant" in any meaningful sense is likely to involve more self-deception than scientific rigor in my opinion! Only in those rare situations where the variables are very well defined and correspondingly well behaved will the idea of describing relations within tiny segments of the population make sense. However, significant segments of the population can occur at combined values of Xs when the Xs are categorical with few categories. For example, if X_1 has three categories and X_2 has two, there are only six values of x_1, x_2. In such cases, it may be sensible to conditionalize on the combinations of values. "X" can be defined in terms of categories defined jointly across two, or even more, categorical variables. Even here, caution is called for because the number of joint categories increases exponentially with the number of variables, so some joint frequencies will become correspondingly small. An investigator is better off as a general rule if he or she looks at the joint frequencies, rather than blindly applying some conditionalizing procedure, and only conditionalizes as deeply as makes sense. Otherwise, we may think the data is telling us more than it is capable of saying.

SPEARMAN RANK CORRELATION

Definition of Rank Correlation

The Spearman rank correlation ρ_S is probably what most people think of as an ordinal correlation. The most direct way of describing ρ_S is as a Pearson correlation between ranks, although we will see that the presence of ties makes it necessary to modify this description. It is the process of conversion to ranks that leads to describing ρ_S as an ordinal measure. The reasoning is that, no matter what the form of the original data, we always end up with ranks as the basis for the correlation; therefore, ranks are ordinal. A second aspect of the rationale is explained best by thinking of an infinite population with scores on two variables X and Y. Assuming no ties, the scores on X and Y can be converted to "proportion-below" scores; these are the same as percentile ranks except that they are proportions instead of percentages. The correlation between these proportion-below scores is obviously the same idea as the Spearman rank correlation, although it happens that in the statistical literature it is called the "grade correlation." An ordinal justification for the rank correlation is that it is a Pearson correlation between the ordinal positions on the variables, with most of the strengths and many of the drawbacks of Pearson correlation.

Formulas for Spearman Rank Correlation

Tau requires examining all pairs of scores on the two variables, whereas other measures of correlation are computed more simply from the individual scores, and those formulas are the ones typically presented. However, for some conceptual purposes ρ_S should be conceived as being based on comparing ranks of pairs of individuals. This is seen most clearly through a rank-difference analogue of (2.13). Before illustrating that, we present the general formula for ρ_S without ties. In the formula, q_{ix} is the rank of x_i and μ_{qx} is the mean rank on X (μ_{qx} rather than m_{qx} because the mean rank is a fixed number not an estimate), and the symbols involving Y are corresponding.

$$r_{Sxy} = \frac{12\Sigma(q_{ix} - \mu_{qx})(q_{iy} - \mu_{qy})}{n^3 - n}. \tag{2.17}$$

The formula is formally identical to various formulas for Pearson correlation when they are applied to ranks, being most directly related to

$$\frac{\Sigma(x_i - m_x)(y_i - m_y)}{[\Sigma(x_i - m_x)^2 \Sigma(y_i - m_y)^2]^{1/2}}.$$

It takes this form (2.17) because, with no ties, $\Sigma(q_{ix} - \mu_{qx})^2 = (n^3 - n)/12$, and the same for the q_{iy} deviations. This formula could be further simplified by noting that $\mu_{qx} = \mu_{qy} = \frac{1}{2}(n + 1)$. Also, $(q_i - \mu_q)/[n(n + 1)/12]^{1/2}$ makes ranks into standard scores. The formula for r_S usually given in textbooks,

$$r_S = 1 - \frac{6\Sigma(q_{ix} - q_{iy})^2}{n^3 - n} \tag{2.18}$$

is equivalent to (2.17) because of the algebraic identities involving sums of ranks and sums of squared ranks that are presented at the end of the chapter.

But much data includes ties, so a question becomes how to adjust for them in r_S. One approach is to make no adjustment, using (2.17) or (2.18) whether there are ties or not, provided the average of the tied ranks is used for q_i. Such a coefficient is analogous to τ_a, and Kendall (1970) does refer to it as ρ_a. It might be thought of as a covariance between ranks, where average ranks are used when scores are tied. One can also construct an analogue of τ_b by directly substituting ranks into the usual formulas for the correlation coefficient. Some older sources, such as Kendall (1970), detail ways of correcting the denominator of (2.17) for the number of ties to this end, but there seems little use for following so explicit an approach in the age of computers; it is simpler just to compute the variances of the ranks whether there are ties or not. Spearman analogues of τ_d or τ_Q are possible, but they do not seem to occur in the literature.

In normal populations, there is a functional relation between ρ_S and ρ, just as there was for τ. In fact, it too involves the sine function:

$$\rho_S = \frac{2}{\pi} \sin^{-1}(\tfrac{1}{2}\rho).$$ (2.19)

Evaluation of this function shows that it means that ρ and ρ_S are very close in the normal case, the ρ_S being .01 or .02 smaller over the middle range one usually encounters in data, and that τ is then about $2\rho_S/3$, and that all three are equal at 0 and 1.0. The close relation between ρ_S and ρ in normal populations does not necessarily occur in non-normal populations or even in samples from normal ones. The relative values of the three coefficients depend on the nature of the bivariate data, particularly on the behavior of the extreme values. Also, it will be seen in the next chapter that r_S is a biased estimate of ρ_S, regardless of the nature of the population.

Spearman Correlation and Rank Differences

Just as it is sometimes conceptually useful to think of products of differences in standard scores as the basis for Pearson r itself, it can be useful to think of r_S as being based on products of rank differences. Specifically, it can be shown that (2.17) is equivalent to

$$r_{Sxy} = \frac{6\sum\sum_{i \neq h}(q_{ix} - q_{hx})(q_{iy} - q_{hy})}{n^4 - n^2}.$$ (2.20)

Like (2.13) this is a formula that no one would use for computational purposes, but it can provide the basis for some useful conceptual relations. Relating back to the dominance variables which form the basis of tau, r_S can be thought of as weighting the direction of differences by the product of the differences in standardized ranks, just as r itself weights them by the differences in standard scores.

Rather oddly, a coefficient that looks like a hybrid between τ and ρ_S turns out to be just ρ_S. Suppose we construct the dominance variables d_{ihx} on x and the rank differences on Y. This may seem a peculiar thing to do, but the result turns out to have several useful applications. The sum, across pairs, of products d_{ihx} with $q_{iy} - q_{hy}$ could be calculated. Such a sum has a maximum when all the positive dominances d_{ihx} go with positive rank differences, and it will be a minimum when all the positive d_{ihx} go with negative ones. Some algebra (see the end of the chapter) shows that the maximum possible value for the sum is $(n^3 - n)/3$, which is indeed a compromise between the maximum of $n^2 - n$ for the sum of products of dominances and the $(n^4 - n^2)/6$ that appears in (2.17). We could use $(n^3 - n)/3$ as a denominator and define the following coefficient: ·

$$r_? = \frac{\sum_i \sum_h d_{ihx}(q_{iy} - q_{hy})}{(n^3 - n)/3}. \tag{2.21}$$

It is shown in the Appendix that $r_?$ is really ρ_S. This definition of rank correlation is useful for studying inferences about ρ_S and in a form of ordinal multiple regression.

Concordance

Sometimes one has several sets of rankings of the same objects or subjects and wishes to have a summary statistic to describe the consistency of the sets of rankings. Examples of this situation abound. A set of judges or observers may all rate a group of subjects on some behavior, such as observers rating the play behavior of children or the supportiveness of husbands of pregnant women. A class of children may be given a set of test items where the quality of their answers to each item can be rank-ordered, including just being divided into two categories, right and wrong. Judges may rate the quality of samples of pizza dough made by different processes. A group of turtles may be raced numerous times, with the order of finish recorded each time. In all these cases, the data either are, or can be converted to, a set of g rankings of n things, allowing tied ranks.

One would like to know two things about such a set of rankings. First, what summary scores for the n things best represent their g rankings? Second, how consistent are the g rankings? The two answers turn out to be closely related, and they both can be derived simply from the average ranks of the n things. The average ranks have several desirable properties as summary scores. First, as averages, they provide the closest possible least-squares approximation to the matrix of ranks. This property may not seem very important if we take a view of the data that is at all strict because least squares may not seem like a very appropriate way to measure agreement with ranks, given the somewhat arbitrary nature of transforming to ranks, but is it still useful as a criterion. Second, and this may sound like almost the same thing but is not quite, the averages have the highest possible average ρ_S with the g rankings. The difference in the two properties is that in the second point we are talking about an average *rank order* correlation. Third, and this is a little surprising (and perhaps esoteric), the differences on the average ranks provide the best possible agreement (in one sense) with the dominances derived from the individual rankings.

With respect to these latter two points, it may be worthwhile to elaborate the description a bit. What is meant is that the averages are rank-ordered, giving a $(g + 1)$th ranking. This new ranking has a higher average rank order correlation with the g other rankings than any other set of ranks. With respect to the second, one can use the ranks on each of the g to make $\frac{1}{2}n(n-1)$ dominances, and one can make the $\frac{1}{2}n(n-1)$ rank differences of the averages. These rank differences have the highest possible sum of products with the dominances from the original rankings. Thus, the average ranks best represent the original rankings in two ordinal senses as well as in the least-squares sense.

The consistency of the g rankings, expressed as the average ρ_s between pairs of rankings, can be derived rather simply from the variance of the average ranks. Let $\bar{r}_{i.}$ stand for the average rank of object i across the g raters. Then

$$\rho_{av} = \frac{12[\sum_i \bar{r}_{i.}^2 - g^2 n(n+1)^2/4]}{g(g-1)(n^3-n)} - \frac{1}{g-1} \qquad (2.22)$$

Rank consistency is sometimes expressed numerically as the "coefficient of concordance," W, (Kendall, 1970) where

$$W = \frac{(g-1)\rho_{av}+1}{g}. \qquad (2.23)$$

W can be computed from the average ranks as well:

$$W = \frac{12[\Sigma \bar{r}_{i.}^2 - n(n+1)^2/4]}{n^3-n} \qquad (2.24)$$

when there are no tied ranks. If there are ties, then the denominator of (2.24) needs to be corrected for that fact, becoming $\Sigma_i\Sigma_j(q_{ij}-\mu_j)^2/g$. In analysis of variance terms, gW is the ratio of "sum of squares for subjects (or objects)" to "total sum of squares" when the data are expressed as ranks; it is used in "Friedman's test" (Friedman, 1937). To me, the average rank correlation (2.22) is much more meaningful than W itself.

A different kind of quantity is the average rank order correlation of a set of ranks with an outside variable (Lyerly, 1952). For example, suppose we have repeated observations of scores on some variable, such as a developmental score of some kind on a group of children, or a degree-of-pathology score on a group of patients. Then the average rank order correlation of the scores with time is a very useful descriptive quantity because it reflects an average trend. Similarly, in the case of multiple judges ranking objects, there may be an outside variable on which the objects have scores. The average rank order correlation of the rating with the judges scores would be useful. This, too, is available from the average ranks. The quantity $12\sum_i(r_{it} - \mu_r)(r_i - \mu_r)/(n^3 - n)$ is the average correlation between ranks on variable t and the average of g other ranks.

Average Taus

There are no major simplifications to formulas if one wants to find the average tau correlation among several variables or the average tau between several variables and another one. If one did want to write a computer program to find average taus of this kind while avoiding knowing what the individual taus were, some efficiencies can be introduced into such a program. However, they seem not to be of very general interest, so we will not explore them here. Given modern computer facilities, it seems straightforward enough just to compute the average.

CONCLUSION

In considering ordinal measures of correlation, we can take several points of view. However, the feeling here is that ordinal correlation is best represented by Kendall's tau. Tau has several interpretations, or can be looked on as directly representing several aspects of the data. First, it has a probability interpretation: if one samples a pair of members of the population at random, τ represents the probability that their direction of difference is the same on both variables, minus the probability that it is opposite (2.1). Equivalently, it reflects the number of interchanges of adjacent elements that are necessary to get two variables into the same order (2.2). Finally, for many purposes it can be thought of in a numerical way as representing the average product of dominance variables (2.3). In all these guises, it seems to be a good representation of what we mean by "similarity of order" when we are trying to describe the extent of the relation between two variables.

There are several ways of adjusting τ in the presence of ties on the variables. One way is not to adjust it, retaining the simplest interpretational versions, both in the probabilistic and the average-product-of-dominances senses. In this case, the coefficient is called τ_a. Other versions delete from consideration the pairs that are tied on one of the variables (Somers's d, τ_d) or either of them (the Goodman–Kruskal gamma, τ_Q). Formulas for these in terms of dominance variables were given as (2.8) and (2.10), respectively, but they also have probability interpretations, the probability being conditioned on the absence of ties on one variable (τ_d) or both variables (τ_Q). A variation that has a cosine-of-the-angle-between-dominance-vectors interpretation, if that is deemed appropriate, is τ_b. It is equivalent to treating the dominance vectors as variables and computing the Pearson correlation between dominance variables. Which approach to the treatment of ties is taken will depend on what aspect of the data the investigator is most interested in preserving, balanced against the mathematical properties of each. As a general rule, τ_a is preferred here because its simple probability interpretation is usually desirable, and it is much easier to work with theoretically.

The main alternative to Kendall's tau is the Spearman rank coefficient, ρ_s. It is the Pearson correlation between observed scores that have been converted to ranks. It is an ordinal measure of correlation in the sense that the variables are converted to ranks, so any monotonic transformation of the variables leads to the same value for the correlation. In a sense, the investigator is choosing one of the infinity of possible monotonic transformation of his or her data, and then treating the transformed data (ranks) as if it were on an interval scale. The agreement between ranks is measured in a sum-of-squared-differences sense. As long as it is clear that this is the case, then ρ_s has a valid interpretation.

The algebraic identities involving sums of ranks and sums of squares of ranks lead to the simplified formulas for Spearman's coefficient, (2.17) and (2.18).

Tau measures consistency of ordinal relations of pairs of subjects, yet any form of ρ seems to be based on considering subjects one at a time. However, both ρ_s and ρ itself, and their sample estimates, can be thought of as based on sums of products of *differences* of scores on variables. This has no practical utility because it greatly enlarges the computations involved, but it does have some conceptual value in that it supplies avenues of comparison of correlational coefficients. In tau, all the directions of difference are equally weighted, regardless of size, whereas in the Pearson coefficient, including its Spearman variation, the direction of difference is weighted by the difference in standard scores of each pair of subjects on the two variables. This relation is captured in (2.11) for Pearson and (2.19) for Spearman.

SOME MATHEMATICAL RELATIONS

Pearson Correlation and Standard Score Differences

The relation between (2.13) and the more typical formula for Pearson r (2.12) can be spelled out rather easily. The relation makes use of some of the basic principles involving the summation operator. The difference formula (2.11) can be expanded:

$$\frac{\sum\sum\limits_{i<h}(z_{ix}-z_{hx})(z_{iy}-z_{hy})}{n(n-1)}=\frac{\sum\sum\limits_{i\neq h}(z_{ix}z_{iy}-z_{ix}z_{hy}-z_{hx}z_{iy}+z_{hx}z_{hy})}{2n(n-1)}. \tag{2.24}$$

We have also changed the range of summations to run over all pairs except self-differences ($i = h$), so each difference is included twice, and we made the denominator $2n(n-1)$ to compensate for the doubling of the number of terms in the summation. One further adjustment is to realize that we can include the self-differences, $z_i - z_h$, in the summations without affecting the summations' values because all these differences are, by definition, zero. Taking this into account and summing each term separately (i.e., removing parentheses), we can write the right-hand side of (2.24) as

$$\frac{\sum\limits_i\sum\limits_h z_{ix}z_{iy}-\sum\limits_i\sum\limits_h z_{ix}z_{hy}-\sum\limits_i\sum\limits_h z_{hx}z_{iy}+\sum\limits_i\sum\limits_h z_{hx}z_{hy}}{2n(n-1)}. \tag{2.25}$$

Now the principles involving double summations can be applied to each of the four terms. In the first one, z_{ix} and z_{iy} are both constant relative to summing over h, so this means that the first term is equivalent to $n\sum_i z_{ix}z_{iy}$. In the second term, z_{ix} is constant relative to summing over h, so it can come outside the h summation: $\sum_i z_{ix}\sum_h z_{hy}$. But by the definition of standard scores, each sum is zero, so the term disappears. In the third, we can do a similar thing, but first we need to remember that the order of summation can always be reversed; the i summation can be on the right and the h summation on the left. Now it is the h terms that can be brought outside one summation, giving $\sum_h z_{hx}\sum_i z_{iy}$, but sums of z scores are zero, so this term is zero also. The last term can be made into $n\sum_h z_{hx}z_{hy}$ because summing over i just means summing over h n times, similar to the first term. Now all that is necessary is to realize that summing over i and over h are really the same thing because both subscripts refer to individuals. In summary, the two middle terms are zero because the sum of z scores is zero, and the two end terms are both $n\sum_i z_{ix}z_{iy}$, so (2.24) ends up as

$$\frac{\sum\sum\limits_{i<h}(z_{ix}-z_{hx})(z_{iy}-z_{hy})}{n(n-1)}=\frac{2n\sum z_{ix}z_{iy}}{2n(n-1)}. \tag{2.26}$$

Canceling $2n$ out of the numerator and denominator of the right side leaves (2.12).

Sums and Sums of Squares of Ranks

The simplifications that underlie formulas for r_S follow from formulas for the sum and sum of squares of the first n integers. The sum of the first n integers (denoted j) is given as

$$\sum_{j=1}^{j=n} j = \frac{n(n+1)}{2}. \tag{2.27}$$

This formula can be proved by mathematical induction. First note that it is correct for $n = 1$. If the formula is correct for some value of n, and the next integer is added, the sum must go up by $n + 1$:

$$\sum_{j=1}^{j=n+1} j = \frac{n(n+1)}{2+(n+1)}. \tag{2.28}$$

Now the sum runs to $n + 1$ instead of n, so $n + 1$ should be substituted for n in (2.27) if one is now to get the sum of the first $n + 1$ integers since n there really refers to the number of integers added. If the formula (2.27) is correct, doing that should be the same as (2.28). Substitution of $n + 1$ into (2.27) gives

$$\sum_{j=1}^{j=n+1} j = \frac{(n+1)(n+2)}{2} = \frac{n^2+3n+2}{2}. \tag{2.29}$$

Putting all the right-hand side of (2.28) over 2 gives $[(n^2 + n) + 2(n + 1)]/2$, which simplifies to $(n^2 + 3n + 2)/2$, which is just the same as in (2.29). This proves that (2.27) is the right formula for the sum of n integers because (a) if it is correct for some value of n it is correct for the next value of n, and (b) we saw it was correct for $n = 1$, so it must be right for $n = 2, 3, \dots$.

The same process can be used to prove that the sum of the first n squared integers is

$$\sum_{j=1}^{j=n} j^2 = \frac{2n^3+3n^2+n}{6}. \tag{2.30}$$

The formula is correct when $j = 1$. If the square of the $(n + 1)$th integer is added, the sum must go up by $n^2 + 2n + 1$. Replacing n by $n + 1$ in (2.27) gives a numerator of $2(n^3 + 3n^2 + 3n + 1) + 3(n^2 + 2n + 1) + n + 1$. These terms can be collected into $(2n^3 + 3n^2 + n) + 6(n^2 + 2n + 1)$. Because this is all divided by 6, the last part becomes just exactly the increment that is necessary when the sum includes $n + 1$. So, in the same way as with the sum of integers, we have shown that (2.30) is the sum of squared integers.

But we are really interested in the sum of squared deviations of integers from their mean in order to get the variance of ranks. From the formula for the sum of integers, μ_q, the mean of the n ranks, is $\Sigma q_i/n = [n(n + 1)/2]/n = (n + 1)/2$. One formula for $\Sigma(x - m_x)^2$ is $\Sigma x^2 - nm_x^2$. Therefore,

$$\Sigma(q_i - \mu_q)^2 = \Sigma q_i^2 - n\mu_q^2 , \qquad (2.31)$$

but since ranks are integers $\Sigma q_i^2 = (2n^3 + 3n^2 + n)/6$ and $\mu_q = (n + 1)/2$, so

$$\Sigma(q_i - \mu_q)^2 = \frac{2n^3 + 3n^2 + n}{6} - \frac{n(n + 1)^2}{4} , \qquad (2.32)$$

which can be put over a denominator of 12, giving

$$\Sigma(q_i - \mu_q)^2 = \frac{4n^3 + 6n^2 + 2n - 3n^3 - 6n^2 - 3n}{12} , \qquad (2.33)$$

which reduces to $(n^3 - n)/12$. This is the reason for the presence of $n^3 - n$ in the denominator of the formula for r_S (2.15) as well as the 12 in the numerator. Dividing by n (rather than the more usual $n - 1$ because this is an exact formula not an estimate of a population variance) gives

$$\sigma_q^2 = \frac{n^2 - 1}{12} \qquad (2.34)$$

as the variance of ranks in the untied case.

This section has provided some of the origins of some of the formulas that have been developed in this chapter. The treatment has been far from complete, but nevertheless may help to suggest some of the framework that underlies them.

3

Inferences About
Ordinal Correlation

WHAT INFERENCES DO WE WANT TO MAKE?

Bivariate Estimation Versus Randomization Tests

In statistical inference, it is often necessary to exercise some care in applying a method that sounds like it is doing what one intends because the method may be doing something a bit different. Otherwise, a conclusion may be correct statistically but inaccurate substantively, or inappropriate statistical theory may have been applied so that probability statements are inaccurate. It often seems that a combination of tradition and convenience can lead to this kind of suboptimal methodology.

Procedures used with ordinal correlations provide a case in point. Most texts provide "tests of significance" for ordinal correlations that take the form of critical values that must be obtained in small samples at a given alpha level, and standard errors that can be used, along with assumed sampling normality for the estimates, in large ones. When such methods are applied, the hypothesis that is being tested is that the two variables are *independent*, which is a more general conclusion than that they have zero correlation. Zero correlation can occur in populations where there is some degree of curvilinear dependence between the two variables, and very often it seems implausible that two empirical variables will be completely independent. If the variables are not independent, then the procedure for testing independence can lead to inappropriate conclusions regarding the presence or absence of an ordinal relation between variables because the sampling behavior of the estimates will not behave in the way that is assumed under independence. If the null hypothesis is rejected, the investigator is undoubtedly going to conclude that there is some *correlation* in the linear sense that is reflected by the correlation coefficient being tested, but the sampling behavior of the coefficient may not be correctly reflected by the independence-testing procedure.

Such independence-assuming methods are described here, but the emphasis will be on other methods that treat the empirical questions like any other bivariate inference context: the ordinal correlation between two variables can have any value, including zero. Our research goal is to infer what it is (point estimate) and establish boundaries within which we can be quite confident that the true value falls (confidence interval), and test a null hypothesis that it has some particular value, usually zero. We do this not by assuming some particular form for the bivariate distribution but by estimating, from the sample, the distributional characteristics that are relevant to such inferences, similar to the way in which one uses a sample estimate of the variance to make inferences about a mean rather than than making an assumption about the population variance.

We will think of sample tau as a statistic being used to estimate its population counterpart in the same sense that a sample mean estimates its population counterpart, so we briefly review the properties of estimators.

Sample Estimates of τ and ρ_S

A sample value of any form of tau (we use t to refer to it and hope that confusions with Student's t will not arise) will have descriptive properties that parallel those of the population value. That is, it counts the number of times that pairs of cases are in the same ordinal relations on both variables, compares it to the number that are opposite, and divides by the number of comparisons that have been made. This means that many of the formulas presented in the previous chapter, such as (2.4), can be applied without modification to compute t. Furthermore, in the absence of ties, the descriptions of tau as the number of interchanges necessary to bring one array into the same order as the other and as the number of intersecting lines that connect the same objects will apply to the sample t.

However, the sample formulas that are most useful for expository purposes, and that are most readily programmed, are those based on dominance variables, so they are repeated here as formulas for forms of t. Only the necessary half of the pairs is considered in each formula; that is, the Σ represent double summations that include only those d_{ih} where $i > h$, so this fact is not repeated in the summations.

$$t_a = \frac{\Sigma d_{ihx} d_{ihy}}{\frac{1}{2} n(n-1)}, \tag{3.1}$$

$$t_{dyx} = \frac{\Sigma d_{ihx} d_{ihy}}{\Sigma d_{ihy}^2}, \tag{3.2}$$

$$t_Q = \frac{\Sigma d_{ihx} d_{ihy}}{\Sigma d_{ihx}^2 d_{ihy}^2}, \tag{3.3}$$

$$t_b = \frac{\Sigma d_{ihx} d_{ihy}}{(\Sigma d_{ihx}^2 \Sigma d_{ihy}^2)^{1/2}}, \tag{3.4}$$

Unbiasedness and Consistency

These formulas can readily be shown to be consistent estimates of the corresponding population coefficients, and t_a is, in addition, unbiased as an estimate of τ. The basis of the reasoning about t_a can be seen by, first, noting that it is a proportion of pairs. A bivariate population is assumed to exist in which each member has values on X and on Y. For each pair i,h of elements—persons, say—of the population, there exists a d_{ihy} and a d_{ihx} showing the relation of the pair on each of the two variables, and so there is also a value of the product $d_{ihx} d_{ihy} = t_{ihxy}$. In the population, there is a probability that a random pair has $t_{ihxy} = 1$, a probability that it has $t_{ihxy} = -1$, and a probability that it has $t_{ihxy} = 0$. When a sample is taken from the population, the proportion of sample pairs of each kind has expected value equal to each of the respective population probilities, and by the usual considerations about sample proportions, these will tend to differ less and less from the population probabilities as the sample size increases. (It is true we are referring to pairs, whereas sampling applies to individual elements, but the logic can readily be extended to take this into account; we are avoiding the complexity of the details by not spelling them out, but the idea is the same as used here.) Thus, as a sample function of these proportions, t_a is unbiased and "consistent," consistent in the technical sense in statistics, which means that the probability of any specific size of difference, $t - \tau$, becomes vanishingly small as the size of the sample becomes indefinitely large.

In fact, t_a is a member of the family of generalized averages known to statisticians as U statistics (Hettmansperger, 1984; Randles & Wolfe, 1979) because, since t_{ihxy} is itself a random variable, t_a is the average of these in the sample. This property is one of the reasons for preferring it as a measure of ordinal correlation.

If the numerators and denominators of t_d and t_Q are each divided by $\frac{1}{2}n(n - 1)$, it can be seen that their components are each unbiased and consistent estimates of the corresponding population quantities, as in t_a. Deciding whether the denominator of t_b is unbiased is beyond our scope, but at least its two parts are each consistent. By standard statistical theory (Kendall &

Stuart, 1958) the consistent nature of the numerators and denominators means that t_d, t_Q, and t_b are all consistent estimators of the corresponding population taus. It makes good intuitive sense that they are consistent in that one would expect that coefficients calculated in this way would tend to deviate less and less from the population counterparts as the sample size increases. We will make use of this consistency property in deriving large-sample estimates of the standard errors of t_d, t_Q, and t_b from the variance of t_a. Whether the three forms of t other than t_a are unbiased as well as consistent is an issue that is beyond our scope. As a general rule, such ratios of unbiased estimates tend not to be unbiased, however, although the bias can be expected to be small in cases like those here.

VARIANCE OF t_a

Goal and Orientation

The main orientation here is that the most common situation faced by an investigator is one where she or he has data on a sample and wants to estimate the ordinal correlation in the population, including testing hypotheses about it and forming confidence intervals (c.i.) for it. Having seen in the previous section that t_a is unbiased and consistent, the next important question is the size of its standard error. Not only does the size of the standard error give a measure of how far the estimate will be expected to deviate from the parameter, but it is the key part of the process of finding c.i. and testing hypotheses.

Corresponding to the previous chapter, t will be used to refer to t_a unless the context makes the subscript necessary. Also, until it becomes necessary to distinguish among several variables, the xy subscript will not be used either.

The sampling variance of any statistic v that is an unbiased estimate of a parameter η is $\sigma_v^2 = E(v - \eta)^2$, which is then, because of unbiasedness and the rules regarding expectations, $\sigma_v^2 = Ev^2 - \eta^2$. This means that $\sigma_t^2 = Et^2 - \tau^2$, so the variance of t can be found if Et^2 can be found.

The formula will be given shortly, and its source at the end of the chapter, but it involves a variable that should be introduced beforehand. This variable is $t_i = E_h t_{ih}$, the expected consistency of person i across all other persons h. At first thought this may seem like it should be the same for all members of the population, but reconsideration suggests that, in the population, some individuals will be in very similar positions on the two variables and have relatively high t_i values, whereas others will be quite different, and have lower ones. This is analogous to ordinary regression where some individuals are near the regression line and some far from it. The value of t depends on the relative numbers of each kind of t_i that happen to occur in the sample. Furthermore, the amount of such variability will itself be higher in some populations than in others. Sampling from a population where there is much variability in the t_i leads to more uncertainty about the value of τ inferred from t than in the case of a population where there is less variability. The variability in the t_i is constrained to some extent by the value of τ, because if τ is near unity almost every t_i must likewise be near unity, but the dependence is far from complete.

Table 3.1 illustrates the values of t_i in a small population having only eight members. There are three variables, X, Y, and Z, and the scores on each, shown as ranks for simplicity, are given in the uppermost section. The t_{ihxy} and t_{ihxz} matrices are shown. Both values of τ are seen to be .50. Also given are the average values of t_{ih} for each i; these are the t_i in this small population. The t_{ixy} are seen to vary from $-.14$ to .71, whereas the t_{ixz} vary only from .43 to .71, even though both $\tau = .50$. On sampling from the populations, we would likewise expect samples to yield more variable values of t_{xy} than t_{xz}.

More explicitly, carrying out the expectations process leads (Daniels & Kendall, 1947; Kendall, 1970; modified in Cliff & Charlin, 1991) to the following expression for σ_t^2:

$$\sigma_t^2 = \frac{4(n-2)\sigma_{ti}^2 + 2\sigma_{tih}^2}{n(n-1)}. \tag{3.5}$$

The formula indicates that the sampling variability of t depends on the variance of the t_i and on the variability of the t_{ih} themselves.

The notation in (3.5) differs from previous sources such as Kendall (1970) and Cliff and Charlin (1991) in using σ_{tih}^2 rather than $1 - \tau^2$ (Kendall, 1970), which does not allow for ties, or $v - \tau^2$, where v is the proportion of pairs that are not tied (Cliff & Charlin, 1991). Parallel to other definitions of variance, σ_{tih}^2 represents $E(t_{ih} - \tau)^2$, and this definition holds whether ties are present or not. When there are no ties, as with continuous variables, $\sigma_{tih}^2 = 1 - \tau^2$. The same principle is followed when dealing with the variance of the d statistic for location comparisons in chapters 5 and 6.

The relative influence of the two variance terms in (3.5) will depend on their relative magnitudes and on the sample size, σ_{ti}^2 becoming dominant in large samples, but the other term is not negligible unless $n > 100$, in my experience.

Judging from data seen so far, σ_{ti}^2 for the most part lies between about .25 and .05, depending partly on how high τ is. In Table 3.1, assuming it is possible to think of such small groups as populations, $\sigma_{ti}^2 = .0969$ for X versus Y (a fairly typical value) and it is .0153, a very low value, for X versus Z. In both cases, $\sigma_{tih}^2 = .75$. For comparison, normal populations in which $\tau = 0$, have $\sigma_{ti}^2 = .11$ (Kendall, 1970), and in that situation σ_{tih}^2 would equal 1.0. However, the main

TABLE 3.1
Illustrations of Components of the Variance of t

Scores								
i:	1	2	3	4	5	6	7	8
X:	1	2	3	4	5	6	7	8
Y:	3	1	4	5	8	2	6	7
Z:	3	2	1	6	5	4	8	7

t_{ihxy}

$i\backslash h$	1	2	3	4	5	6	7	8	
1	0	−	+	+	+	−	+	+	
2	−	0	+	+	+	+	+	+	
3	+	+	0	+	+	−	+	+	
4	+	+	+	0	+	−	+	+	
5	+	+	+	+	0	−	−	−	
6	−	+	−	−	−	0	+	+	
7	+	+	+	+	−	+	0	+	
8	+	+	+	+	−	+	+	0	
Σ	3	5	5	5	1	−1	5	5	
$\hat{t}_i$	.43	.71	.71	.71	.14	−.14	.71	.71	$.50 = t_{xy}$

$s_{ti}^2 = .0969;\ s_{tih}^2 = .7500.\ \hat{\sigma}_{ti}^2 = .1108;\ \hat{\sigma}_{tih}^2 = .7636.$

t_{ihxz}

$i\backslash h$	1	2	3	4	5	6	7	8	
1	0	−	−	+	+	+	+	+	
2	−	0	−	+	+	+	+	+	
3	−	−	0	+	+	+	+	+	
4	+	+	+	0	−	−	+	+	
5	+	+	+	−	0	−	+	+	
6	+	+	+	−	−	0	+	+	
7	+	+	+	+	+	+	0	−	
8	+	+	+	+	+	+	−	0	
Σ	3	3	3	3	3	3	5	5	
$\hat{t}_i$	.43	.43	.43	.43	.43	.43	.71	.71	$.50 = t_{xy}$

$s_{ti}^2 = .0153;\ s_{tih}^2 = .7500.\ \hat{\sigma}_{ti}^2 = .01749;\ \hat{\sigma}_{tih}^2 = .7636.$

point to consider is that, in any population, σ_t^2 depends on the two characteristics of the population indicated in (3.5) as well as on the sample size.

The reader may recall that the usual formulas for inferences about ρ from r do not seem to involve such complication. The reason, of course, is that those common formulas assume bivariate normality. If populations are not normal, then the standard error of r is a complex function of the fourth moments of the populations in large samples (Kendall & Stuart, 1958, p. 236) and virtually unknown in small ones. The consequences of ignoring nonnormality in making inferences about correlations is unknown in any application, but the lack of robustness of r is substantial (e.g., Long & Cliff, 1995).

If one is only concerned with testing whether two variables are independent, then things are simpler with tau as well. The variance of t in that case is given in a formula presented later as (3.14), but then the inferences are very narrow, as discussed in that section.

Sample Estimates of σ_t^2

For any practical application such as testing a hypothesis about τ or forming a c.i. for it, a way of estimating (3.5) is necessary. Since the sample analogues of the quantities in (3.5) are all consistent estimates of their population counterparts, it would be feasible to substitute them directly into it. This seems to be what was done by Yu and Dunn (1982). However, Daniels and Kendall (1947; see Kendall, 1970) have derived a formula that is an unbiased estimate of σ_t^2, and Cliff and Charlin (1991) have generalized it to allow for ties on the variables. In a sample, $\sum_h t_{ih}/(n-1) = \hat{t}_i$ is an unbiased estimate of t_i, and so it is used in the estimate of σ_t^2. Then, using $s_{ti}^2 = \sum(\hat{t}_i - t)^2/n$ and $s_{tih}^2 = \sum\sum(t_{ih} - t)^2/n(n-1)$, the latter double summation excluding $i = h$, the following is an unbiased estimate of σ_t^2:

$$\hat{\sigma}_t^2 = \frac{4(n-1)s_{ti}^2 - 2s_{tih}^2}{(n-2)(n-3)}. \tag{3.6}$$

The formula can be illustrated by treating the data of Table 3.1 as sample data. Then $s_{tixy}^2 = .0969$ and $s_{tihxy}^2 = .75$, giving $\hat{\sigma}_{txy}^2 = [4(7)(.0969) - 2(.7500)]/(6)(5) = .0905$, so the estimated standard error of t_{xy} is .301.

Note that the s_{tih}^2 term in (3.6) is subtracted, whereas in (3.5) the analogous σ_{tih}^2 is added. This is a result of requiring an unbiased estimate of σ_t^2 and the way in which the counterparts of the terms in (3.5) are confounded with each other in sample computations. This confounding is made more salient in the section where we derive the formulas. However, this subtraction leads to the possibility that (3.6) can be negative, which a variance is not allowed to be. Therefore,

$$\min(\hat{\sigma}_t^2) = \frac{2s_{tih}^2}{n(n-1)} \tag{3.7}$$

is recommended as the minimum usable value of the estimated variance of t.

Negative variance estimates can occur in other applications where unbiased estimates are used. For example, the estimated variance due to regression can also be negative. In such cases it is generally effective to substitute the minimum estimate for the unbiased estimate (Browne, 1975).

A negative estimated variance is illustrated in the example for X versus Z, where $s_{ti}^2 = .0153$ (the $\hat{t}$s in this example were deliberately made as similar to each other as is possible with $n = 8$ and $t = .50$), so (3.6) is negative: $[4(7)(.0153) - 2(.7500)]/6(5) = -.0357$. Using (3.7), therefore, instead of (3.6) gives $2(.75)/8(7) = .0268$, so the standard error of τ_{xz} is estimated as .164.

Formula (3.6) gives a clear impression of the factors in the data that determine the sample estimate of the variance of t, but it is not the most convenient for computing or programming $\hat{\sigma}^2$. The form of (3.8) is better for that purpose.

$$s_t^2 = \frac{4\Sigma[(\Sigma t_{ih}^2) - n(n-1)^2 t^2] - 2(\Sigma\Sigma t_{ih})^2 - n(n-1)n^2}{n(n-1)(n-2)(n-3)}. \tag{3.8}$$

The use of the formulas for the estimated variance is illustrated in Table 3.2.

The behavior of (3.6) was evaluated extensively by Long and Cliff (in press) and found to be fairly good, but c.i. coverage was found to be less than $1 - \alpha$ when parent correlations were moderately high. A modified version of the population expression (3.5) was also investigated as an estimator, and it was found to behave better. The modification was to estimate the two parts, σ_{ti}^2 and σ_{tih}^2, separately and substitute them into (3.5):

$$\hat{\sigma}_{ti}^2 = \frac{\Sigma(\hat{t}_i - t)^2}{n-1} \tag{3.9}$$

and

TABLE 3.2
Computation of Estimated Variances

---

1. Using the unbiased estimate (3.6) with the variances s_{ti}^2 computed in Table 3.1:

$$s_{xy}^2 = \frac{4 \times 7 \times .0969 - 2 \times .75}{6 \times 5} = .0404. \quad s_{xz}^2 = \frac{4 \times 7 \times .0153 - 2 \times .75}{6 \times 5} = -.0356$$

Because s_{xz}^2 is negative, the minimum formula (3.7) is used as the estimate:

$$\hat{\sigma}_{xz}^2 = \frac{2 \times .75}{8 \times 7} = .0268.$$

2. Using the consistent estimate (3.11) with the variances $\hat{\sigma}_{ti}^2$ computed in Table 3.1:

$$\hat{\sigma}_{xy}^2 = \frac{4 \times 6 \times .1108 + 2 \times .7636}{8 \times 7} = .0748. \quad \hat{\sigma}_{xz}^2 = \frac{4 \times 6 \times .0179 + 2 \times .7636}{8 \times 7} = .0348$$

$$\hat{\sigma}_{tih}^2 = \frac{\Sigma\Sigma(t_{ih} - t)^2}{n(n-1)-1},\tag{3.10}$$

giving

$$\hat{\sigma}_t^2 = \frac{4(n-2)\hat{\sigma}_{ti}^2 + 2\hat{\sigma}_{tih}^2}{n(n-1)}.\tag{3.11}$$

The reason that c.i. formed using (3.11) behaved slightly better than those using (3.7) seemed to be that (3.11), though slightly biased, was considerably less variable than (3.7). This standard error was found to give appropriate c.i. under all circumstances of parent correlation and sample size, so it is the one recommended here. The reason for its better behavior than (3.6) seemed to lie in the latter's tendency to be quite small on occasion as a result of subtracting the second part of the expression. An additional, and surprising, finding of the study was that the "Fisher z" transformation of t, $[\frac{1}{2}\ln(1 + t)/(1 - t)]$, improved the behavior of t when it was close to 1.0.

Other findings of the research (Long & Cliff, 1995) had to do with the behavior of r. In contrast to the t procedure, none of several procedures based on r was found to behave well under all circumstances of sample size and parent population, even when populations were normal. Moreover, their behavior deteriorated further when the populations were not normal.

Maximum Possible σ_t^2

Kendall (1970) presents a maximum possible value for σ_t^2, perhaps partly as an alternative to estimating it from the sample in an era when such a computation was demanding. Another motive could be the concern that the variance estimated from the sample data may itself be subject to uncertainty, so an investigator who wanted a highly conservative approach to testing the null hypothesis, or who wanted to be assured that his or her c.i. would contain τ with probability no less than $1 - \alpha$, would have a conservative estimate available (Kendall & Gibbons, 1991). He derives the maximum by assuming that σ_{ti}^2 has the largest possible value, given τ^2. Under this assumption,

$$\sigma_t^2 = 2(1 - \tau^2)/n.\tag{3.12}$$

This seems like a highly conservative estimate. It is more than twice the variance of τ under normality, which is about $(1 - \tau^2)^2/n$. Beyond that, examination of the maximum for σ_{ti}^2 shows that it occurs only if the relation between the two variables is a very odd one, illustrated in Fig. 3.1. For

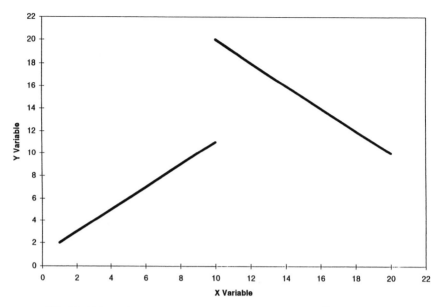

FIG. 3.1. Relation between two variables that must occur if σ_t^2 is to take on its maximum value.

maximum σ_{ti}^2, there must be a perfect ordinal correlation between the two variables over an interval, followed by a second interval in which there is again a perfect ordinal correlation *in the opposite direction*. Furthermore, there is an extreme discontinuity at the point where the two intervals meet. For example, if X has in the population a set of values 1, 2, 3, 4, 5, 6, 7, 8, 9, and $\tau = .667$, then the order on Y must be 1, 2, 3, 4, 5, 9, 8, 7, 6 in order for σ_{ti}^2, and consequently σ_t^2, to reach its maximum. This is such an unlikely kind of relation for two variables to have that it seems quixotic to guard against it, so it seems undesirable to use this estimate as a general practice. However, if you are the type who has more life insurance than you can afford, you may want to use it. If so, its unbiased estimate can readily be found to be $2(1 - t^2)/(n - 2)$. A related idea will be suggested here for use when $t = 1.0$.

Confidence Intervals and Hypotheses About τ

Estimated variances of t can be used to test hypotheses about τ or to form confidence intervals for it. In all such cases, an assumption must be made about the form of the sampling distribution of the statistic. Since t is a U statistic, as noted earlier, its sampling distribution approaches normality asymptotically with increasing sample size. Such a property provides theoretical comfort, but for practical applications it is important to know whether the approach to normality can be expected to be sufficient to make the assumed probabilities in inferences reasonably accurate in a given-size sample. In the case of many statistics, such as r when ρ is moderately high, the sample size required for this property is quite large.

The most serious effect of non-normality of the sampling distribution is through its skewness, and t is skewed unless $\tau = 0$, but this seems not to present a serious problem for t unless τ is quite close to the limits. Long and Cliff (in press) found good coverage assuming normality for t unless τ was above .7 (remember that this corresponds to ρ of about .9) and n was 10, so assuming normality seems likely to give good results. Daniels and Kendall (1947; Kendall, 1970) derive the skewness of t and show how to estimate it, thus allowing a correction on confidence intervals and tests of hypotheses, but this seems unnecessary in view of the results of Long and Cliff (in press). The latter also investigated methods for trying to adjust c.i. for the association between σ_t^2 and τ^2, but these, too, turned out to be unnecessary. Assuming normality for the sampling distribution of $\hat{t}$, approximate .95 c.i. are thus available as $t \pm 1.96\hat{\sigma}_t$, and .99 c.i. as $t \pm 2.58\hat{\sigma}_t$, and the degree of approximation seems quite good (Long & Cliff, in press).

In the examples, the .95 and .99 c.i. are $.50 \pm .59$; that is, $-.09$ to 1.00 and $.50 \pm .78$ ($-.28$ to 1.00), respectively, for τ_{xy}, and $.50 \pm .32$ ($.18$ to $.82$) and $.50 \pm .42$ ($.08$ to $.92$), respectively, for τ_{xz}. Thus, t_{xy} would not be significantly different from zero at either .05 or .01, but t_{xz} would be significant at either level, even though both are .50.

The foregoing c.i. can be improved slightly in small samples by taking the discreteness (discretion?) of t into consideration. It can only go from -1 to 1 in steps of $4/n(n - 1)$, when there are no ties. (The presence of ties complicates the possibilities, but the same considerations apply.) The discreteness suggests that adding half of the step size [i.e., $2/n(n - 1)$] to each end of the c.i. will result in more realistic c.i. This extends each end of the c.i. in the example by about .04 at each end, giving $.50 \pm .63$ and $.50 \pm .81$ as the c.i. for τ_{xy} and $.50 \pm .36$ and $.50 \pm .46$ for τ_{xz}.

The inferential strategy I have espoused here is one in which the hypothesis $\hat{\tau} = 0$ is tested by $z = (t - 0)/\hat{\sigma}_t$, and c.i. are formed as $t - z_{\alpha/2}\hat{\sigma}_t$ to $t + z_{\alpha/2}\hat{\sigma}_t$. It is based on the idea that it is better to estimate σ_t from the sample than to make some fairly arbitrary assumption about it. This is clearly necessary, as I have just argued, in the case of the c.i., and seems desirable when testing the hypothesis because it frees us from making any possibly misleading assumptions about the nature of the relation between the variables. The overall principle is that we should use procedures that are sensible, given what we expect data to be like, rather than being merely ritualistic.

The example just used should be taken as merely illustrative; these inferential procedures should not be used in samples this small. Perhaps one should never try to make inferences of any kind with samples below 10 in any context. Too many odd things can happen.

One special situation in which the estimated standard error cannot be used does need to be considered, and that is finding $t = 1$. When that happens, $s_t = 0$, so the c.i. would be the point $\tau = 1.0$, but it is unreasonable to conclude that 1.0 is the only conceivable value, for t can equal 1.0 when τ does not, and this can happen fairly readily in small samples if τ is fairly high. Thus, in this special case, a variation on the foregoing procedure seems called for. This is to use the conservative value (3.12) as the assumed variance of t for finding a c.i. when $t = 1.0$. Then the boundaries for the c.i. are found as the solutions for τ of

$$z_{\alpha/2}{}^2 = \frac{(t - \tau)^2}{2(1 - \tau^2)/n}.$$
(3.13)

When $t = 1.0$, the solutions are $(n - 2z^2)/(n + 2z^2)$ and 1.0. This provides a lower bound for τ when $t = 1.0$, but it is a very conservative one. Zero always will be in the .95 c.i. unless $n > 7$. Some more realistic estimate for the variance might be used instead in the same approach of solving for the lower limit of the c.i.

Testing the Hypothesis of Independence

As mentioned, the most common sources on tau recommend testing it for significance under the null hypothesis of complete independence. This procedure, and others like it, such as group comparisons that assume a null hypothesis of identical distributions or of randomization, is not recommended here for two main reasons. First, it encourages the kind of conceptual inconsistency that plagues much of statistical practice. Although it may be sensible under some circumstances to entertain the hypothesis that two variables are completely independent, the inconsistency comes when the hypothesis is rejected. What does the investigator conclude? Simply deciding that the variables are not independent, which is the logically consistent decision, seems unsatisfactory, and observation shows that the investigator rarely limits her conclusion to this simple choice. It is quite reasonable to ask, "What is the nature of the independence?" One common recourse seems to be to conclude that $\tau = t$, but we know that that cannot be literally true. How should the remaining uncertainty about the value of τ be expressed? Using the standard error that results when assuming independence can hardly be appropriate if one has just concluded that the variables are not independent.

After rejecting independence, one seemingly would have to fall back on one of the following strategies, none of which seems logically consistent. One approach is to test independence and then use the standard error from (3.6) to form a c.i. when independence is rejected. But if this variance is appropriate when independence was rejected, it should be appropriate beforehand. A second approach is to use a variance estimated by assuming that the variables were normal. But if normality is assumed after rejection, one might as well have assumed it beforehand and computed and tested r instead of t in the first place. A more logically consistent approach is to make no assumptions about distributions at any point and to express the uncertainty about τ using (3.6), making inferences about τ using it.

A second kind of reason for not using a test of independence is that τ can be zero without the variables being independent. The extreme is the situation in Fig. 3.1. In that case—which is admittedly unusual—the variance of t is about $2/n$, about four times as large as that given for the independence case in (3.14). More generally, a test of independence makes a very specific assumption about the sampling behavior of the statistic, an assumption that may well be highly incorrect, leading to erroneous inferences. Let us be realistic: If the null hypothesis of independence is rejected on the basis of a test for correlation, the investigator is very rarely going to confine his or her conclusion to the statement that "the variables are not independent." Rather, she or he will make some conclusion about the direction, and probably the degree, of correlation present. In such a conclusion, it is wisest to use the estimated standard error rather than one derived on the basis of assuming independence.

Nonetheless, independence may be a plausible null hypothesis sometimes, or some readers may want to follow tradition—wherever it leads—and there may be some advantages to retaining a connection to standard sources. The procedure for testing t against the null hypothesis that the variables are independent will therefore be presented here. There are several possible verbalizations of the null hypothesis, depending on the nature of the empirical context. "X and Y are independent random variables" is the most obvious. It might be encountered in a context where subjects are sampled and their paired values of the two variables are observed. Alternatively, Y could be the value of a dependent variable in an experiment in which xs represent values of the independent variable. An alternative null hypothesis is, "Given the order on X, all possible orders on Y are equally likely." This again could be in an experimental context in which X is manipulated and Y is observed, or one could have stimuli ordered on some character by two judges. Finally, the null hypothesis could be "X and Y are independent normal variables." Leaving the consideration of what one is going to do after the null hypothesis is rejected, any of these might be legitimate questions to ask about data. They amount to statements that "absolutely nothing is going on here."

The standard approach to this test uses the fact that t is close to normally distributed, even in quite small samples, when an H_0 of independence is true. The variance of t under independence is

$$\sigma_t^2 = \frac{4n + 10}{9n(n - 1)}. \tag{3.14}$$

Then t^2/σ_t^2 can be treated in moderate-sized samples as a single-degree-of-freedom chi-square variate, or its square root can be treated as a normal deviate. *This test is used in all major statistics packages to give the significance or tau.* Many texts use the disorder count S as the thing to be tested rather than t itself. Why S is tested rather than t is hard to understand. Perhaps it is to protect the user from the knowledge of t's value when it is nonsignificant, which might tempt him or her into some kind of statistical sin, or to save one or two strokes on a hand calculator.

When samples are quite small, less than a dozen, then nonnormality of the distribution of t, even under the independence null hypothesis, is usually felt to be a problem, and lists of critical values of t, or more often S, that are needed to reject H_0 are usually given (cf. Kendall, 1970). However, most of the distortion in the size of a test using (3.14) in small samples results from the fact that t can take on only discrete values, as noted in the previous section. Applying a correction for continuity in the form of using $[|t| - 2/n(n - 1)]^2$ instead of t^2 as the numerator results in tests that have appropriate size as long as $n > 4$. With n of 4 or fewer, the issue becomes moot. When $n = 4$, only a t of 1 or -1 can be significant at $\alpha = .05$, and only if it is one-tailed, because the number of "equally likely" permutations is $4! = 24$, so the probability of getting $t = 1$ by chance is .042. If $n = 3$, there are only six possibilities, so no result can reach conventional levels of significance. These facts about very small ns, along with the satisfactory behavior of the ratios when the correction for continuity is used with n at least 5, make tables of the values of t or S that are required for significance unnecessary.

The independence test can be applied to the example data where both ts are .5 and $n = 8$. Using the correction for continuity with the variance defined in (3.14) gives a chi-square of 2.587, corresponding to a normal deviate of 1.608. This clearly does not exceed the conventional two-tailed critical value of 1.96, and just misses the one-tailed one of 1.645 as well. This result contrasts, it will be remembered, with the results using sample-estimated variances, where t_{XY} was far from the .05 significance level but t_{XZ} was signficant at the .01 level.

As a matter of passing interest, the obtained normal deviate of 1.608 cuts off the upper .053 of the normal distribution. The exact probability of obtaining a t of .50 or greater with $n = 8$ under the assumption that all possible permutations are equally likely is .054. The smallness of this discrepancy in the probabilities exemplifies the accuracy with which the correction for continuity in conjunction with (3.14) approximates the probability of obtaining a given result under independence, even in very small samples.

OTHER INFERENCES ABOUT τ

Other Research Questions About Ordinal Correlation

In investigations involving correlation or prediction, the researcher often has research questions beyond those answerable from inferences about individual τs. For example, one might want to know whether τs are equal in two populations or whether two predictors correlate equally with a criterion variable in a single population or whether the average τ among a set of variables is zero. We will see, in the chapter on a tau-based analogue of multiple regression, that we will be concerned about inferences relating to a certain linear combination of taus between predictors and a criterion. Other possible questions arise, depending on the context and on the ingenuity of the investigator.

These questions can usually be cast as being about the difference between two taus or about the sum, or even weighted sum, of two or more taus. The ts used to estimate the τs are either independent (comparing samples from different populations) or correlated (comparing different taus in the same sample). In these cases, the suggested procedures to use are based on very elementary statistical considerations. For example, as with any other estimator, the variance of the difference between two independently estimated τs, t_1 and t_2, is[1]

$$\text{var}(t_1 - t_2) = \sigma_{t1}^2 + \sigma_{t2}^2, \tag{3.15}$$

just as the variance of the difference between the means of two independent samples is $\sigma_{m1}^2 + \sigma_{m2}^2$, as is familiar from elementary statistics and mentioned in chapter 1.

If one is wanting to investigate a hypothesis about the *average* tau in two subpopulations, males and females, say, the situation is similar. The variance of $(t_1 + t_2)/2$ is $(\sigma_{t1}^2 + \sigma_{t2}^2)/4$. This variance can also be used as a way of combining the significance of ts in two samples, but then it is more efficient to weight the ts by their respective sample sizes. In that case, the formula for the variance must take the weights into consideration. A general

---

[1]In (3.14) and a number of formulas used subsequently, var(·) is used to stand for "the variance of whatever is in the parentheses" in order to avoid complicated subscripts on σ. Also, cov(·,·) will be used in later formulas to stand for "the covariance between the two statistics in the parentheses" for the same reason.

formula for the variance of a weighted combination of independently estimated ts is estimated as

$$\text{var}(\Sigma w_s t_s) = \Sigma w_s^2 \hat{\sigma}_{ts}^2, \tag{3.16}$$

where w_s is the weight applied to the t from sample s, and $\hat{\sigma}_{ts}^2$ is the estimated variance of t in sample s. In the case of a simple sum the weights in (3.16) are 1 and 1; in the case of a simple difference they are 1 and -1.

More complex weight patterns are also possible. For example, to see if the ordinal correlation between two variables changes as a function of age, one might have young children (6–8 years old), preadolescents (9–11), and adolescents (12–14). The ts between the same two variables are computed within each age group, and the question is whether the correlations are the same in the groups. The ts are computed and their variances are estimated using (3.8) in each group. The standard error of the three pairwise differences in ts can be estimated by substituting the respective variance estimates in (3.16), using a Bonferroni correction on the α level if analysiswise Type I errors are to be controlled.

The investigator's interest may focus on whether adolescents differ from both younger groups. In that case, a contrast strategy can be employed to investigate, first, whether correlation in the 12–14-year-olds differs from the average correlation in the other two, and, second, whether the latter two correlations differ from each other. The first question implies using (3.16) with weights for the groups of -1, -1, and 2, respectively, for the 6–8, 9–11, and 12–14 groups; the second is again a simple difference, so weights of 1 and -1 can be used for the two youngest.

Categorical Data

These methods can be adapted to categorical data. Where there are two variables, X and Y, consisting of ordered categories, one can obviously compute the tau between them and the corresponding standard error. Any third categorical variable, Z, ordered or not, can be used to subdivide the data. Then, within each category on Z, a tau and the corresponding standard error can be computed. These are conditional taus, $t_{XY|Z}$, and each can be tested for significance, and so on.

In methods for analyzing multivariate categorical data, such as loglinear analysis, associations between variables are often investigated in terms of dependence/independence conditional on some other variable(s). This can take the form of a summary chi-square statistic testing the hypothesis of independence, or it can reflect some more narrow aspect of the dependence represented by a contrast among the categories. Some such contrasts are referred to as "ordinal," but these often (e.g., Agresti, 1984) actually reflect an equal-interval assumption on the categories.

Where the investigator's interest lies in the degree to which monotonic (rather than equal-interval) relations between some X and Y exist, conditional on some Z, the methods described here seem closer to her or his purpose than a typical loglinear analysis. Testing for differences among different t_{XYZ} by using their combined respective variances will indicate whether this X,Y relation "interacts" with Z (i.e., differs according to levels on Z).

The control variable, Z, can actually consist of two or more categorical variables with their category-definitions combined. For example, if Z_1 has two categories and Z_2 has three, then "Z" could be defined in terms of all six crossed categories of Z_1 and Z_2, and the procedure can be extended to multiple Zs. Such a process can easily result in some t_{XYZ} being based on very few cases, so it may not be sensible to interpret or even compute all the t_{XYZ}. If this seems like a limitation of the procedure, it may be a blessing in disguise because it is informing the user about what is actually going on in the data rather than allowing him or her to make generalizations that may be quite misleading. In any event, the idea of conditional taus, and inferences about them, can be applied quite directly to categorical data.

Nonindependent ts

Different sorts of questions can arise when ts are from the same sample. For example, the question might be, "Does X_1 or X_2 correlate more highly with Y?" A number of other, sometimes more complex ones, are suggested in the next section. In all these, hypotheses about sums or differences—or differences of sums—must take into consideration the nonindependence of the ts. This is conceptually fairly simple in simple cases. For example, the variance of the difference between the taus of two variables with a third, such as a criterion, is

$$\text{var}(t_{1y} - t_{2y}) = \sigma_{t1y}^2 + \sigma_{t2y}^2 - 2 \, \text{cov}(t_{1y}, t_{2y}). \tag{3.17}$$

The generalization of (3.17) to the case of any weighted combination of nonindependent ts is

$$\text{var}\left(\sum_u w_u t_u\right) = \sum_u w_u^2 \sigma_{tu}^2 + \sum_{u \neq v} \sum w_u w_v \, \text{cov}(t_u, t_v). \tag{3.18}$$

In (3.18), the subscript u stands for a *pair* of variables, and v is a different pair. If the general formula (3.18) is applied in the simpler case depicted in (3.17), $u = 1,y$ or $u = 2,y$; the first weight is 1 and the second is –1; there are two covariance terms, $\text{cov}(t_{1y}, t_{2y})$ and the equivalent $\text{cov}(t_{2y}, t_{1y})$. The way to estimate the covariance terms is described in the next section.

A second kind of simple application is one where the research question is whether, in a single sample, the correlation between two variables, say, τ_{12}, is different from the correlation of two others, say τ_{34}. Again, the weights are 1 for t_{12} and -1 for t_{34}, so the form of (3.18) applies.

A more complicated situation might arise when a collection of variables is divided into clusters on a priori grounds. For example, seven variables might be divided into one cluster of three and one of four. If the data support the existence of clusters, then the average within-cluster correlation should be larger than the average between-cluster correlation. Specifically, the average of the three taus within cluster 1 and the six ($4 \times 3/2$) within cluster 2 should be larger than the average of the 12 (3×4) between-cluster taus. Averaging the nine within-cluster and comparing that average to the average of the 12 between-cluster means that the 9 should get weights of 1/9, and the 12 get weights of $-1/12$. The reason is that the null hypothesis is

$$(\tau_{12} + \tau_{13} + \tau_{23} + \tau_{45} + \tau_{46} + \tau_{47} + \tau_{56} + \tau_{57} + \tau_{67})/9$$
$$- (\tau_{14} + \tau_{15} + \tau_{16} + \tau_{17} + \tau_{24} + \tau_{25} + \tau_{26} + \tau_{27} + \tau_{34} + \tau_{35} + \tau_{36} + \tau_{37})/12$$
$$= 0.$$

Application of the formula is rather complex because there are now 441 terms to be summed in (3.18), 21 involving the variances of the individual ts and 420 involving the covariance of one t with another, but the principle is simple enough, and a computer will not mind doing the calculations. Compared to other things we might ask it to do, the work is rather minor.

Formulas similar to (3.15), (3.16), 3.(14), and (3.18) have very general application; any other independent statistics could be used for the variance of the difference in (3.15), and any two nonindependent statistics could be used in (3.17) instead of ts. The formula for the variance of the difference between the means of two scores obtained from the same subjects is like (3.17), for example. Analogous formulas are applied later for comparing d statistics that represent separations between distributions of different groups.

COVARIANCES OF ts

Population Covariances of ts

Inferences about ts from the same sample thus involve the sampling covariances between ts as well as their variances, as just noted, so it is necessary to have the expressions for these and for their unbiased estimates. The covariances also provide the basis for deriving approximate standard errors for t_b and t_d.

The methods used to derive (3.5) lead (Cliff & Charlin, 1992) to

$$\text{cov}(t_u, t_v) = \frac{4(n-2)\text{cov}(t_{iu}, t_{iv}) + 2\,\text{cov}(t_{ihu}, t_{ihv})}{n(n-1)} \tag{3.19}$$

as the expression for the covariance between two ts. Here, u and v again refer to pairs of variables. If u and v are the same, then this becomes the variance of t, (3.5). The covariance is seen to depend, first, on the tendency of the t_i underlying the two ts to covary and, second, on the tendency for the individual t_{ih} to covary. In large samples, this latter effect is negligible.

Sample Estimate of Covariance of ts

The unbiased[2] sample estimate can be found by the same methods used before to be

$$\text{Est}[\text{cov}(t_u, t_v)] = \frac{4(n-1)\text{Est}[\text{cov}(t_{iu}, t_{iv})] - 2\,\text{Est}[\text{cov}(t_{ihu}, t_{ihv})]}{(n-2)(n-3)}. \tag{3.20}$$

This formula is analogous to (3.6); however, the results of Long and Cliff (in press) suggest that, instead of generalizing (3.6), one should generalize (3.11) to

$$\text{Est}[\text{cov}(t_u, t_v)] = \frac{4(n-2)\text{Est}[\text{cov}(t_{iu}, t_{iv})] + 2\,\text{Est}[\text{cov}(t_{ihu}, t_{ihv})]}{n(n-1)}. \tag{3.21}$$

using

$$\text{Est}[\text{cov}(t_{iu}, t_{iv})] = \Sigma(t_{iu} - t_u)(t_{iv} - t_v)/(n-1), \tag{3.22}$$

which for computational purposes is best expressed as

$$\frac{\sum_i [(\sum_h t_{ihu})(\sum_h t_{ihv})] - n(n-1)^2 t_u t_v}{(n-1)^3}, \tag{3.23}$$

---

[2]Here, and at later places, the abbreviation "Est" stands for "an estimate of," analogous to the way $\hat{\sigma}^2$ was used for the estimate of σ_t^2.

and

$$\text{Est}[\text{cov}(t_{ihu},t_{ihv})] = \frac{\Sigma\Sigma(t_{ihu} - t_u)(t_{ihv} - t_v)}{n(n-1)-1}, \tag{3.24}$$

which is likewise most easily computed as

$$\frac{\Sigma\Sigma t_{ihu} t_{ihv} - n(n-1)t_u t_v}{n(n-1)-1}. \tag{3.25}$$

It is clear that estimating these covariances is even more computationally demanding than estimating the variances because there will be two pairs of pairs of variables involved. However, assuming access to reasonable computing capacity and the availability of suitable computer programs, this is not a reason to hesitate to use them when they are called for. Moreover, simplified versions are justifiable in large samples because the influence of the $\text{Est}[\text{cov}(t_{ihu},t_{ihv})]$, which is the most arduous term to compute, then becomes negligible relative to the other one.

These computations can be illustrated with the data from Table 3.1. From there, using computations summarized in Table 3.3, it can be found that $\text{Est}[\text{cov}(t_{ixy},t_{ixz})] = .01749$ and $\text{Est}[\text{cov}(t_{ihxy},t_{ihxz})] = .1818$, leading to $\text{Est}[\text{cov}(t_{xy},t_{xz})] = .0140$ via (3.21).

The calculations from Tables 3.2 and 3.3 can be combined to provide a c.i. for the difference, $\tau_{xy} - \tau_{xz}$, based on substituting the sample estimates obtained so far in (3.17). Thus, the estimated variance of the difference is $.0748 + .0348 - 2 \times .0140 = .0816$, so the standard error of the difference is .286. This could be used as the denominator of the difference in the ts to test the hypothesis of zero difference in τs, but it seems pointless to do so when the sample difference is zero. This estimated standard error can, however, be used in the .95 c.i., $t_{12} - t_{13} \pm z_{\alpha/2}s_{\text{diff}}$, which here is $0 \pm 1.96 \times$

TABLE 3.3
Computation of Covariance between Two ts Using Formula (3.27)

From Table 3.1

$$\Sigma(\hat{t}_{ixy} - t_{xy})(\hat{t}_{ixz} - t_{xz})/(n-1) = .01749$$

$$\Sigma\Sigma(t_{ihxy} - t_{xy})(t_{ihxz} - t_{xz})/[n(n-1)-1] = .1818$$

$$\text{Est}[\text{cov}(t_{xy},t_{xz})] = \frac{4 \times 6 \times .01749 + 2 \times .1818}{8 \times 7}$$

$$= .0140$$

.286, or $0 \pm .560$. Thus, with this small sample, the obtained difference of zero could be masking a substantial difference in the population.

Extended Applications

The availability of the formulas for variances and covariances of taus permits a wide variety of applications, including alternatives to a fair proportion of applications of confirmatory factor analyses. The cluster analysis application suggested is one example, and it can clearly be extended to multiple clusters.[3] Where there is an a priori expectation that certain variables will cluster, the between-cluster taus can be compared to within-cluster, either as parts of averages or as individual coefficients, and the plausibility of the hypothesized clustering can thus be evaluated, and aberrant members of proposed clusters can be identified by noting that a within-cluster correlation is significantly too low or that a between-cluster is too high.

The multitrait–multimethod matrix (MTMMM) is another example. Campbell and Fiske's (1959) original formulation was more qualitative than the highly parametric version usually studied by covariance structure analysts. In it, monotrait–heteromethod correlations (t_{mh}) should be higher than heterotrait–monomethod (t_{hm}) and heterotrait–heteromethod (t_{hh}) coefficients. The significance of the differences between such individual correlations, and between averages of correlations of a given kind for a given trait, can be determined using the formulas here. Given the nature of most of the psychometric instruments and crude operational indices to which the MTMMM is applied, ordinal correlations are more generally applicable than Pearson's, and the comparisons of the size of different kinds of coefficients in the matrix can be made. That is, each t_{mh} can be compared to the relevant t_{hm} and t_{hh}. For inferential purposes, the significance of the differences can be evaluated using the method outlined here for comparing nonindependent ts.

Such a procedure seems preferable to hammering the data into the mold that covariance structure analysis (CSA) requires. It has the additional advantage of not requiring the endless adjustment of the status or value of parameters in the CSA model being fit that seems to characterize many such analyses. It also avoids the seemingly endless debate over how to evaluate overall goodness of fit of such models, a debate whose basis is suspect due

---

[3]Where the investigator has only weak expectations concerning the nature of the clusters of variables, any of the standard exploratory cluster procedures can be employed to define clusters. Binclus (Cliff, McCormick, Zatkin, Cudeck, & Collins, 1986), which allows overlapping clusters, might be particularly adapted to that role when taus are the basis of the clustering. A good strategy is a cross-validation method, dividing the sample in half randomly. The cluster procedure is applied in one half. Then the statistical reliability of the clusters can be assessed in the other, independent, half of the data by the methods suggested here.

to the nature of the true distributions of the variables involved. A drawback, of course, is that using these ordinal methods would require one to forgo the pleasures of drawing arrows between circles and boxes, with its attendant feelings of mastery and power.

Sometimes CSA methods are applied in a group-comparison fashion, testing whether the structures are the same in different subpopulations. Obviously, one can always test the differences between taus individually, using (3.11) in (3.15), but the equality in different groups of the average correlation in a given cluster can be done by generalizing (3.15). The variance of the average tau in a cluster can be found by employing (3.18) within each group. Then the difference between the averages in different groups has a sampling variance that is the sum of these for the two groups, just as in (3.15). The question of whether there are differences between groups in their levels on the variables can be investigated by using the methods in chapter 5.

Questions of longitudinal (sometimes called cross-panel) homogeneity of correlational pattern can be investigated as well. The variances of differences in nonindependent taus between particular variables can be put into the framework provided by (3.18), just by using weight of 1 for one panel and −1 for the other. Likewise, the cross-time correlation between two variables can be compared to one or the average of both of the within-time correlations of the same two variables. This process can be generalized to the average taus within a cluster. Comparing the average within-time correlations at different times would mean using weights of $1/p(p-1)$ for all the taus in one panel and $-1/p(p-1)$ for those in the other. On the other hand, comparing between-time taus to those within time would use $1/p^2$ for the between-time coefficients and $-1/p(p-1)$ for those within if the comparison is to one time, and $1/2p(p-1)$ if the comparison is to the average of both sets of within-time correlations.

These suggestions include only a few of the questions that it is possible to answer by formulating them as equalities or differences in correlations. Others that are suggested by one's theories, expectations, or data can be answered as readily, requiring only a modest degree of ingenuity. Such formulations are often closer to the investigator's intent than are those that require him or her to answer the question using CSA, which often will be answering a different question.

Linear Models and Taus

The foregoing suggestions do not include the application of standard linear model techniques to matrices of taus. What I *have* tried to suggest is that one's research questions can often been investigated with these alternative methods.

The direct application of multivariate methods to tau correlations can lead to erroneous results or interpretations. The difficulty lies in two things. The fundamental one is that standard models such as factor analysis are based on weighting scores. Parallel models for ordinal variables are not possible because they would not be invariant under monotonic transformation. It also seems implausible to consider the dominance relations on one variable to be a linear function of dominance relations on other variables. Thus, linear models cannot be expected to apply to dominance data.

A more direct difficulty lies in the partialing process that is part of standard linear model techniques. As indicated in chapter 2, partial tau cannot be viewed as a correlation between X and Y when Z is held constant, even under ideal (i.e., multinormal) circumstances. For that reason, path analysis and factor analysis, which are based on partialing techniques, or which assume certain partial correlations in the models, can lead to misleading results when applied to taus. However, as noted, research questions investigated with path analysis can often be formulated in such a way as to permit their evaluation using taus and their differences, and such formulations are often more representative of the investigator's interest.

The reader may have observed that the chapter following is apparently about an ordinal version of multiple regression, and suspect some inconsistency with the previous paragraph. However, on reading chapter 4 it will be seen that the kind of multiple regression that can be applied to taus has a more limited interpretation than is often standard in multiple regression.[4] The coefficients that correspond to regression weights, for example, cannot be viewed as either partial regression weights or as structural coefficients that explain the dependent variable in terms of the independent ones. Instead, they are simply coefficients that optimize prediction. Thus, in the case of multiple regression, as well as others, the analysis of taus can be adapted to serve many, but far from all, of the goals that an investigator has. Additionally, the results are likely to be less prone to the kind of inappropriate interpretation that seems to accompany many linear model analyses.

VARIANCES OF MODIFIED ts

Ties and ts

Several forms of tau modified to take account of ties were noted in the previous chapter. Deriving sampling variances for them from first principles is a task beyond the capability of the author, and, as far as is known, no one else has done so, except in cases where the data are reducible to a few categories (cf. Agresti, 1984; Yu & Dunn, 1982).

---

[4]Bear in mind that I feel that such interpretations of multiple regressions are often ill-founded (Cliff, 1983, 1991).

What can be done instead is to use methods that derive the variances of these taus for very large samples—that is, "asymptotic" variances. These are values that the variances are guaranteed to approach as the sample becomes infinitely large. One might well wonder about the importance of sampling error estimates when the sample is very large, because then the sample estimates will be very close to the population values anyway, but the assumption is that values derived in this way will often adequately represent matters in empirical samples that are not very large.

The difficulty posed by the tau estimates that adjust for ties is that they are a function not only of the $t_{ihjk}s$, as t_a is, but also of the number of ties on one or both variables. This number of ties is itself subject to sampling fluctuation, so now there are two or three influences on the value of the tau estimate, and so on their sampling error. Furthermore, the number of ties is in the denominator of all these coefficients, and so may have quite an influence on the value of the ratios.

A commonly used approach to estimating the variance of a random variable that is a function of two or more other random variables is the "delta method." Descriptions of it can be found in various statistical sources, Kendall and Stuart (1958, p. 231) and Agresti (1984) being examples. The sample counterparts of τ_{bjk} and τ_{djk} can both be thought of as ratios, each having t_{ajk} in the numerator and "self-taus," that is, proportions untied on the variable, t_{ajj}, in the case of t_d, or $(t_{ajj}t_{akk})^{1/2}$, the case of t_b, in the denominator. This is because $t_{ajk} = Et_{ihjk}$, even when $j = k$; all the t_{ihjj} are ones, except for the pairs that are tied, where they are zeros.

Application of the delta method (some details are sketched by Cliff & Charlin, 1991) leads to the following expression for the asymptotic variance of t_d:

$$\mathrm{var}(t_{djk}) = \frac{\sigma_{jk}^{2}}{\tau_{jj}^{2}} - \frac{2\tau_{jk}\mathrm{cov}(t_{jk},t_{jj})}{\tau_{jj}^{3}} + \frac{\tau_{jk}^{2}\sigma_{jj}^{2}}{\tau_{jj}^{3}}. \tag{3.26}$$

The variance of t_{ajj} in (3.26) can be estimated by the same formula as the variance of t_{ajk}, (3.6). Here, there will be t_js, just as in the more ordinary case; their variation represents the differential tendency for different individuals to be involved in ties. What is also necessary in the variance of t_d is the covariance between t_{ajj} and t_{ajk}, which can be estimated by adapting (3.23). The powers of t_{jj} would need to be substituted in the denominators in (3.26).

Thus, it is possible, but complicated, to find the variances of t_ds. It is prudent to use such a formula with considerable caution because there are so many terms in it that need to be estimated.

It is even more complex to find the variances of t_bs because they involve the proportions of ties in two variables. Using the same methods as before, it can be found that

$$\text{var}(t_{bjk}) = \sigma_{jk}^2 - \tau_{jk}\left(\frac{\sigma_{jk,jj}}{\tau_{jj}} + \frac{\sigma_{jk,kk}}{\tau_{kk}}\right) + \tau_{jk}^2\left(\frac{\sigma_{jj}^2}{4\tau_{jj}^2} + \frac{\sigma_{kk}^2}{4\tau_{kk}^2} + \frac{\sigma_{jj,kk}}{2\tau_{jj}\tau_{kk}}\right) \quad (3.27)$$

is the variance of t_{bjk}.

Thus, asymptotic variances for these derived forms of tau can be found, although they are complex due to the necessity of incorporating the effects of sampling of the proportions of tied pairs into them. In applications the unbiased estimates of all the quantities would be substituted into the formulas. The result would not itself be unbiased, but such biases would probably be small, and the task of deriving unbiased estimates is too daunting to undertake.

These formulas are completely general, applicable no matter what the nature of the data. However, a special situation occurs when the variables are dichotomous because then the data consist of proportions. This permits the application of other methods that can then be applied. Agresti (1984) and Yu and Dunn (1982) provide some discussion of t_b and t_d in this case, but space will not be taken for it here.

OTHER APPLICATIONS OF TAU

Some suggestions concerning types of applications have been made in this chapter, but some further observations can be made on the utility of methods for making inferences about taus and their differences and averages. Most obviously, whenever inferences are to be made about correlations, the standard error formulas provided here permit the investigator to make the corresponding inferences about the taus. This can be preferable for any of the motives presented in Chapter 1: concern about the measurement status of the variables, concern about the assumptions underlying the inferences in Pearson correlation, or simply preference for an ordinal measure of degree of relation.

Use of the sampling-based formulas, rather than simply relying on tests of independence, greatly broadens the range of applications of tau. For example, it permits one to test whether taus are equal in several populations. Formula (3.15) can be used to test the hypothesis $\tau_1 = \tau_2$; one simply uses $(t_1 - t_2)/[\text{var}(t_1 - t_2)]^{1/2}$ as a normal deviate. For example, Stallings (1993) used this procedure in a behavior genetics application to test whether twin-pair correlations (i.e., the correlation between one twin and the other on a variable) were the same in identical twins as in fraternals to test the hypothesis of greater resemblance in twins. He also divided the twins into subgroups on the basis of their reported frequency of contact, and tested the differences in correlations between those with more contact compared to those with less. He did similar analyses involving comparisons between twin-pair correlations in male and female pairs, as well as several involving other family members.

Since there were tests of this kind involving several traits on the twins, and the differences between fraternals and identicals (or males and females) were significant on some and not on others, an omnibus test of the average difference might have been desirable in order to be sure of controlling the analysiswise alpha level. Several taus here come from the same individuals, so the taus' covariances must be taken into account in assessing the difference in their averages in a manner parallel to what was suggested in the case of comparing intracluster to intercluster taus.

In other applications one might want to test whether p variables are independent, and this could be done using their average t and the formula for the variance of t under independence, (3.14). This can actually be done in two ways. If there are p variables (so that there are $p(p-1)/2$ different pairs of variables) and the variables are all independent, each t_{jk} is an independent random variable with variance (3.14). Then the sum of the $p(p-1)/2$ of them is normal with variance $\frac{1}{2}p(p-1)(4n+10)/9n(n-1)$, so

$$\chi_1^2 = \frac{\left(\sum_{j>k}\sum t_{jk}\right)^2}{\frac{1}{2}p(p-1)(4n+10)/9n(n-1)} \tag{3.28}$$

is a 1-df chi-square variate under the hypothesis of complete independence. Alternatively, each t_{jk} can be squared and then summed. Under the hypothesis of independence, each of these is an independent normal deviate with variance (3.14), so

$$\chi^2 = \frac{\sum_{j>k}\sum t_{jk}^2}{(4n+10)/9n(n-1)} \tag{3.29}$$

is a chi-squared variate with $\frac{1}{2}p(p-1)$ df.

I believe that this kind of hypothesis testing should be carried out only after careful consideration of the plausibility of the null hypothesis that all the variables are independent. If an investigator really wants to test the hypothesis that the average τ is zero and expects that some individual ones may not be zero, then (3.28) and (3.29) do not employ an appropriate variance for the sum or average. The more complex version (3.18), using unit weights, with the variances of all the taus estimated from (3.11) and their covariances estimated from (3.21), is the appropriate denominator. However, given the scarcity of computer routines for estimated variances of t, much less the covariances, these procedures offer an alternative to apply if the situation seems to justify it.

Taus With an External Variable

Taus can be used in a repeated-measures design where, for example, one is looking for trends in individual subjects across time, as in a study of development or aging. That is, one has scores of n individuals for each of p occasions and wishes to estimate the extent to which the scores seem to show a trend across time and to assess its statistical reliability. There are several ways in which this can be done ordinally, and the most common one is probably Friedman's test (Friedman, 1937), which uses average ranks. It will be discussed in the section on r_S and the coefficient of concordance. The approach suggested here is different.

Friedman's test is of the omnibus variety in the sense that it looks for any systematic deviation from equiprobable permutations. In looking for trends across time, one is usually expecting a monotonic relation between the scores of individuals and the order provided by time, not just *any* relation with time, so it seems that a sharper test of the research hypothesis might be desirable and possible. This should be provided by computing the τ between each individual's scores and the temporal order. The average of these τs is then a useful descriptive statistic, reflecting the degree to which individuals display monotonic trends. Then, rather than assuming that each of these τ_i reflects independent random permutations, it seems more plausible to believe that each is a number that, at least approximately, reflects some characteristic of the individual. The individuals can be considered a sample from some population, where there is a mean of all the τs, μ_τ, and a null hypothesis might be $\mu_\tau = 0$. The τs can thus be considered to be like any other score, and their sample mean and variance computed and used in an ordinary Student's t test of $\mu_\tau = 0$. The single-sample Student's t has been found to be rather insensitive to distributional assumptions, so we need not be very concerned on the score of distributional concerns about the distribution of the τ in the population.

This kind of analysis need not be confined to applications involving temporal orders. Any other external variable that provides an order can be used instead. The subjects could be rating stimuli on some property, and the order could be any physical characteristic of the simuli. Or it could be a theoretical order or one observed in the past. In any of these cases, the average t with the standard order would be of interest, and inferences about it could be made by just considering that one has sampled n ts from a population. A more elaborate approach to multiple repeated-measures designs is discussed in chapter 6, which is on the repeated-measures version of the d statistic.

An additional application of these formulas is found in the next chapter on ordinal analogues of multiple regression.

INFERENCES ABOUT ρ_S

One reason for focusing on τ instead of ρ_S in this book is the complication in the latter's sampling properties. The first aspect of this is the observation that r_S is a biased estimate of its population counterpart. Furthermore, the bias involves τ! Kendall (1970) shows that $E(r_S) = [(n - 2)\rho_S + 3\tau]/(n + 1)$, which is clearer if it is rearranged into $\rho - 3(\rho - \tau)/(n + 1)$. If one wants an unbiased estimate of ρ_S, therefore, it is necessary to use

$$\hat{\rho}_S = r_S + 3(r_S - t)/(n - 2). \tag{3.30}$$

Note that the correction will usually be quite small because the two coefficients are typically very comparable in size. That is not always the case, though, so with a small sample the correction could be appreciable.

The larger complication concerning inferences about ρ_S is that there is no general expression for the variance of r_S comparable to (3.5). In fact, Kendall (1970) asserts that no such expression is possible "in terms of elementary functions." There are some possibilities if one is willing to assume bivariate normality. In that case, the variance of r_S has been shown to be a complex power series function of the Pearson ρ^2. (See David & Mallows, 1961 and Fieller & Pearson, 1961 and their references for this topic.) Kraemer (1974, 1975) provides a more easily used approximation for the normal case based on the Student t distribution. Using these might be dismissed on the grounds that one might as well use r itself if bivariate normality is assumed, but these methods can provide at least approximate bases for inferences in more general cases. However, the behavior of these methods seems not to have been as extensively investigated as they may have deserved, so their applicability remained speculative until the study by Caruso and Cliff (1995).

That work examined several candidates for inferences about ρ_S with bivariate normal data under a variety of conditions of sample size and level of parent population. Rather surprisingly, they found that the most effective inference procedure to use for inferences about ρ_S was the "Fisher z" transformation of r_S. All the other suggested formulas for the standard error of r_S showed poor performance in terms of size, power, or coverage under at least some of the conditions. One reason this is surprising is that this transformation has been found to have problems in the case for which it is ordinarily used, inferences about Pearson r (e.g., Long & Cliff, 1995). Note that Caruso and Cliff's (1995) results, although obtained under the assumption of bivariate normality, have more generality. They apply to any data that is monotonically transformable to bivariate normality since r_S and ρ_S are invariant under such a transformation.

Kendall (1970) furnishes a maximum possible value for $\sigma_{r_S}^2$, comparable to the maximum that he suggested for σ_t^2, and that I argued against as unrealistically conservative. This expression is $\sigma_{r_S}^2 \leq 3(1 - \rho_S^2)/n$. In general inferences about ρ_S the choices are to assume that the data are normal or transformable to bivariate normality and use the Fisher z transformation, or to use the conservative expression for the variance. Otherwise, all that one can seemingly do is to test the hypothesis that the two variables are independent, in spite of the limitations that have been suggested here for such an approach. This independence test can be done in small samples using available tables of "significant" values of r_S, such as Table 2 in the Appendix or for n above 20, r_S is adequately normally distributed around zero (Kendall, 1970) under independence, with

$$\sigma_{r_S}^2 = 1/(n - 1). \tag{3.31}$$

DERIVATIONS OF FORMULAS

The formulas in this chapter can be derived by elementary methods, although sometimes in complex ways, using the principles of expected values. The main aspects used are the following:

1. The definitions of variances and covariances of estimates v or u of η or θ in terms of expected values: $\sigma_v^2 = E[v - E(v)]^2$ and $\text{cov}(u,v) = E[uv - E(u)E(v)]$.
2. The consequence that, if u and v are unbiased estimates of η and θ, respectively, then $\sigma_v^2 = E(v^2) - \theta^2$, and $\text{cov}(u,v) = E(uv) - \eta\theta$, and the algebraically equivalent statements about $E(v^2)$ and $E(uv)$.
3. The principle that if estimators u and v are independent, then $E(uv) = E(u)E(v)$.
4. The expected value of a sum is the sum of the expected values: $E(u + v) = E(u) + E(v)$, elaborated to $E\sum_m u_m = \sum_m E(u_m)$.

A few other characteristics of expected values are used from time to time, but these are the main ones employed here. The other aspect that is important is a very tedious and sometimes eye- or mind-straining, attention to subscripts.

Variance of t

Since t is an unbiased estimate of τ,

$$\sigma_t^2 = E(t^2) - \tau^2.$$

By definition of t,

$$t^2 = \frac{(\sum\sum_{i \neq h} t_{ih})^2}{[n(n-1)]^2}.$$

The squared term in the numerator means that every element in the t_{ih} matrix is to be multiplied by every other one, and the resulting $n(n-1) \times n(n-1)$ products are summed: $\sum\sum\sum\sum t_{ih}t_{pq}$. The products in the quadruple sum are of different kinds, and they will have different expectations. We have to recognize the different kinds, figure out what the expectation of each is, and deduce how many there are of each kind.

The different kinds are defined by how many subscripts are shared between t_{ih} and t_{pq}. In the first kind the subscripts are the same in both. Since the t_{ih} matrix is symmetric, this can happen in two ways. One is the obvious one where $p = i$ and $q = h$, so that the product is clearly t_{ih}^2, but there is a parallel instance where t_{ih} is matched with its symmetrically placed counterpart, t_{hi}, so there are for each t_{ih} two ways to get t_{ih}^2. There are $n(n-1)$ t_{ih} terms, so the quadruple sum has $2n(n-1)$ terms that have expectation $E(t_{ih}^2)$. By the principle about variances of unbiased estimates, $E(t_{ih}^2) = \sigma_{tih}^2 + \tau^2$.

The second kind of term has one subscript in common between t_{ih} and t_{pq}. That is, $p = i$ or h or $q = i$ or h, but not both. These are products of terms in the same row or column or in the same row as column or column as row, but not in the same position in the row or column. Again due to the symmetry of the t_{ih} matrix, it does not matter which of these four possibilities occurs. For example, considering t_{12}, we could have $t_{12}t_{13}$ or $t_{12}t_{32}$ or $t_{12}t_{31}$ or $t_{12}t_{23}$. Two of these four, $t_{12}t_{13}$ and $t_{12}t_{31}$, have expectation t_1^2, and the other two have expectation t_2^2. The reason can be seen as follows. Take the first possibility, $E(t_{12}t_{13})$. Each of the two multiplied elements is independently sampled, except that the elements have to be connected to subject 1, so $E(t_{12}t_{13}) = E(t_{12})E(t_{13})$; however, for any h, $E(t_{1h}) = t_i$, so $E(t_{12}t_{13}) = t_1^2$. The subscript 3 could be replaced by any other number except 1 or 2, so $t_{12}t_{1q}$ has $n - 2$ possibilities, each with expectation t_1^2, and we remember there are actually four ways in which one subscript could match. There are $n(n-1)$

terms like t_{12}, each with $4(n-2)$ matches, that is, with expectation t_i^2, so there are $4n(n-1)(n-2)E(t_i^2)$ terms. As in other expected values of squared random variables, $E(t_i^2) = \sigma_{ti}^2 + [E(t_i)]^2$, and we know that $E(t_i) = \tau$ because t_i is an average, over h, of the t_{ih}.

The third kind of term has no subscripts in common, such as $t_{12}t_{34}$. This type is easier to deal with because sampling persons 1 and 2 is independent of sampling 3 and 4, so t_{12} and t_{34} are independent, each having expectation τ. There are $n(n-1)(n-2)(n-3)$ such terms because all the subscripts have to be different; each such term has expectation τ^2.

Collecting all the terms into one expession, we have

$$E(\Sigma\Sigma\Sigma\Sigma t_{ih}t_{pq}) = 2n(n-1)(\sigma_{tih}^2 + \tau^2) + 4n(n-1)(n-2)(\sigma_{ti}^2 + \tau^2)$$
$$+ n(n-1)(n-2)(n-3)\tau^2.$$

Collecting all the terms involving τ, one finds that there are $[n(n-1)]^2$ of them, so

$$\frac{\Sigma\Sigma\Sigma\Sigma t_{ih}t_{pq}}{[n(n-1)]^2} - \tau^2 = \frac{2n(n-1)\sigma_{tih}^2 + 4n(n-1)(n-2)\sigma_{ti}^2}{[n(n-1)]^2}.$$

On the right-hand side, $n(n-1)$ cancels out of numerator and denominator, and we can change the order of the two terms in the numerator, so

$$\sigma_t^2 = \frac{4(n-2)\sigma_{ti}^2 + 2\sigma_{tih}^2}{n(n-1)},$$

which is the formula we were looking for, (3.5).

Unbiased Estimate of σ_t^2

The methods by which one can arrive at (3.6) as the unbiased estimate of σ_t^2 are rather roundabout. A simpler approach is to start from the equation and show that (3.5) is its expectation. The methods involve noting what subscripts are in common and what the expectations are of different terms.

The process can start from the definition of s_{tih}^2,

$$s_{tih}^2 = \frac{\displaystyle\sum_{i \neq h}\sum (t_{ih} - t)^2}{n(n-1)},$$

and finding its expectation. Expanding the numerator and noting that $\sum\sum t_{ih}/n(n-1) = t$ leads to $\sum\sum t_{ih}^2 - n(n-1)t^2$. Then $E(t_{ih}^2) = \tau^2 + \sigma_{ih}^2$ and $E(t^2) = \tau^2 + \sigma_t^2$, by the principle about expectations of squared unbiased estimates. Putting these together in the numerator gives

$$E[\sum\sum t_{ih}^2 - n(n-1)t^2] = n(n-1)(\sigma_{tih}^2 + \tau^2) - n(n-1)(\sigma_t^2 + \tau^2),$$

and substituting the already derived expression for σ_t^2, $[4(n-2)\sigma_{ti}^2 + 2\sigma_{tih}^2]/n(n-1)$, means that

$$E[\sum\sum t_{ih}^2 - n(n-1)t^2] = n(n-1)\sigma_{tih}^2 - 4(n-2)\sigma_{ti}^2 - 2\sigma_{tih}^2$$

$$= (n^2 - n - 2)\sigma_{tih}^2 - 4(n-2)\,\sigma_{ti}^2.$$

We put this aside for the moment and turn to finding the expectation of s_{ti}^2. Its definition is $\sum_i(\hat{t}_i - t)^2/n$, which can be rearranged as $[\sum\hat{t}_i^2 - nt^2)]/n$ by using the fact that $t = \sum\hat{t}_i/n$. Now, $\hat{t}_i = \sum_{i\neq h}t_{ih}/(n-1)$, so $\hat{t}_i^2$ will have in its numerator $n-1$ terms like t_{ih}^2 and $(n-1)(n-2)$ like $t_{ih}t_{im}$. The expectation of each of those of the first kind is, as before, $\sigma_{tih}^2 + \tau^2$, whereas that of the second is t_i^2 because t_{ih} and t_{im} are independent within t_i, each having t_i as its expectation. Putting the two kinds of terms together and noting that there are n terms in the summation, each having this expectation, gives

$$E(\sum\hat{t}_i^2) = \frac{n[(n-1)(\sigma_{tih}^2 + \tau^2) + (n-1)(n-2)(\sigma_{ti}^2 + \tau^2)]}{(n-1)^2}.$$

Collecting the terms in the numerator gives $n(n-1)\sigma_{tih}^2 + n(n-1)(n-2)\sigma_{ti}^2 + n(n-1)^2\tau^2$.

From this, we need to subtract n times the expectation of t^2, which is, as with the expectations of other squared unbiased estimates, $\tau^2 + \sigma_t^2$, and we have already worked out that $\sigma_t^2 = [4(n-2)\sigma_{ti}^2 + 2\sigma_{tih}^2]/n(n-1)$. There are exactly the same number of τ^2 terms in $\sum\hat{t}_i^2$ as there are in nt^2, so they cancel out, leaving

$$E(\sum\hat{t}_i^2 - nt^2) = \frac{n(n-1)(n-2)\sigma_{ti}^2 + n(n-1)\sigma_{tih}^2}{(n-1)^2}$$

$$-\frac{n[4(n-2) + 2\sigma_{tih}^2]}{n(n-1)}.$$

The factor $n - 1$ can be canceled in numerator and denominator of the first term, and likewise n in the second, so both have denominator $n - 1$. Putting both over this leads to

$$E(\Sigma \hat{t_i^2} - nt^2) = \frac{n(n-2)\sigma_{ti}^2 + n\sigma_{tih}^2 - 4(n-2)\sigma_{ti}^2 - 2\sigma_{tih}^2}{n-1}.$$

Collecting terms and dividing by n to arrive at s_{ti}^2 gives

$$E(s_{ti}^2) = \frac{(n-2)(n-4)\sigma_{ti}^2 + (n-2)\sigma_{tih}^2}{n(n-1)}.$$

Putting together this expected value with the previously developed value of s_{tih}^2 leads to

$$E[4(n-1)s_{ti}^2 - 2s_{tih}^2] = \frac{4(n-1)(n-2)[(n-4)\sigma_{ti}^2 + \sigma_{tih}^2]}{n(n-1)}$$

$$-\frac{2[(n^2-n-2)\sigma_{tih}^2 - 4(n-2)\sigma_{ti}^2]}{n(n-1)}.$$

Note that the coefficients of σ_{ti}^2 from the two terms are $4(n-1)(n-2)(n-4)$ from the first term and $8(n-2)$ from the second. Factoring out the $4(n-2)$ leads to $(n-1)(n-4) + 2$ or $n^2 - 5n + 6$, which again factors into $(n-2)(n-3)$, so the coefficient of σ_{ti}^2 is $4(n-2)^2(n-3)$. The coefficients of σ_{tih}^2 are $4(n-1)(n-2)$ and $-2(n^2 - n - 2)$, but we note that the second polynomial factors into $(n+1)(n-2)$. Putting the two together and factoring out $2(n-2)$ give $2(n-2)[2(n-1) - (n+1)]$, which reduces to $2(n-2)(n-3)$.

Putting these parts together and seeing that both contain the factor $(n-2)(n-3)$ means

$$E[4(n-1)s_{ti}^2 - 2s_{tih}^2] = \frac{4(n-1)(n-2)[(n-4)\sigma_{ti}^2 + \sigma_{tih}^2]}{n(n-1)}$$

$$-\frac{2[(n^2-n-2)\sigma_{tih}^2 - 4(n-2)\sigma_{ti}^2]}{n(n-1)}.$$

This expression is the same as σ_{ti}^2 except for the extra factors $(n-2)(n-3)$, so dividing by this we finally arrive at

$$E\left[\frac{4(n-1)s_{ti}^2 - 2s_{tij}^2}{(n-2)(n-3)}\right] = \sigma_t^2,$$

which was what we wanted to show.

Thus we see that rather tedious and fussy processes lead to the overall expression for σ_t^2 and for its unbiased estimate. One reason for going about it in this way is that it has not been necessary to assume continuity for the variables involved. The formulas just follow from the definition of d_{ihx} and $t_{ihxy} = d_{ihx}d_{ihy}$, and from the definitions of variance and the properties of expected values. Thus, the formulas apply to any kinds of variables that provide orders, including those on which there are ties.

4

Predicting Ordinal Relations: Ordinal Analogues of Multiple Regression[1]

SCARCITY OF MULTIVARIATE METHODS

Ordinal methods are used for analyzing data in only a few instances, becoming almost unknown once the data go beyond the simplest kinds of bivariate correlations or one-way comparisons of location. Part of the reason for not treating data ordinally is that there is inherently less that we can do with ordinal data. Multivariate models are almost always based on additive assumptions that can at best be only crudely valid when the data are ordinal. But part of the answer is also that less methodology has been developed for analyzing ordinal data, and what there is is sometimes obscure.

One approach to more sophisticated analyses of ordinal data, dating from the early 1960s, has been to *assume* a particular model fits the data and then *transform* the observed scale so that it optimally fits the model. The earliest suggestion of this kind was perhaps Anderson's (1962), who suggested—but did not implement with a public algorithm—the possibility in the two-way ANOVA case. The development that provided the greatest stimulus to this kind of work was undoubtedly Shepard's (1962) demonstration that it could be implemented in the context of multidimensional scaling—that is, the fitting of the euclidean distance model to data on the pairwise similarity of stimuli—and that such an implementation would make the interpretation of some data sets simpler and more satisfying. The outcome of such an analysis is a ratio scale for the similarity, and the spatial coordinates of the stimuli

---

[1]This chapter is based on Cliff (1994), published in the *British Journal of Mathematical and Statistical Psychology*.

provide multiple interval scales for the stimuli. Thus, the process of fitting the model provided the constraints necessary to define the interval scales.

These procedures were rapidly extended to multivariate models other than the one for euclidean distance, and packages became, and still are, available to perform such analyses. Notable examples include the the Alscal series (Takane, Young, & de Leeuw, 1977; Young, de Leeuw, & Takane, 1976), and several others are described in books, such as Young and Hamer (1987), and review articles such as Young (1984). Some of these programs are in widely marketed computer packages.

The methods have had considerable application, but have never replaced the traditional, normal-based ones to any large degree. The reasons for the limited application are not completely clear because the methods seem to offer considerable advantage over assuming that the data come to us on what are already interval scales, as is required by the standard linear models that are so widely used. One possible reason is the methods' near divorce from inferential issues; the results are typically used only descriptively, and issues such as providing standard errors for scale values, determining whether structures for stimuli are "significantly different," and the like are difficult to integrate into this methodology. Some exceptions do exist. Takane (1981, 1982) and Ramsay (1978, 1980, 1982) have based methods on the maximum likelihood principle, so they provide inferential information. However, these inferential methods are exceptions, and they never "caught on" to the same extent that the more purely data-descriptive ones did. Also, rough-and-ready methods based on replicability of results or on adaptation of standard statistical methodology are perhaps possible, but again they have never had widespread adoption. The lack of influence by these empirical methods for defining the nature of scales has been an impediment to the advancement of psychology, in my opinion, one comparable to the corresponding failure of the abstract measurement theories (Cliff, 1992).

Two other possible reasons for the circumscribed effect of the "nonmetric revolution" come to mind. One is the apparent reluctance of those who apply the methods to believe the results of a nonmetric analysis in terms of its definition of the nature of the response variable that has been observed. That is, it was almost never concluded that the transformed version of the response scale was its "real" form, one that could be carried over into other contexts. Attempts were sometimes made (e.g., Cliff, 1972) in that direction, but even those tended to be half-hearted. We who used the methods never quite believed their results, it seems. This is in part because the models themselves that furnish the basis for the definition of the scales were rarely thought to be any more than convenient mechanisms for providing the scales, and the scales were only looked on as heuristics to help the substantive psychologist or marketer to think about the stimuli. In most applications, the models were models in the sense of toys, not models as serious attempts at descriptions of reality. Thus, the scales that resulted from fitting them could hardly be considered to represent reality either.

Also influential may have been the methodologists' obsession with maximizing goodness of fit at the expense of cross-study consistency. The transformation that allowed the best fit to the data was the "correct" one, no matter how odd it looked. This can contribute to a seeming inconsistency in the results of different applications in a given area, when in reality the same, or a very similar, transformation might have done almost as well as the seemingly different ones. Whatever the reasons have been, it is safe to say that, without important exception, the "nonmetric revolution" did not result in the use of its methods to transform ordinal data into scales of any generality that have well-defined interval properties. Such a development might have gone far toward justifying the use of standard multivariate statistical models of the general linear model variety to a wider range of variables.

I wish that development had taken place. It would have provided the basis for a much more sophisticated behavioral science than we now have. The fact that it has not provides a good deal of the motivation for this book. If we do not have interval-scale data, then let us at least adopt some less-than-primitive statistical methods that are appropriate to the data that we have. There is a scarcity of such methods. Some possibilities have been suggested (Cliff, 1991; Ferguson, 1965; Hawkes, 1971), but they have limited application or have been criticized on interpretational grounds (Somers, 1974; Wilson, 1971, 1974; Winship & Mare, 1984).

Although it is generally hard to justify multivariate methods for ordinal data (Kim, 1975; Somers, 1974), the contention in this chapter is that there is a sense in which one *can* legitimately do a kind of multiple regression. That is, information about dominances or even differences on several predictor variables can be combined to optimize accuracy of prediction of the dominances on a dependent variable. The methods that result from this reasoning share some, but not all, of the characteristics of ordinary multiple regression. The results have a narrower interpretation than do those of the standard methods. That is a price paid for only making use of ordinal properties. The gains lie in the ability to generalize the results because of their insensitivity to scale transformations and in the more direct validity to the goal of predicting ordinal relations.

MOTIVES FOR AN ORDINAL REGRESSION ANALYSIS

Ordinary least-squares multiple regression (LSMR) has the goal of predicting scores on a dependent variable as accurately as possible in a least-squares sense. Regression weights b_j to apply to predictor variables X_j, along with an intercept b_0, are chosen so as to minimize a sum of squared deviations:

$\phi = \Sigma(\hat{y}_i - y_i)^2$, where $\hat{y}_i = \Sigma_j b_j x_{ij} + b_0$. The values of the b_j depend on the covariances of the predictors X_j, with the dependent variable Y and their variances and covariances with each other through the well-known matrix equation $\mathbf{b} = \mathbf{S}_{xx}^{-1}\mathbf{s}_{xy}$, where $\mathbf{S}_{xx}$ is the variance–covariance matrix of the predictors and $\mathbf{s}_{xy}$ is their covariances with Y. The main foci of interpretation in LSMR are the "squared multiple correlation," in behavioral science usually denoted R^2, which is $1 - \phi/\Sigma(y_i - \bar{y})^2$, and on ϕ's sensitivity to the presence or absence of a particular X_j (usually expressed in terms of the statistical significance of the weights) and on the values of the different b_j, particularly in standardized form.

But if Y is ordinal, transformation of it will change its covariances with the X_j in an unpredictable manner, and consequently R^2 is unlikely to remain constant under such a transformation. Likewise, the b_j will change, even in standardized form and so will their significance or the sensitivity of ϕ to the presence of any variable. Thus, when Y has only ordinal status, the interpretation of any given set of results becomes questionable, at both the descriptive and inferential levels.

The possibility of transforming Xs has similar consequences. Monotonically transforming X_j changes not only its covariance with Y but its covariances with the other predictors as well, and such transformation is likely to do so in unpredictable or irregular ways. This will alter its coefficient b_j and affect ϕ and X_j's contribution to its reduction. Thus, OMR results are not invariant if the variables are transformed. On the other hand, if there were an ordinal alternative to it, the alternative would not have this sensitvity to transformations of variables.

Another issue arises from the nature of the loss function ϕ. Based, as it is, on squared deviations, it, and the b_j as well, are most sensitive to the most extreme values of the variables. The squaring process means that a small change in one of the most extreme values has a much greater effect than an equally small change of a more central value. This is the basis of "sensitivity analysis" that quantifies the extent to which regression results are differentially affected by the presence of different cases. Alternative methods of analysis, such as absolute values regression and various robust forms (Wilcox, 1996) that reduce this differential sensitivity are available, but a more purely ordinal form of regression analysis should also serve such a function. Among the work cited earlier on optimal transformation of variables is some on multiple regression (Young, 1972; Young, deLeeuw, & Takane, 1976).

An additional motive for a more purely ordinal analysis lies in the observation that the investigator's goal in prediction is frequently formulated at the outset of an analysis as "predicting the order on Y," or "predicting which individuals will score higher on Y." Thus, the goal of a regression analysis is often an ordinal one. An LSMR analysis may satisfy the ordinal goal reasonably, or it may not, but a more strictly ordinal analysis, designed to minimize an ordinal loss function, seems more likely to do so.

The ordinal form of multiple regression suggested below has many of the kinds of benefits that have been cited as motives for ordinal analysis in earlier chapters: It is invariant under scale transformation; it is less sensitive to extreme values in the data; it satisfies the often-ordinal motives of the investigator more directly. It applies whether the variables are quasi-continuous or consist of a few ordered categories.

What about the additional desire of not relying on normality assumptions in making inferences? With respect to this motive, it will be seen that ordinally based inferential methods are available. They are based on the results in the previous chapter. Their rationale is not completely developed, but they provide useful answers to many inferential questions.

PREDICTING DOMINANCES

Explanatory Linear Models and Ordinal Variables

Multiple regression analyses are carried out from two stances. One is that the investigator intends to use the multiple regression model to *explain* the dependent variable in terms of the regression weights of the independent variables. This does not seem justifiable in the case of ordinal variables (Kim, 1975; Somers, 1974; Wilson, 1971, 1974; Winship & Mare, 1984). One difficulty with attempting to apply multiple regression to ordinal variables in an *explanatory* way lies in the linear model itself. When the equation $y_i = \sum b_j x_{ij} + b_0 + e_i$ is used in the explanatory sense, one is, in effect, using the equation as a kind of literal recipe for concocting values of Y out of the values of the Xs. The additivity implied in the function cannot logically be applied to the variables when either the dependent or independent variables are ordinal. Furthermore, as noted, there is the practical consequence that the b_j will change under monotonic transformation of the variables. Thus, the "recipe" will change, with no change in the data other than the kind of transformation that is legitimate; the "explanation" of Y in terms of the Xs will be different, surely an undesirable state of affairs. This means that there is a kind of fundamental inconsistency in in applying this linear model to ordinal variables. This is an issue with rather far-reaching implications because many such explanatory analyses, including latent variable regressions and other forms of covariance structure analysis, have been carried out on variables that can only be considered ordinal and interpreted in a rather literal fashion.

In this context, one of the ironies of recent behavioral science is the inconsistency of its dominant psychometric models—covariance structure analysis and item response theory. The former assumes that all the relations between variables, whether observed or latent, are linear, whereas the latter implies that the relations between observed and latent variables, and by implication among observed variables, are nonlinear. This is not to be interpreted as an endorsement of item response theory, which I believe has its own internal contradictions, but simply to point out that one who adopts one should be constrained to abandon the other for the sake of consistency.

As an alternative to applying LSMR to variables that are ordinal, several writers (Hawkes, 1971; Reynolds & Suttrick, 1986; Smith, 1972, 1974) proposed applying LSMR methodology to tau correlations. The rationale was based on treating dominance variables as if they were ordinary variables in that the least-squares criterion would be applied to predicting u_{ih}, the dominance on Y, from a weighted combination of the d_{ihj}; the model would be $u_{ih} = \sum_j w_j d_{ihj} + e_{ih}$. The weight vector $\mathbf{w}$ that minimized $\sum_{i,h}(u_{ih} - \sum_j w_j d_{ihj})^2$ could then be found from the taus, $\mathbf{w} = \mathbf{T}_{xx}^{-1}\mathbf{t}_{xy}$, which is directly analogous to the LSMR equation, because of the direct relation between taus and dominances. We will see that there is a sense in which this approach gives the correct results if the goal is *predictive* rather than *explanatory*; however, the reasoning was inappropriate as originally presented (Kim, 1975; Somers, 1974; Wilson, 1971, 1974; Winship & Mare, 1984).

There are several basic criticisms of this "least-squares" approach based on dominance relations as an explanatory method. One has to do with the very idea of minimizing a sum of squared differences between the actual u_{ih} and the $\hat{u}_{ih}$ that are estimated from $\sum_j w_j d_{ihj}$. Since the u_{ih} are 1, −1, or 0, whereas $\sum_j w_j d_{ihj}$ is on a continuum, there is an "apples and oranges" character to their comparison. Furthermore, using their squared differences as a loss function seems even more arbitrary here than it is in LSMR. Thus, applying least-squares reasoning to dominances seems out of place.

An even more serious criticism of making explanatory interpretations of the "ordinal regression coefficients" w_j lies in the discrepancy between partial regression coefficients, as they are derived in LSMR, and "partial tau" that was noted in chapter 2 (Donoghue & Cliff, 1991; Somers, 1974). The fact that it is the *dominance* on the variable rather than the value of the variable itself that is held constant in the partialing process makes the interpretation of partial tau regression coefficients difficult. The parallel fact that residualized dominances on predictors are themselves no longer dominances because they are not 1, −1, or 0 makes structural interpretation of tau-based regression coefficients additionally questionable. The inappropriateness of partial tau is also reinforced by the fact that if one takes normally distributed variables with a known regression structure, transforms the Pearson correlations to taus, and does the least-squares-like analysis, the resulting partial taus are not simple transformations of the corresponding true regression coefficients.

Finally, there is simply a lack of plausibility in the linear model applied to dominances in an explanatory way. Can one really entertain the idea that a dominance on Y is *explained* as a sum of fractional dominances on Xs? To do so treats the signs of differences—which is all that dominances are—as if they could be constructed out of fractional parts of other dominances. This seems clearly to be an inappropriate treatment of dominances as if they were true quantities, mistaking the fact that, like any numbers, they can be added up for their behavior as the outcome of relations in the natural world. For all such reasons, there seems to be no justification for analyzing ordinal variables from an explanatory or structural point of view via least-squares-based methods.

Predicting Dominances

The other way multiple regression is used is from a simply practical prediction stance. We want to predict Y "as accurately as possible," given several Xs. There are several ways of measuring accuracy of prediction. When asked to express what he or she wants to do with multiple regression, an investigator often replies with something like, "Given any two cases, I would like to predict which will score higher on the criterion. I would also like to know which variables are most important to that prediction."

This is an ordinal goal. If LSMR is the analytical method, its goal is somewhat different from the one the investigator framed, and the two goals will coincide only under a limited set of circumstances. The purpose of the present chapter is to present several approaches to predicting ordinal relations, of the kind described by the hypothetical investigator, on a dependent variable Y from several predictor variables.

Rationale

The reasoning is sketched here in a rather intuitive way, but the reader may see that it can be given a more rigorous justification. In LSMR, we usually think of predicting Y for each individual, and we measure accuracy in terms of squared differences between predicted and actual Ys. However, we might also think of trying to predict the differences in Ys for *pairs* of persons. Indeed, sometimes this is the way our intuitions run when we are thinking about or trying to describe regression. What if one took the sum of squared discrepancies between actual differences and predicted differences on Y as the loss function instead of the sum of squared discrepancies between actual and predicted scores?

Although not widely appreciated, it is known that variances and covariances are proportional to sums of squared differences and sums of products of differences, respectively:

$$s_j^2 = \frac{\sum_i \sum_h (x_{ij} - x_{hj})^2}{n(n-1)}, \tag{4.1}$$

$$s_{jk} = \frac{\sum_i \sum_h (x_{ij} - x_{hj})(x_{ik} - x_{hk})}{n(n-1)}. \tag{4.2}$$

This means that the same equations for regression coefficients will hold whether we are trying to minimize squared discrepancies between actual and predicted score differences for every pair of persons or between actual and predicted raw scores for every person. That is, a multiple regression system that had the goal of predicting differences between scores on Y leads to the same weights as trying to predict the actual scores, with the one exception that there would be no intercept term involved when predicting differences.

If variables are ordinal, then it makes little sense to predict raw differences, but the description of regression as predicting differences from differences can be adapted to the ordinal case. When an investigator is loosely describing a correlational relation such as "people who score higher on X tend also to score higher on Y," such a statement is, of course, not strictly true when the correlation coefficient is the Pearson r. But it *is* strictly true if the correlation is tau (Kendall, 1970).

The goal in predicting order on Y is to combine information on the Xs—leaving "combine" and "information" undefined for the moment—in order to predict the u_{ih}, the dominances on Y, as accurately as possible. We need first to deal with the issue of what is meant by "predicting as accurately as possible." That is, we need to define the *objective function*, or loss function, that is used to measure how accurate the predictions are. Such objective functions are part of any optimizing process, and to some extent determine the values of the fitted parameters (Guttman, 1971).

There are many possible objective functions in this context, but only two are considered here. We want to measure the agreement between u_{ih} and a value of it predicted from paired scores on the Xs, $\hat{u}_{ih}$. The most familiar objective function is the average squared deviation, which here would be

$$\phi_1 = \Sigma(u_{ih} - \hat{u}_{ih})^2/n(n-1),$$

where the sum runs over *pairs* of scores. As noted, this function is not ideal if u_{ih} is 0, 1, or −1, so measuring quantitative differences from it remains awkward unless the $\hat{u}$ are also made ternary.

A second possibility, the one pursued here, is to look for agreement between the *direction* of differences on Y and the direction of *predicted* difference. That is, the objective function is

$$\phi_2 = \sum u_{ih}[\text{sign}(\hat{u}_{ih})]/n(n-1), \tag{4.3}$$

where sign($\cdot$) is 1, 0, or -1. This is a tau-like measure in that it is comparing the direction of difference on Y (represented in u_{ih}) with the direction of the predicted dominance $\hat{u}$ for that pair. The idea is that we have $\hat{u}$s that are derived in some way from the scores of the pairs on the predictors, and we want to maximize the proportion of pairs where the direction of $\hat{u}$ is the same as that of u for the pair. If there are ties on Y, then some modification of ϕ_2 may be necessary, depending on whether we want to predict that some pairs will be tied and how we think the success and failure of such predictions should be scored in the objective function. For now, this is not a concern, but we will return to it.

Sources of $\hat{u}$

We consider three of the many possible bases for constructing the $\hat{u}$. First, one could predict the direction of difference on Y from the *raw differences* on the Xs. This assumes that there is valid information in the relative sizes of differences on a given predictor variable—that is, that the predictor is an interval scale. Alternatively, we could predict the us from *rank* differences on the Xs. Rank differences are really just one form of a priori transformation of the scale, and others could be used instead, but variables transformed to ranks may present a useful compromise between raw differences and signs of differences in predicting direction of difference on Y. Finally, one could use simply the *directions* of the differences on the Xs to predict the us. This is in many ways the most consistent approach if we consider the predictor variables to be ordinal as well as Y. Thus, we can can consider predicting direction of difference on Y from raw differences on Xs, from rank differences on Xs, or from directions of differences on Xs.

The next question is how to combine the information about differences on several predictors to get the overall prediction. Again there are many possible approaches, but we will examine only one, the use of a linear weighting system, familiar from multiple regression. That is, $\hat{u}$s will be constructed as linear combinations of raw differences, or of rank differences, or of signs of differences:

$$\hat{u}_{ih1} = \sum w_{j1}(x_{ij} - x_{hj}), \tag{4.4}$$

$$\hat{u}_{ih3} = \Sigma w_{j3}(r_{ij} - r_{hj}),$$ (4.5)

$$\hat{u}_{ih2} = \Sigma w_{j2}[\text{sign}(x_{ij} - x_{hj})].$$ (4.6)

Whichever kind of difference on predictors is being used, we want to choose the weights so as to maximize sign agreement between u and $\hat{u}$ (i.e., the objective function ϕ_2). (Note that $u_{ih} = -u_{hi}$, and the same is true for any of the $\hat{u}$.) The interpretation of the relative sizes of weights is purely pragmatic. If one variable has a higher weight than another, this simply means that a difference (or dominance or rank difference) of a given size on the first variable will predictively override a difference of the same size but opposite direction on the other.

EFFECT OF WEIGHTS

Arbitrary Weights

Methods for literally maximizing ϕ_2 turn out to be feasible only in the case of predicting from the dominances, but approximate solutions are possible in all three cases, and the approximations seem satisfactory in practice. We first concentrate on these approximate solutions.

The solutions follow from recognizing the current concern as a discriminant analysis problem, one where the goal is to discriminate as many as possible of the pairs with $u = 1$ from those with $u = -1$ (leaving aside for the moment the question of ties on Y). As in any discriminant analysis, this can be done, at least approximately, by making the means of the $\hat{u}$s for positive and for negative us have a large separation relative to the variances of the $\hat{u}$, and this goal can be accomplished using any of the three types of differences.

The results are rather simple, but the reasoning that leads to them may seem rather roundabout. First, consider predicting from the raw differences. Arrange all the $n(n-1)$ differences on the p predictors into an $n(n-1)$-by-p matrix $\mathbf{A}$ in such a way that all the pairs with $u = 1$ are in the top half and those with $u = -1$ in the lower half. This is illustrated with some simple data where $n = 5$ in Tables 4.1 and 4.2. Table 4.1 shows the data, including the ranks of the scores, and Table 4.2 shows the raw differences, the dominances, and the rank differences. It will be assumed at first that there are no ties on Y; later the adjustments to the formulas that are necessary with ties are introduced.

The mean of the $\hat{u}_1$ for those pairs with $u = +1$ is defined as

TABLE 4.1
Example Data

i	Raw Data				Ranks			
	X_1	X_2	X_3	Y	r_1	r_2	r_3	r_y
1	8	8	4	8	3	5	3.5	5
2	9	2	5	6	4.5	2	5	4
3	9	4	0	5	4.5	4	1	3
4	6	0	4	2	1.5	1	3.5	2
5	6	3	2	1	1.5	3	2	1

$$\mu_{\hat{u}+} = \Sigma \hat{u}_{ih1}/\tfrac{1}{2}n(n-1) \tag{4.7}$$

(where this summation runs over the half of the pairs that have $u = 1$). But, according to its definition (4.4), $\hat{u}_{ih1} = \Sigma w_{j1}(x_{ij} - x_{hj})$, and the mean of a weighted average is the weighted sum of the averages of the components. To simplify the formulas a bit, let $a_{ihj} = x_{ij} - x_{hj}$. (Again, $a_{hij} = -a_{ihj}$.) There will be a mean

TABLE 4.2
Raw Differences, Dominances, Rank Differences, and u

Pair	Raw Differences			Dominances			Rank Differences			u
	a_1	a_2	a_3	d_1	d_2	d_3	c_1	c_2	c_3	
1,2	−1	6	−1	−1	1	−1	−1.5	3	−1.5	1
1,3	−1	4	4	−1	1	1	−1.5	1	2.5	1
1,4	2	8	0	1	1	0	1.5	4	0	1
1,5	2	5	2	1	1	1	1.5	2	1.5	1
2,3	0	−2	5	0	−1	1	0	−2	4	1
2,4	3	2	1	1	1	1	3	1	1.5	1
2,5	3	−1	3	1	−1	1	3	−1	3	1
3,4	3	4	−4	1	1	−1	3	3	−2.5	1
3,5	3	1	−2	1	1	−1	3	1	−1	1
4,5	0	−3	2	0	−1	1	0	−2	1.5	1
μ_{j+}	1.4	2.4	1.0	0.4	0.4	0.3	1.2	1.0	0.9	—
2,1	1	−6	1	1	−1	1	1.5	−3	1.5	−1
3,1	1	−4	−4	1	−1	−1	1.5	−1	−2.5	−1
4,1	−2	−8	0	−1	−1	0	−1.5	−4	0	−1
5,1	−2	−5	−2	−1	−1	−1	−1.5	−2	−1.5	−1
3,2	0	2	−5	1	−1	−1	0	2	−4	−1
4,2	−3	−2	−1	−1	−1	−1	−3	−1	−1.5	−1
5,2	−3	1	−3	−1	1	−1	−3	1	−3	−1
4,3	−3	−4	4	−1	−1	1	−3	−3	2.5	−1
5,3	−3	−1	2	−1	−1	1	−3	−1	1	−1
5,4	0	3	−2	0	1	−1	0	2	−1.5	−1
μ_{j-}	−1.4	−2.4	−1.0	−0.4	−0.4	−0.3	−1.2	−1.0	−0.9	—

of the as of variable j for the pairs whose $u = 1$, that is, in the upper half of the matrix. This mean will be denoted μ_{aj+}. Thus we have found that

$$\hat{\mu}_{u+} = \sum_j w_{j1} \mu_{aj+}, \tag{4.8}$$

where μ_{aj+} is the mean of the score differences on X_j for the pairs with $u = 1$. There will likewise be a mean of the as in the $u = -1$ half of the matrix, μ_{aj-}. The mean of the $\hat{u}$ for the pairs having $u = -1$ is identical to $\hat{\mu}_{u+}$ except in sign because every a_{ihj} in the upper half will have a counterpart $a_{hij} = -a_{ihj}$ in the lower, so

$$\hat{\mu}_{u-} = -\hat{\mu}_{u+}. \tag{4.9}$$

Thus, with sufficient computing resources, $\hat{\mu}_{u+}$ and $\hat{\mu}_{u-}$ can be computed for any vector of weights, but we will see that it is possible to get optimum values of them more simply.

The variance of the $\hat{u}$ corresponding to the pairs where $u = 1$ can be found fairly easily because $\hat{u}_+ = \sum w_{j1} a_{ihj}$, and the sum of squares of the $\hat{u}_+$ is therefore $\sum_{i,h} \hat{u}_{ih+}^2 = \sum_{i,h} (\sum w_{j1} a_{ihj})^2$. The variance of the $\hat{u}_+$ (and of the $\hat{u}_-$ because of the equivalence of the two halves of the matrix of as) is the average squared $\hat{u}$ minus the squared average:

$$\sigma_{\hat{u}+}^2 = (\sum \hat{u}_{ih+})^2 / \tfrac{1}{2} n(n-1) - \hat{\mu}_{u+}^2. \tag{4.10}$$

Now we have, for any vector of weights $\mathbf{w}_1$ that are applied to the raw differences, the means of the $\hat{u}$ that go with positive and negative u as given by (4.8) and (4.9), respectively, and their common variance is (4.10). If the difference between $\hat{\mu}_{u+}$ and $\hat{\mu}_{u-}$ is large relative to (4.10), then most of the $\hat{u}$ will have the same sign as the corresponding u, and ϕ_2 will be close to 1.0.

Earlier we noted the relation between sums of products of differences on variables and the corresponding covariances (4.2), so that $(\sum w_{j1} a_{ihj})^2$ is proportional to the ordinary covariance matrix of the predictors, pre- and postmultiplied by the vector of weights. A less obvious relation is that

$$\sum_{i<h}\sum a_{ihj} = 2\sum_i (r_{iy} - \mu_r)(x_{ij} - m_j), \tag{4.11}$$

where r_{iy} is the rank of y_i, from lowest to highest, μ_r is the mean rank, $(n + 1)/2$, and m_j is the mean of X_j. Therefore, $\mu_{aj+} = 4s_{jry}/n$, where s_{jry} is the covariance between the scores on X_j and the ranks on Y. These algebraic relations mean that $\mu_{\hat{u}+}$ can be calculated from

$$\mu_{\hat{u}+} = 4\Sigma w_j s_{jry}/n, \tag{4.12}$$

and $\sigma_{\hat{u}+}^2$ from

$$\sigma_{\hat{u}+}^2 = 2\Sigma\Sigma w_{j1} w_{k1} s_{jk} - \mu_{\hat{u}+}^2. \tag{4.13}$$

Optimal Weights

The preceding section has been simply a set of algebraic identities that hold for any arbitrary weight vector, but our purpose is to find the optimal one. This is the vector that maximizes the ratio $\mu_{\hat{u}+}^2/\sigma_{\hat{u}+}^2$ because we can thereby expect the most $\hat{u}$s to have the correct sign. In a discriminant analysis, the optimal vector of weights for maximizing such a ratio is the one that solves the eigenproblem

$$\mathbf{G}_w^{-1}\mathbf{G}_a\mathbf{w} = \mathbf{w}\beta \tag{4.14}$$

where $\mathbf{w}$ is an eigenvector and β an eigenvalue, and the two matrices contain the sums of products of deviations within and among groups and the total sums of squares and products matrix $\mathbf{G}_t = \mathbf{G}_b + \mathbf{G}_w$. In the present context, the "groups" are the sets of pairs with $u = 1$ and with $u = -1$; $\mathbf{G}_t = \mathbf{A}'\mathbf{A}$, where $\mathbf{A}$ is the complete matrix of all the $n(n-1)a_{ihj}$; $\mathbf{G}_a$ comes from the μ_{aj+} defined earlier. Arranging these means in a vector μ_{a+},

$$\mathbf{G}_a = n(n-1)\mu_{a+}\mu_{a+}'. \tag{4.15}$$

When $\mathbf{G}_a$ is of rank 1, as when there are only two groups, there is only one solution to (4.14), and the discriminant analysis is equivalent to a multiple regression predicting a dichotomous variable denoting group membership. The optimal weights can be found from

$$\mathbf{w}_1 = (\mathbf{A}'\mathbf{A})^{-1}\mathbf{A}'\mathbf{u}, \tag{4.16}$$

which, because of the relations described earlier, is equivalent to

$$\mathbf{w}_1 = 2\mathbf{S}^{-1}\mathbf{s}_{ry}/n, \tag{4.17}$$

where $\mathbf{S}$ is the sample variance–covariance matrix of the predictors and $\mathbf{s}_{ry}$ is the vector of covariances between the scores on the Xs and the ranks on Y. That is, the optimal weights for predicting the ordinal relations on Y from the differences on the Xs can be found from the inverse of the predictor variance–covariance matrix and the covariances of the predictors with the ranks on Y. Using either (4.16) or (4.17) to define the weights, we can find $\mu_{\hat{u}+}$ from (4.12); when there are no ties (4.13) reduces to

$$\sigma_{\hat{u}+}^2 = \mu_{\hat{u}+}(1 - \mu_{\hat{u}+}). \tag{4.18}$$

Estimating Accuracy of Prediction

Once having $\mathbf{w}_1$, the formula for $\hat{u}$ can be applied to the score differences on the predictors, and ϕ_2 itself can be evaluated by noting the proportion of pairs where $\hat{u}$ has the same sign as u. It is possible to estimate the value of ϕ_2 without calculating all the $\hat{u}$ by assuming that the $\hat{u}$ will be approximately normally distributed within the two groups of pairs. If this is so, and we have found it to be reasonably so in practice with a limited number of applications, then ϕ_2 can be estimated from $\mu_{\hat{u}+}$ and $\sigma_{\hat{u}+}^2$:

$$\phi_2 \approx 2F(\mu_{\hat{u}+}/\sigma_{\hat{u}+}) - 1, \tag{4.19}$$

where $F(\cdot)$ is the integral of the standard normal distribution up to $\mu_{\hat{u}+}/\sigma_{\hat{u}+}$. The reason for (4.19) is that if the $\hat{u}_+$ are reasonably normally distributed, the proportion of them that are positive depends on how far zero is from $\mu_{\hat{u}+}$ relative to $\sigma_{\hat{u}}$. This relation was used by Cliff (1989) and Cliff and Donoghue (1992) in formulations of ordinal test theories.

Thus we have an optimal way of predicting the ordinal relations on Y from the raw differences on the Xs. Strictly speaking, the weight vector is an optimum only if the $\hat{u}$ are normally distributed within each group of pairs, because it is only in that case that we can be sure that maximizing the probability that $\hat{u}$ has the right sign is the same as maximizing the ratio of its mean to its standard deviation. However, in practice the two may be equivalent even when $\hat{u}$ is not normal, and we have found it to be approximately normal in several examples.

Predicting From Rank Differences

Predictions about ordinal relations can also be constructed from rank differences, that is, according to (4.5). Ranks can, at the level of the data, just be considered one kind of score, so the equations developed so far apply quite directly, with the difference that the equations for $\mu_{\hat{u}+}$ and $\sigma_{\hat{u}+}$ can be expressed in terms of the generalized Spearman rank coefficient,

$$\rho_{jk} = \frac{12(\Sigma r_{ij} r_{ik} - n(n+1)^2/4)}{n^3 - n}, \tag{4.20}$$

in which the average of the tied ranks is substituted when there are tied scores. It can also be shown that for any weight vector $\mathbf{w}_2$,

$$\mu_{\hat{u}+} = (n+1)\Sigma w_{j2}\rho_{jy}/3 \tag{4.21}$$

and

$$\sigma_{\hat{u}+}^2 = n(n+1)\Sigma\Sigma w_j w_k \rho_{jk}/6 - \mu_{\hat{u}+}^2. \tag{4.22}$$

The weight vector to optimally separate $\mu_{\hat{u}+}$ and $\mu_{\hat{u}-}$ can be found by using rank differences in (4.16), which can be simplified to

$$\mathbf{w}_2 = \mathbf{P}^{-1}\boldsymbol{\rho}_y, \tag{4.23}$$

in which $\mathbf{P}$ is the matrix of coefficients (4.20) among the predictors and $\boldsymbol{\rho}_y$ is the vector of coefficients with Y. Again, an approximate ϕ_2 can be calculated indirectly, this time from the Spearman rank coefficients, making use of (4.23) in (4.21) and (4.22) to substitute in (4.20).

PREDICTING ORDER FROM DOMINANCES

Predicting From Dominances on Xs

The preceding method was based on using raw or rank differences on predictors to predict directions of difference on Y under the assumption that there was valid information in those differences. However, if the Xs are themselves ordinal, this would not be legitimate; we should use only the ordinal information from them, and transformation to ranks may not be appropriate either.

The ideas presented in the raw-difference case can be adapted when predicting from dominances as well. Now, we make a $\mathbf{D}$ matrix, similar to the raw-difference matrix $\mathbf{A}$ but with the ternary dominance scores d_{ihj} instead of the raw differences a_{ihj}. This matrix is again divided into two sections, one whose rows correspond to the positive us and one to the negative. (See the middle section of Table 4.2 for the dominances in the small example.) Then $\hat{u}_{ih3} = \Sigma w_{j3} d_{ihj}$, and again ϕ_2 will tend to be maximized if we make the differences in the means $\mu_{\hat{u}+}$ and $\mu_{\hat{u}-}$, defined by equations parallel to (4.8) and (4.9), large relative to the variances within the two sets, which would be defined by an equation parallel to (4.10).

The statistics derived from dominances can be derived quite directly from the tau correlations:

$$\mu_{dj+} = \tau_{jy} \tag{4.24}$$

and

$$\frac{\sum_{i}\sum_{h} d_{ihj} d_{ihk}}{n(n-1)} = \tau_{jk}. \tag{4.25}$$

The weights can be applied to the predictor dominances, and ϕ_2 can be calculated for this system, just as from the raw differences. As before, the discrimination of the positive u from the negative will be good insofar as $\mu_{\hat{u}+}/\sigma_{\hat{u}+}$ is large. For any vector of weights $\mathbf{w}_3$,

$$\mu_{\hat{u}+} = \Sigma w_{j3} \tau_{jy} \tag{4.26}$$

and

$$\sigma_{\hat{u}+}^2 = \Sigma\Sigma w_{j3} w_{k3} \tau_{jk} - \mu_{\hat{u}+}^2. \tag{4.27}$$

Reasoning parallel to that used above to define the optimal weights to apply to the a_{ihj} leads to

$$\mathbf{w}_3 = (\mathbf{D}'\mathbf{D})^{-1}\mathbf{D}'\mathbf{u} \tag{4.28}$$

as the optimal weight vector to apply to the dominances on the Xs. Due to (4.24) and (4.25), they can be computed from the taus:

$$\mathbf{w}_3 = \mathbf{T}^{-1}\tau_y, \tag{4.29}$$

where $\mathbf{T}$ contains the tau correlations among the predictors, the diagonal, τ_{jj}, being the proportion of pairs not tied on X_j, and τ_y is the vector of their taus with Y. When the optimal weights are used, (4.18) holds here as well. Equation (4.29) is the same as the solution for the optimal weights proposed by Hawkes (1971), already cited, for minimizing the least-squares criterion ϕ_1.

Assuming normality for these $\hat{u}$ also, which is likely to be less true than when the prediction was from the raw differences because of the ternary nature of the d_{ihj}, an approximate value of ϕ_2 can be found without calculating the $\hat{u}$ directly by putting this mean and variance in (4.19).

In the case of predicting from dominances, there is a true solution for the optimal weights as well as the approximate one given by (4.28) or (4.29). It has interesting properties that point up the differences between using ϕ_1 and ϕ_2 as objective functions. It will be discussed more fully later.

Illustration

The data of Tables 4.1 and 4.2 can be used to illustrate the operation of the methods. The example is artificial and the sample size is extremely small, so this serves only to illustrate the operation of the equations in a concrete manner; no conclusions about the way the methods operate in practice can be drawn here. A second, real data example which is more useful in that respect is provided later.

Table 4.3 shows the matrices of covariances, τs, and ρs, and the respective weight vectors that result from them in the upper section and lower shows the $\hat{u}$ for the three methods, the values of ϕ_2, and the corresponding $\hat{\mu}_u$s, $\hat{\sigma}_u$s, and the ϕ_2s estimated from (4.19).

TABLE 4.3
Illustrative Analysis

	Covariances				Taus				Rhos			
	X_1	X_2	X_3	$r(Y)$	X_1	X_2	X_3	Y	X_1	X_2	X_3	Y
X_1	2.30	1.70	-.25	1.75	.80	.20	.10	.40	.90	.30	.08	.60
X_2	1.70	9.05	-.75	3.00	.20	1.00	-.30	.40	.30	1.00	-.40	.50
X_3	-.25	-.75	4.12	1.75	.10	-.30	.90	.30	.75	-.40	.95	.45
w_j	.246	.102	.160		.325	.471	.464		.152	.271	.292	

Pair	1,2	1,3	1,4	1,5	2,3	2,4	2,5	3,4	3,5	4,5	ϕ_2
$\hat{u}_{ih1}$	.21	.80	1.31	1.32	.60	1.10	1.12	.51	.52	.01	1.00
$\hat{u}_{ih2}$	-.32	.61	.80	1.26	-.01	1.26	.32	.33	.33	-.01	.40
$\hat{u}_{ih3}$	.15	.77	1.31	1.21	.63	1.16	1.06	.54	.44	-.10	.80

	$\hat{\mu}_{u+}$	$\hat{\sigma}_{u+}^2$	Est(ϕ_2)
w_1	.75	.188	.92
w_2	.46	.251	.64
w_3	.72	.204	.89

TIES ON Y

The previous discussion has been under the assumption that there are no ties on Y. Ties on the Xs are automatically handled in the computing formulas. The question we now turn to is what to do if there are ties on Y. If there are, then the formulas for $\mu_{\hat{u}+}$ have to be modified to take account of the reduced number of pairs where $u = 1$. This is rather simple. In the formulas for computing $\mu_{\hat{u}+}$ directly, the mean is computed only for the untied pairs, so the expressions for computing $\mu_{\hat{u}+}$ from the covariances, rhos, and taus, (4.12), (4.21), and (4.26), respectively, remain unchanged except that each needs to be divided by g, the proportion of pairs not tied on Y.

Formulas for $\sigma_{\hat{u}+}^2$ do not require modification if one is willing to assume that the variance of the $\hat{u}$ is the same in the tied pairs as in the untied. If there is reason to expect heterogeneity, then there is no substitute for computing the $\hat{u}$ for untied and tied pairs separately, including both $\hat{u}_{ih0}$ and $\hat{u}_{h i0}$ in the latter, and calculating the variances directly from them.

The solutions for the optimal weights remain the same whether or not there are ties and whether or not one wants to predict them. It is true that there are now three groups of pairs, according to whether the u are 1, 0 or -1, and in the usual three-group discriminant analysis there will be two solutions to the characteristic equation (4.11), but in the present case the $\mathbf{G}_a$ matrices turn out still to be rank one. The reason is that the mean μ_{j+} for any variable equals $-\mu_{j-}$, and the means for the sections where $u = 0$ are all zero. Therefore, the matrix of means of the three groups of pairs is rank 1, so $\mathbf{G}_a$ must be also. This unit rank condition means that there is only one eigenvalue not equal to zero, so the solutions for the $\mathbf{w}$s are the same as those presented previously: (4.16) or (4.17); (4.23); or (4.28) or (4.29). The weight vectors are defined only within a multiplying constant anyway, and once they have been calculated, the $\mu_{\hat{u}+}$ and $\sigma_{\hat{u}+}^2$ can be calculated by using the shortcut formulas under the assumption of variance homogeneity or directly from the $\hat{u}$.

However, attention must be paid to the prediction process itself, including a strategic decision about whether to predict that any pairs are tied. If not, then literal application of ϕ_2 means that its maximum is the proportion of untied pairs, g, rather than unity. Its approximation (4.19) needs to be multiplied by that factor as well. If some pairs are to be predicted to be tied, then a decision system can be developed, parallel to those used in ordinary discriminant analysis, which would define a band of $\hat{u}$ around zero that are predicted to be ties. In that case, ϕ_2 would need to be modified to reflect the proportion of correct classifications, whether 1, 0, or -1, along with a system of penalties for the different kinds of misclassification. This complication is not pursued here. Instead, the simpler approach that was mentioned first is used: A direction of difference is predicted for all pairs and

ϕ_2 is used directly. This corresponds to constructing a dominance variable from $\text{sign}(\hat{u})$ and calculating a τ_a between it and u. The $\text{sign}(\hat{u})$ would not be zero except under unusual circumstances, such as a pair being tied on all predictors. Sometimes, it may be preferable to convert ϕ_2 so as to count only the pairs not tied on Y, making it a kind of Somers' d.

ODDS FOR RELATIONS

We have concentrated on comparing the sign of $\hat{u}$ to the direction of differ-ence on Y, but it is reasonable to expect some patterns of differences on the Xs to lead to greater confidence about the predicted direction of differ-ence on Y than others. Simply considering a vector of d_{ihj}, if we find one member of a given pair ranks ahead of the other on all predictors, we might feel pretty confident that that person will rank ahead of the other on Y as well, assuming positive relations between predictors and criterion. On the other hand, if one person is ahead on some predictors, but behind on several, and it turns out that, using the weights, $\hat{u}$ is positive although close to zero, then we might feel less confident that its sign will predict the direction of difference on Y directly.

There is a way to formalize this expression of confidence, and again it is similar to an aspect of discriminant analysis. If one assumes that the distri-bution of the $\hat{u}$ is approximately normal within the pairs that have $u = 1$ and within those with $u = -1$, then one can compute an odds ratio for the likelihood that a given pair has their Y difference in one direction as opposed to the other.

Under this normality assumption, the probability density in the $u = 1$ pairs corresponding to a given $\hat{u}$ is

$$k \exp[-\tfrac{1}{2}(\hat{u} - \mu_{\hat{u}+})^2/\sigma_{\hat{u}}^2], \tag{4.30}$$

k being the constant $1/\sigma_{\hat{u}}(2\pi)^{1/2}$, whereas its corresponding density for the $u = -1$ pairs is

$$k \exp[-\tfrac{1}{2}(\hat{u} - \mu_{\hat{u}-})^2/\sigma_{\hat{u}}^2]. \tag{4.31}$$

The odds that the given $\hat{u}$ belongs to the $u = 1$ as opposed to the $u = -1$ are given by the ratio of the densities (4.30) and (4.31). Collecting some terms and using the fact that $\mu_{\hat{u}-} = -\mu_{\hat{u}+}$ allow (4.31) to be simplified to

$$\exp -(2\hat{u}\mu_{\hat{u}+}). \tag{4.32}$$

Thus, given a $\hat{u}$ from any of the three prediction systems, we can give the odds concerning the direction of their difference on Y. These odds are, of course, only approximate because the $\hat{u}$ distributions are not truly normal. The approximation should be fairly good if the predictions are from raw-score differences that are themselves fairly normal, and reasonably so for the rank-difference case, the approximation tending to improve in both of these as the number of predictors increases. For predictions based on dominances, the approximation is likely to be poor (see the example to follow), but these odds can be calculated directly for any pattern of d_{ihj}, without the need to assume normality for the $\hat{u}$, because there are only a finite, perhaps small, number of possible $\hat{u}$, for reasons that become clearer in the example.

Separate variances for tied and untied pairs might be one case where it is desirable to calculate odds analogous to (4.32) on whether a given pair is expected to be tied or not on Y. In discriminant analysis, we compute the density for a case under the assumption that it comes from each of the groups, take account of the sizes of the respective groups and their relative within-group variances, and classify the case into the groups where the result is highest. The same can be done here.

However, to simplify matters in discussing the odds, it is assumed initially that the variances are homogeneous. Obviously, if $\hat{u} > 0$, the choice is between classifying the pair as a 1 and as a 0. The density for $u = 1$ is that given by (4.30), multiplied by the factor $g/2$ to represent the relative frequency of these pairs. Using $\sigma_{\hat{u}}^2$ for the pooled variance estimate from one of the expressions for variance, the density for the tied pairs is

$$k(1 - g)\exp[-\tfrac{1}{2}(\hat{u} - 0)^2/\sigma_{\hat{u}}^2]. \tag{4.33}$$

The odds on tied versus untied are the ratio of this to $g/2$ times (4.30):

$$\text{odds} = \frac{g}{2(1-g)} \exp \frac{\mu_{\hat{u}+}\hat{u} - \tfrac{1}{2}\mu_{\hat{u}+}^2}{\sigma_{\hat{u}}^2}. \tag{4.34}$$

The reasoning leads to the conclusion that a tie should be predicted for a certain pair if the ratio (4.34) is less than 1.0. Where there are only a few ties, as in the subsequent example, we have found that this ratio is not less than 1.0 for any obtained $\hat{u}$, so it would not be optimal to predict a tie for any pair. When separate variances are computed for tied and untied pairs, (4.34) would need to be modified in the same way as is usually done in discriminance analysis.

APPLICATION

These procedures are applied to an empirical example in this section. The basic data are in Table 4.4, taken from Wong and Mason's (1985) analysis of data by Entwisle, Hermalin, and Mason (1982) in a study of contraceptive behavior in 15 countries. The goal in the present analysis is to predict the ordinal relations between the countries on "Percent Ever Practicing Contraception," (Y), from four other national characteristics: Average Years of Education (X_1), Percent Urbanized (X_2), Gross National Product Per Capita (X_3), and Expenditures on Family Planning (X_4), using the methods described before.

The results of the analyses are shown in Table 4.5 and Figure 4.1. Table 4.5 is divided into three sections, one for each treatment of the data. Section A shows the covariances among the four predictors and their covariances with the ranks on Y. Below that matrix are the weights found using (4.17), followed by $\mu_{\hat{u}}$, $\sigma_{\hat{u}}$, and the estimate of ϕ_2 from (4.19) and the actual value of ϕ_2. The line below that gives the weights, standardized to correlation metric so that comparison of their relative sizes are more meaningful. We see that X_4 has the highest weight. The value of ϕ_2, .581, reflects the fact that, of the $15 \times 14/2 = 105$ relations, 82 were predicted in the right direction (that is, had $\hat{u}$s with the right sign), 21 had the wrong sign, and 2 were ties on Y. Thus, $(82 - 21)/105 = .581$. The estimated value of ϕ_2 from (4.19) is fairly close, .663.

The other two sections of the table give the corresponding information for the dominances and the rank differences. Section B gives the τs and the

TABLE 4.4
Selected Characteristics* of 15 Countries

Country	X_1	X_2	X_3	X_4	Y
Lesotho	3.9	4	73	0	6
Kenya	0.9	4	108	6	9
Peru	2.7	17	367	0	14
Sri Lanka	3.8	20	142	12	22
Indonesia	1.2	9	61	14	25
Thailand	2.1	8	142	20	36
Colombia	2.7	47	284	16	37
Malaysia	1.6	29	313	18	38
Guayana	6.1	20	318	0	42
Jamaica	6.9	8	593	23	44
Jordan	1.4	53	197	0	44
Panama	5.3	50	570	19	59
Costa Rica	4.7	18	464	21	59
Fiji	3.7	15	321	22	60
Korea	4.5	15	188	24	61

*See text for definitions of variables.

TABLE 4.5
Covariances, Correlations, Weights, and Accuracy of Prediction

	X_1	X_2	X_3	X_4	$\hat{\mu}_\mu$	$\hat{\sigma}_\mu$	Est. ϕ_2	ϕ_2
A. Raw Differences								
X_1	3.395							
X_2	−1.598	268.8						
X_3	205.483	888.0	28666					
X_4	4.271	−6.8	584	86.57				
Y	3.832	26.2	420	25.39				
w_{j1}	.875	.110	−.000	.261	3.458	3.703	.638	.581
std. wt.	.361	.405	−.014	.544				
B. Dominances								
X_1	.990							
X_2	.057	.962						
X_3	.467	.248	.990					
X_4	.229	−.086	.267	.943				
Y	.267	.257	.438	.562				
w_{j2}	.024	.259	.217	.552	0.488	0.495	.663	.619
C. Rank Differences								
X_1	.998							
X_2	.075	.993						
X_3	.614	.391	.998					
X_4	.331	−.134	.357	.982				
Y	.462	.387	.588	.681				
w_{j3}	.159	.436	.080	.670	4.055	3.702	.713	.676

weights derived from these through (4.29). Again, X_4 gets the highest weight (it has the highest correlation with Y), but there are some changes in the relative size of the other weights, compared to the results in section A. The value of ϕ_2 is a little higher than it was above, reflecting the fact that 84 of the untied pairs have their ordinal relation on Y correctly predicted from the rank differences. The implication of the relative accuracies of prediction based on interval interpretation of the predictors and the purely ordinal one is that, here, taking interval size into account makes prediction of order worse than when it is ignored.

The last section gives the information for the analysis based on rank differences. Presented in the table are the Spearman coefficients (4.20) among the four predictors and with Y as the last row. The weights derived using (4.23) are below those coefficients. The weights are similar to the ones obtained by the other analyses, although ϕ_2 is somewhat higher here, .676, because 87 of the predictions are correct. The implication is that the transformation of the scores to ranks improved the prediction of the ordinal relations on Y, not only over using the raw scores themselves but over just using dominance information (the τ analysis). Some other transformation might have been even more successful.

A: Raw Differences:

Not Tied on $\underline{Y}$: $\mu_{\hat{u}} = 3.458$; $\sigma_{\hat{u}} = 3.703$

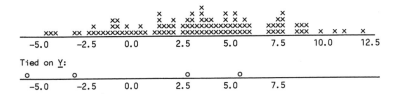

Tied on $\underline{Y}$:

B: Dominances

Not tied on $\underline{Y}$: $\mu_{\hat{u}} = .488$; $\sigma_{\hat{u}} = .495$

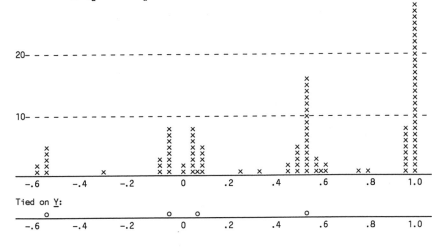

C: Rank Differences

Not tied on $\underline{Y}$: $\mu_{\hat{u}} = 4.055$; $\sigma_{\hat{u}} = 3.703$.

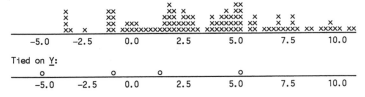

FIG. 4.1. Distributions of the $\hat{u}$ for (A) raw differences, (B) dominances, and (C) rank differences. Pairs not tied on Y are (x) and tied pairs are (o), the latter represented with both positive and negative signs.

The results are illustrated graphically in Fig. 4.1, which include μs and σs. The main parts of the figures, in which the pairs are represented by xs, show the distributions of the $\hat{u}$ for the pairs with $u = 1$. The distributions for those with $u = -1$ will be mirror images of these, reflected around zero. We see in the top section, for example, that there are indeed 19 $\hat{u}$ that are negative, most of them only mildly so. The distributions for the tied pairs are given also, even though there are only four such pairs (four pairs rather than two because we have to count h,i as well as i,h).

The normality of the distributions may be of some interest since our maximizing principle strictly maximizes only if the distributions are normal. The distribution for the data based on raw differences is reasonably normal, and that derived from rank differences somewhat less so. The distribution for the dominance data is clearly non-normal with a strong mode at the upper end of the distribution. This is a rather common result in our experience. These modal pairs are those that are in the "correct" direction on all four predictors, which is a common pattern when there are generally positive correlations with Y. In spite of the departures from normality, the values of ϕ_2 estimated from (4.19) are reasonably accurate in all three cases.

MAXIMIZATION OF ϕ_2 IN THE DOMINANCE CASE

It was mentioned that a truly optimal solution for the weights could be found in the dominance case. This exact solution follows from the fact that, with dominances, there are only a finite number of possible patterns of dominance relations across the predictors. This number is 3^p, where p is the number of predictors, if there can be ties on them because the score of each pair can only be 1, 0, or -1, or 2^p if there cannot.

Consider applying any vector $\mathbf{w}_2$ to the vector of dominances for a given pair. Lesotho versus Kenya in Table 4.4 can be taken as an example, where Kenya > Lesotho on Y. The vector of dominances for the pair is $(-1, 0, 1, 1)$ on the predictors. From the weights from Table 4.5B, $\hat{u} = .024 \times (-1) + .259 \times 0 + .217 \times 1 + .552 \times 1 = .745$. The sign is positive, so the prediction is correct in this case. It will be correct in exactly the same way for every other pair of countries that has the same pattern of dominances. However, if the opposite pattern, $(1, 0, -1, -1)$, occurred in a pair ordered in the same way as Kenya–Lesotho on the criterion, the value of $\hat{u}$ would be $-.745$, opposite in sign to u and therefore would result in a wrong prediction of direction of dominance.

This is an example of a rather obvious general principle and suggests a procedure. Considering only the pairs with $u = 1$, for any pattern vector $\mathbf{d}_q$ of dominances on the predictors, there is an opposite pattern, $-\mathbf{d}_q$. If $\mathbf{w}'\mathbf{d}_q > 0$, that is, a correct prediction, then $\mathbf{w}'(-\mathbf{d}_q) < 0$, and $\mathbf{w}$ will give an incorrect prediction if there are any $-\mathbf{d}_q$. If one eliminates the pattern of all ties on the predictors $(0, 0, 0, \ldots)$, one can separate the patterns into two sets, $\{S\}$ and $\{-S\}$, $(3^p - 1)/2$ in each, such that if $\mathbf{d}_q$ is in $\{S\}$, then $-\mathbf{d}_q$ is in $\{-S\}$. Further define the members of $\{S\}$ by requiring $f(\mathbf{d}_q) \geq f(-\mathbf{d}_q)$, where $f(\cdot)$ means "the frequency of."

This process of tabulating patterns and their opposites is illustrated with the data from Table 4.4 in Table 4.6, where, for example, the first pattern (1, 1, 1, 1), meaning one member of the pair is higher on all four predictors, occurs in 27 pairs and its opposite $(-1, -1, -1, -1)$ in none. The Kenya–Lesotho pattern ($q = 4$ in the table) occurs only once, and its negative never does. Some instances are more mixed; the fifth pattern occurs in 16 pairs, and its negative in 5; it also occurs in one of the two ties on the criterion. Pattern 14 is completely ambiguous because it occurs equally often in positive and negative forms.

The patterns and their frequencies provide information about the multivariate prediction of orders. The first pattern shows that, whenever one country was higher than another on all four predictors, it was also ahead on the birth control variable. On the other hand, when the direction of difference on X_4 was opposite to that on the other three predictors ($q = 14$), the direction of difference on birth control was 50–50. Examination of the patterns and their relative frequency can thus provide insight into understanding effects.

TABLE 4.6
Dominance Pattern Vectors $\mathbf{d}_q$ and Their Frequencies

q	$\mathbf{d}_q$				$f(\mathbf{d}_q)$	$f(-\mathbf{d}_q)$	$f(tied)$
1	1	1	1	1	27	0	0
2	-1	1	1	1	8	0	0
3	1	0	1	1	1	0	0
4	-1	0	1	1	1	0	0
5	1	-1	1	1	16	5	1
6	-1	-1	1	1	4	0	0
7	-1	-1	0	1	1	0	0
8	1	1	-1	1	2	0	0
9	0	1	-1	1	1	0	0
10	-1	1	-1	1	3	2	0
11	1	0	-1	1	1	0	0
12*	1	0	1	-1	1	0	0
13	1	-1	-1	1	5	3	0
14	1	1	1	-1	8	8	1
15	1	1	1	0	1	0	0
16	-1	1	1	0	2	0	0
17	-1	1	-1	0	2	0	0
18	1	1	-1	0	1	0	0
$\Sigma f(\mathbf{d}_q)$					85	18	2

*$\mathbf{d}_{12}$ implies an inequality that is inconsistent with those from other patterns.

True Optimal Weights

The relative frequencies of the $\mathbf{d}_q$ compared to the $-\mathbf{d}_q$ determine the effectiveness of a weight vector, because whenever the vector $\mathbf{w}_2$ provides a $\hat{u}$ of the correct sign with $\mathbf{d}_q$, using that vector on $-\mathbf{d}_q$ must give a $\hat{u}$ of the wrong sign. The most effective weight vector is the one that yields the largest number of positive $\hat{u}$. This means that each $\mathbf{d}_q$ furnishes an inequality on the weights. The Kenya–Lesotho dominance vector provides an example. Table 4.6 shows that its frequency (i.e., 1) is higher than that of its opposite (0). Therefore, we want $w_1(-1) + w_2(0) + w_3(1) + w_4(1) > 0$ so that the corresponding $\hat{u}$ will be positive. Another example is the very common vector (1, 1, 1, 1). It implies that $w_1 + w_2 + w_3 + w_4$ should be > 0. Any set of weights that satisfies this inequality will provide positive $\hat{u}$s for all 27 pairs that have this pattern. Each pairing of a prototype vector with its less frequent negative counterpart thus furnishes an inequality on the weights. The optimal $\mathbf{w}_2$ is the one that satisfies the most inequalities. The tabulation in Table 4.6 indicates that these data provide 17 inequalities (pattern 14 providing no information because the frequency of $\mathbf{d}_{14}$ and of $-\mathbf{d}_{14}$ are equal) to be satisfied.

The relative frequencies of the $\mathbf{d}_q$ compared to their negative counterparts also provide an upper bound for ϕ_2. Clearly, weights can do no better than give positive $\hat{u}$ in all 85 pairs corresponding to the more frequent form. They will then necessarily result in negative $\hat{u}$ for their 18 negative counterparts. The sum of the frequencies in Table 4.6 implies that ϕ_2 could be (85 $-$ 18)/105 = .638, slightly higher than the value .619 from Table 4.5B that was found using the the approximate, discriminant-analysis-based, method. However, analysis of the 17 inequalities furnished by the frequencies of the vectors in Table 4.6 shows that they are not consistent. No set of values for the four weights satisfies all 17. If, however, the inequality derived from $\mathbf{d}_{12}$ is excluded, the remainder of them are consistent. Thus, no set of weights can do better than predict the correct direction of difference on Y in 84 pairs, and, therefore, the incorrect one in the remaining 19, or $\phi_2 = .619$.

It happens that $\mathbf{w}_3$ from Table 4.5B satisfies all these inequalities, as would be expected because it, too, gave a value of ϕ_2 of .619, according to Table 4.5B, so that in this case the approximate solution was optimal in the sense of providing the highest possible value of ϕ_2. We have found that the least-squares weights are optimal, in the sense of satisfying the maximal set of inequalities, in a number of the empirical examples we have studied, but not all. However, it has always true so far that the approximate vector came very close to doing as well as the optimal vector.

The fact that the constraints furnished by data are only inequalities means that only ranges of values for the individual weights are implied. Often, quite different-looking weights will have exactly the same effectiveness. Although it is true that sample LSMR weights that are numerically different can have overlapping confidence intervals and that r^2 can be rather insensitive to changes in them, the ambiguity here is greater. Different values for weights can lead to identical values for ϕ_2. It is as if different LSMR weights led to identical r^2.

An extreme case is that of two predictors. When there are no ties on the predictors, there are only two pairs of $\mathbf{d}_q$, so only two inequalities need to be satisfied. Assuming X_1 to be the predictor having the highest tau with the criterion and both predictors to be defined so that their taus are positive, these inequalities are $w_1 + w_2 > 0$ and $w_1 > w_2$. A pair of weights that satisfies these inequalities is $w_1 > 0$ and $w_2 = 0$. That is, the second variable never improves prediction in the sense defined by ϕ_2!

On the other hand, the criterion ϕ_1, like other least-squares criteria, will virtually always be reduced by the addition of another predictor. This contrast shows that the criteria ϕ_1 and ϕ_2 are not always interchangeable. In the sense of the approximate solutions, ϕ_1 and ϕ_2 are equivalent, but there can be situations where a true optimum for ϕ_1 is not the optimum for ϕ_2.

Since the number of inequalities expands exponentially with the number of predictors, the exact analysis is only feasible when there are a few, perhaps up to seven or eight. Even then, an algorithm for finding the maximal set of inequalities to satisfy would be needed in order to find the true optimal weights routinely.

One can wonder whether there are also exact solutions when raw differences or rank differences are the basis of the prediction, and presumably there are. The problem that quickly appears, however, is that the number of possible $\mathbf{a}_q$ or $\mathbf{c}_q$, analogous to $\mathbf{d}_q$, expands rapidly with n. There would typically be nearly as many distinct difference or rank-difference vectors as there are pairs of scores, so finding weights that satisfied as many as possible of the resulting inequalties would be infeasible. Nonetheless, in principle an optimal solution based on rank differences or raw differences would be defined by the same sorts of considerations as were used with dominances.

DISCUSSION

Antecedent Research

The approach presented here avoids many of the difficulties encountered by earlier attempts to develop a multiple regression analogue for ordinal data. The weights are not used in any causal or explanatory way; they simply are viewed as instruments of prediction. Variables with larger weights are more influential in prediction than those with small ones. When two variables have differences, or dominances, or rank differences, that are equal but of opposite sign, the one with the larger weight will determine the sign of $\hat{u}$.

In LSMR, the importance of a variable to prediction in the multipredictor context is assessed by finding the reduction in squared multiple correlation that occurs when only that variable is deleted from the battery. This is proportional to the "F-to-delete" ratio provided in computerized LSMR programs, as well as to the squared semipartial correlation of that variable because of the mathematics underlying LSMR (e.g., Cliff, 1987), so it is not necessary to literally delete the variable to find this reduction in predictive accuracy. The amount of such contribution can be estimated in that way in the cases here of predicting from ranks and from raw scores.

However, this shortcut seems to be inappropriate in the case of predicting from dominances although it would be still be possible to calculate the literal reduction in predictive efficiency when a variable is deleted from the battery by just deleting that variable and finding the corresponding reduction in predictive efficiency. Applying this principle in the present case is interesting. Deleting X_1 has no effect at all, and the same happens if just X_3 is deleted: The same 84 pairs are predicted correctly and the same 19 incorrectly. However, putting X_1 back in and deleting X_2 raises the number predicted incorrectly to 21. Deleting X_4 has the most effect. This raises the incorrectly predicted pairs to 27. Thus, the assessment of the importance of a variable to prediction can take place, even in the case of predicting from dominances.

The difference in interpretation between partial τ and partial ρ, and consequently in the interpretation of the corresponding partial weights, was also salient in criticisms of ordinal multiple regression of the kind suggested by Smith (1972, 1974). As discussed in chapter 2, it is the value of the relation between members of the pair, that is, -1 or 1, that is partialed out in partial τ, not the value of the variable itself. Thus, partial τ and partial ρ can have radically different values, even in cases where both τ and ρ would be appropriate (cf. Somers, 1974). The fact that the formula for partial τ (Kendall, 1970) looks like the formula for partial correlation adds to the confusion. Interpreting weights from ordinal prediction in anything more than a pragmatic, predictive fashion has seemed inappropriate from any point of view. Thus, no direct interpretation of weights obtained from dominances as "partial regression weights" can be made.

The present approach provides a different, and, I believe, more justifiable rationale for the process by which multiple predictors are used to predict order on a dependent variable than has previously been avaliable. Maximizing ϕ_2 seems more nearly what we want to aim for in ordinal prediction than does the least-squares criterion ϕ_1. Furthermore, the method of treating ties on the criterion is more explicit. The odds expressions (4.32) and (4.34) are also useful additions. Perhaps equally important is the fact that this chapter considers all three bases for prediction: raw differences and rank differences, as well as dominances. If the goal really is to predict order on the criterion, as I believe it often is, here are methods for doing so.

Other Issues

There are other methods of analysis that are used in the presence of an ordinal criterion. Prominent among these are the treatment of the variables as categorical and performing a loglinear analysis (Agresti, 1984). Examination of these methods shows that the "ordinal" analysis is actually treating the categories as if they were interval variables with equal spacing of the categories. Thus, these are not ordinal methods in the sense of predicting order that is used here. One adaptation of these loglinear methods that does seem to more completely ordinal is that of Teeuwen (1989), but applications of his methods are extremely rare. It also becomes cumbersome when the number of joint categories on the predictors becomes large, as it must when there are more than a few variables and/or each has more than two or three categories. Logistic regression (McCullagh, 1980) is another approach to such problems, but it suffers from several of the same problems as loglinear analysis in not corresponding very directly to what the objectives of the investigator are when ordinal prediction is the goal. Other methods for seemingly ordinal treatment of data often rest on very strong parametric assumptions, such as the proposals by Terza (1984) and Muthén (1984) to use polychoric correlational analysis, which assume that multivariate normal distributions underlie the observed categorical variables. The present approach seems to offer advantages, both practical ones and in terms of the results more nearly fitting the purpose of the study.

Inferential Methods

The methods for predicting ordinal relations have been presented here from a descriptive point of view, without regard to issues of a hypothesis-testing or confidence-interval-setting kind. Thus, they have most direct application where description is the primary concern, as in the contraception example. The methods would have more utility if they were accompanied by inferential procedures, and some are suggested here.

In the case or predicting from raw differences, it seems that the inferential methods used in LSMR would be directly appropriate. The weights are derived from the same data as form the basis for LSMR, with the exception that the criterion covariances with Y are with the ranks rather than directly with the scores. Standard errors for the weights derived from LSMR algorithms could be used for inferences about them in the usual ways (Cliff, 1987), and the usual F ratio to test the hypothesis that no prediction is possible could be employed. Using LSMR methods on rank correlations may provide a reasonable way of making inferences about the weights used to predict ordinal relations from rank differences.

The case of prediction from dominances is similar, although its basis is less widely known and established. The analysis rests on tau correlations, and, as discussed in the previous chapter, the sample values t can be considered estimates of population counterparts in the same sense as an analysis based on covariances. The sampling properties of t were established by Daniels and Kendall (1947), who provided distribution-free formulas for its variance. The formulas have been elaborated by Cliff and Charlin (1991) to allow for ties on the variables and to include the covariances between taus, as we have seen in chapter 3. Since the weights are linear combinations of the t_{jy}, their variances are the corresponding linear combinations of the covariance matrix among the t_{jy}. Let $\mathbf{V}$ be a matrix whose element v_{jk} is the covariance between t_{jy} and t_{ky}. Then this suggests that

$$\mathbf{Q} = \mathbf{T}^{-1}\mathbf{V}\mathbf{T}^{-1} \tag{4.35}$$

has $q_{jj} = \sigma_{wj3}^2$ as its diagonal elements and $q_{jk} = \mathrm{cov}(w_{j3}, w_{k3})$. Then w_{j3}^2/q_{jj} should be asymptotically a one-degree-of-freedom chi-square variate, thus providing a large-sample way of testing $w_{j3} = 0$ in the population. Extensive simulations by Long (1996) found that this methodology gave appropriate c.i. for weights.

Implications for the Interval-Scale Status of Variables

In the example, it was found that the most accurate prediction was that based on the rank differences, and the least accurate was based on the raw differences. We have found this in other examples as well, but this is not to say that there is a high degree of consistency in this finding about the relative efficacy; dominances or raw differences sometimes work best as well. However, let us consider the finding here that using dominances, which ignore the sizes of differences and attend only to their directions, is more predictive of order than using the actual differences themselves. Common sense might say that if X is related to Y, a large difference on X should be more predictive of the direction of difference on Y than a small one. However, this was found not to be the case overall in the example; on balance, the opposite was true, albeit the difference in correct pairs predicted was small, two pairs. The fact that taking account of the sizes of differences did worse than ignoring them calls into question the interval status of the predictors and can be taken as evidence against that status.

The fact that rank differences did better than simple dominances suggest that there may be interval information in the data; it is just that the data are not appropriately scaled. Ranks are one transformation of the data. Perhaps another transformation would have worked even better. Relations between Xs and Y could be examined graphically to see if some transformed version of an X might be expected to be more closely aligned with Y. Such analyses may help furnish the basis for defining interval properties for variables on the basis of the relations they show with each other.

There may be a more literal interpretation of the success of ranks. Differences in ranks reflect the degree of separation of the ordinal positions of scores. It might just be that larger separations in predictor distributions—larger percentile differences—are more predictive of directions of difference on Y than smaller ones are.

Psychometric Applications

An area of application of the ideas of this chapter is in providing a basis for ordinal theories of mental tests. Cliff (1989; Cliff & Donoghue, 1992) made use of the approximation (4.19) as the basis of estimating the tau correlation between observed test or item scores and the true score that the test estimates. In the second version, which is the more successful theory, it is assumed that the objective of a test score is to estimate the order of the individuals on a universe of test items. The reasoning first formulates a way to estimate the τ between an individual item on the current test and the universe order through estimating (4.26) and (4.27) from observed data to put in (4.19), and then using these estimates in the same way to approximate the relation between observed total score and universe score. The methods agreed well with both simulated and real data. They have the advantage over other psychometric theories of being, on the one hand, more realistic and, on the other hand, less complex.

Approximate Optimality of Weights

A point that deserves mention is that we have referred to the weights derived from (4.17), (4.23), and (4.28) as "approximate" optima, and the discussion of the true solution in the dominance case was in part intended to elucidate the sense in which they are approximate. However, in defense of these approximations it should be borne in mind that they are approximate in the same sense that the weights derived in any linear discriminant analysis are approximate. The objective of a discriminant analysis is the development of an equation for the correct classification of objects. The function maximized by discriminant analysis is the ratio of among-groups sum of squares to within-groups. Maximizing this maximizes probability of correct classification only in the case of equal-variance normal parent distributions for all groups. This assumption is rarely valid in practice. Our procedures at least have the advantage that the distribution for the $\hat{u}_+$ must have the same variance as the $\hat{u}_-$, even if their distributions are not normal.

As a general rule, maximizing the ratio of squared mean to variance works well in the typical application of discriminant analysis. Making the means far apart relative to the variance does have the effect of making the probability of misclassification small. Nevertheless, the possibility always exists that a different set of weights, used instead of the ones that maximize this ratio, would be more effective at minimizing the probability of misclassification. The same heuristic rationale is used here as in the typical discriminant analysis, and a similar degree of success at the true objective, maximizing ϕ_2, can be expected.

The use of (4.19) to estimate the value of ϕ_2 is perhaps more problematical, particularly in the case of predicting from dominances, because its accuracy relies on the literal conformity of the $\hat{u}$ to the normal shape. Inaccuracy of that kind can be expected to diminish as the number of predictors increases and as their correlation decreases, due to Central Limit Theorem considerations, but the accuracy of (4.19) could still be an issue in many applications. This issue may well be moot. Given modern computing equipment, there is little reason not to compute the $\hat{u}$ directly rather than relying on estimates. It is felt that (4.19) is still of theoretical interest, however, as in the psychometric case cited earlier.

Computational Considerations

One of the reasons that ordinal methods have not been more widely adopted may well be their computational demands. Although it is true that in very small data sets the calculations for ordinal statistics can be carried out with paper and pencil, the number of operations required rises more than linearly as samples increase in size. Thus in the initial period of computerization of statistics (the 1950s and early 1960s) they were burdensome to the computers that were available, setting a pattern that was hard to break as computational capacity increased. This should no longer be a consideration, but, due to the historical context, computer programs have been few.

These deficiencies are beginning to be diminished. Dr. S. A. Madigan has developed a PC program for doing most of the analyses described here, as well as calculating the variances and covariances of ts. In addition, M. C. Stallings has found ways of performing them in the SAS system (SAS Institute, 1987) by making use of its matrix and data transformation features. J. M. Long has written FORTRAN programs to perform the least-squares analyses. Although none of these programs are published, they may be available to interested parties. The one by Long is available through the internet address given earlier. Thus, the methods that have been described here are now feasible.

EXTENSIONS

In the context of linear models, the two-group linear discriminant problem is equivalent to a multiple regression predicting the dichotomous group membership variable. If one wants to discriminate two groups just on the basis of their ordinal relations on several variables, there seems to be a direct analogy here to the linear models case. Dominance on Y here means membership in one population rather than the other. These dominances can be predicted from the dominances on predictors using exactly the same equations as were used in the prediction from dominances case, such as (4.29). The relative sizes of the weights indicate which variables are more important in predicting that "order," which here means taking each pair of subjects and predicting which one goes into which group. Members of the same group are "tied" on the criterion and are not of interest. The odds that a given pair will be correctly assigned can be estimated—probably only roughly due to the non-normality of predicting from dominances—using (4.32). More realistically, the likelihood that a given pair will be correctly discriminated by the tabulation of patterns of dominance vectors, $\mathbf{d}_q$. Thus, many of the goals of discriminant analysis can be achieved from ordinal information in the two-group case.

The multiple-group case offers less in the way of direct analogy because the linear models treament makes, in effect, a linear composite of the group membership dummy variables at the same time that it is combining the predictors (Cliff, 1987). This makes less sense in the ordinal case. However, some applications of the ordinal methodology still seem applicable. First, many multiple-group discriminant problems must later be reanalyzed as a series of two-group ones. That is, the real purpose of the analysis is often to discriminate pairs of groups (or see which pairs are discriminable), or this must be done at the end anyway, for practical or substantive reasons. Heterogeneity of variance–covariance matrices within groups can also be a reason.

In that case, the two-group method suggested above can be applied to each pair. In addition, it is often true that the several groups to be discriminated can be arranged a priori into an order. If so, why not use this order as the dependent variable and apply the tau-based multiple regression directly? A useful adjunct to such an analysis would be to tabulate $\mathbf{d}_q$ vectors separately for each pair of groups. In that way, the groups that were easier to discriminate could be identified.

Thus, given that we have a multiple-regression-like procedure that predicts dominances on one variable from dominances on the others, we can apply those methods to the problem of discriminating between groups on the basis of ordinal information.

CONCLUSION

The issue of dealing with prediction of an ordinal criterion has been dealt with here. The specific goal is seen as predicting as many of the ordinal relations on the criterion variable as possible. It turns out to be possible to formulate ways of doing this by treating this as a problem of discriminating those pairs with ordinal relations in one direction on the criterion from those with the other. The basis of the predictions can either be raw differences on the predictors, dominance variables on the predictors, or rank differences on them. The solution for the optimizing weights to apply will involve the variables covariances, tau correlations, or Spearman rank correlations, respectively. Such a system for predicting order is seen as having the advantage of more directly accomplishing the goal that an investigator has in mind than traditional regression methods do while requiring fewer assumptions about the data.

5

Alternatives to Mean Comparisons

DO WE WANT TO COMPARE MEANS?

Why Not Compare Means?

Much behavioral research centers around hypotheses that scores in one group or under one condition tend to be higher than those in another. Such questions are generically referred to as questions of location. The most common methods of investigating these hypotheses are the traditional *t* test for independent groups or for correlated observations, or some form of analysis of variance. There are, however, several reasons for preferring ordinal analyses to these familiar methods.

The reasons are specialized versions of the general ones that have been cited from the outset of this book. One commonly cited motive for using alternatives to mean comparisons is that ordinal methods are more robust than classical methods in the face of violations of the distributional or equivariance assumptions that underlie the traditional inferences, and equally or more, sometimes much more, powerful. A second reason is that much behavioral data can only be given ordinal-scale status, and ordinal statistics are invariant under monotonic transformation, whereas mean comparisons or linear correlations are not. It has been argued, beginning with Lord (1953), that this in itself does not invalidate the use of the classical statistics, but the contention has been here, continued in the present chapter, is that such a conclusion has a very narrow base, and that in fact this is an important issue. A third, less often cited, reason is that, contrary to the usual view, the ordinal statistics here too have *descriptive* superiority in that they often more nearly correspond to the questions the investigator has in mind in carrying out the research than mean comparisons do (Cliff, 1991, 1993a).

The purpose of this chapter is, first, to reinforce these arguments in the case of comparisons in the locations ("location" is used here and in other statistical literature as a generic term to refer to where a distribution generally lies; means, medians, and the like are used as measures of location) of two or more distributions, particularly the last two arguments, and then to describe ways in which ordinal comparisons of location can be made more widely applicable. The discussion focuses on *dominance analysis*, summarized by the *d* statistic, which measures the extent to which one sample distribution tends to generally lie above another, and its use to make inferences about δ, which measures the extent to which that is true in the population.

The δ Measure and the *d* Statistic

If one asks a researcher why she or he compared the means of two groups, the answer often is "to see if scores in this group tend to be higher than scores in that." A well-established, but not widely employed, measure for comparing two distributions that is a very direct translation of that statement is δ^1 (Agresti, 1984; Cliff, 1991, 1993; Hettmansperger, 1984; Randles & Wolfe, 1979; Siegel & Castellan, 1988). For a random variable X_1 sampled from one distribution and an X_2 sampled from the other, δ is the probability that the sampled X_1 is greater than the sampled X_2 minus the reverse probability:

$$\delta = \Pr(x_{i1} > x_{j2}) - \Pr(x_{i1} < x_{j2}). \tag{5.1}$$

Equation (5.1) simply means that each x_{i1} in one population can be compared to each x_{j2} in the other, and that there is a probability that the x_{i1} is the higher and that the x_{j2} is the higher. This difference in probabilities, which can run from −1.0 (nonoverlapping distributions with the x_1s on the left) to 1.0 (nonoverlapping with x_1s on the right), in preference to simply $\Pr(x_{i1} > x_{j2})$ (cf. McGraw & Wong, 1992; Mee, 1990), introduces a slight cognitive complexity. However, given that in much of our data xs can be tied with ys, the form of (5.1) avoids the necessity of modifiers that communicate the probability of ties. Ties are included in defining (5.1), but they are counted as neither higher nor lower rather than discarded. Delta is a form of tau (specifically, τ_d) in which one variable is a dichotomy. Where there are ties

---

[1]The uppercase Δ is used for this measure in the literature, even though the lowercase form δ used here would be more consistent with standard practice of letting lowercase Greek letters stand for population parameters.

on X, and g is the probability that an X_1 is not tied with an X_2, the range for δ is $-g$ to g. Where there are no ties, δ can be translated back into a probability as $Pr(x_{i1} > x_{j2}) = (\delta + 1)/2$.

Discussions and investigations of δ (e.g., Fligner & Policello, 1981; Hettman-sperger, 1984) often focus on using it as a surrogate for the comparison of means or medians, but here the emphasis will be on using it as a basis of distributional comparison in its own right. If we want a quantified expression of the tendency of Xs to be higher than Ys—one that is not dependent on any assumptions whatsoever—then we use δ. It is also true that this is all it provides. In the absence of auxiliary assumptions about the shape and spread of the distributions, it says nothing about where the overlap occurs nor about quantified differences on the original scale. However, if one's primary interest is in a quantification of the statement "Xs tend to be higher than Ys," then δ provides an unambiguous description of the extent to which this is so. In data applications, X and Y would typically represent the same empirical variable, X, and δ then directly measures of the degree to which one population's distribution lies to the right of the other. As is true of the other methods described in this book, dominance analysis can be applied to ordered categories as well as to quasi-continuous variables.

The sample estimate d, corresponding to δ, is the proportion of xs in one sample that are higher than those from the other, minus the reverse proportion. That is, comparing each of the n x_i scores to each of the m x_j scores (# denotes "the number of" or "the number of times"), we have

$$d = \frac{\#(x_i > x_j) - \#(x_i < x_j)}{mn}. \tag{5.2}$$

Equation (5.2) simply means that each of the n xs in one group is compared to each of the m xs in the other, and counts are made of how many times the member of the first group is higher and how many times it is lower. As in τ_a, ties are not counted in the numerator as higher or lower, but are included in the total number of comparisons, mn, in the denominator.

d as a Form of t

In the context of parametric statistics, the reader may be familiar with the connection between differences in means and Pearson correlation, specifically the form of correlation called the point biserial, which is the Pearson correlation between a dichotomous variable that represents group membership and a numerical variable. There is a similar connection between d and t. It is easy to see that one can define a group membership variable; call that variable Y, giving scores of 1.0 to all m members of one group and scores of 0 to the n in the other (or use any other arbitrary numbers) and calculate dominances on that variable. There will be $(m + n)(m + n - 1)/2$ such dominances, but all those involving members of the same group will be zero. One correspondingly finds the dominance on X of the $m + n$ subjects. Then the t_{ih}s between X and Y can be calculated and summed over all pairs of subjects, as is done in the numerator of tau, but all the t_{ih} involving members of the same group will be zero because they are tied on the group membership variable Y. The remaining t_{ihxy}, those involving members of different groups, are identical to the corresponding d_{ihx} because all their d_{ihy} are 1.0. Thus, we could just as well refer to d_{ih}s used to calculate d as t_{ihxy}s.

It will be recalled that the form of tau called Somers' d (Somers, 1968), but here called τ_d (2.8), uses as its denominator the number of untied pairs on one of the variables. In the case of the d statistic, the number of untied pairs on Y is mn. Therefore, the d statistic is identical to t_{dxy}, where Y is a dichotomy representing group membership, and similarly δ is τ_{dxy} under those same circumstances. Stated verbally, δ is a form of tau correlation, specifically τ_d, between a dichotomous and a nondichotomous variable. The use of the letter d in the two contexts seems to be a coincidence.

Evaluation of d

The sample d has attractive characteristics. First, as a descriptive statistic, it is a direct reflection of the overlap in two sample distributions, which is often the main concern of an investigator. Second, d has nice sampling properties. Properly used, it has good robustness and power. Not only is it an unbiased estimate of δ, but its sampling variance depends in a simple fashion on the way the populations overlap, and this variance can be readily estimated from the sample data. Third, it, and inferences about it, are clearly invariant under monotonic scale transformation, so substantive conclusions from it will be invariant under such transformations of the scale originally used.

In addition to estimating δ, d is a simple transformation of the Wilcoxon–Mann–Whitney U statistic (Mann & Whitney, 1947; Wilcoxon, 1945). If there are n observations from one population and m from the other, and the r_1 are the ranks of the first group's scores among all the $n + m$ scores, ties being given the average rank, then $U = \sum r_1 - n(n + 1)/2$, and

$$d = 2U/nm - 1. \tag{5.3}$$

Converting U to a proportion of times a score from the first group is higher than one from the second, $p = U/mn$, was suggested by Birnbaum (1956).

There is a certain amount of literature on inferences about p (e.g., Mee, 1990), as distinct from d, but there is surprisingly little cross-referencing between the literature of d and that on p, in spite of the fact that $d = 2p - $

1. Here, I will refer primarily to to d for simplicity of exposition, but the reader can bear in mind that the discussion applies equally to p.

Inferences About δ

The δ defined by (5.1) seems like a good measure of the separation between groups, one that has a very direct intuitive interpretation but that does not depend on any assumptions about the distributions. The sample d has a similarly straightforward interpretation as a description of the sample. It is seen to be related to a fairly familiar test statistic (5.3). However, the inferential methods for ordinal statistics such as U that are most often encountered in texts, or implemented in computer packages, are tests of the null hypothesis that the two distributions are identical, or of the equivalent randomization null hypothesis that all possible assignments of the observations to two groups, m in one and n in the other, are equally likely. This is similar to the situation with respect to inferences about tau that was described in chapter 3 where the commonly employed tests assume independence of the two variables.

The randomization hypothesis puts a highly limiting constraint on inference, just as it is in the case of using tau to test independence, because the distributions could differ in shape or in spread, with and without having δ equal to 0. Inferences about location differences that are based on assuming identity of distributions may have an erroneous basis because other distributional differences also make it true that not all possible randomizations are equally likely. This has been a concern since early days (e.g., Birnbaum, 1956; Zaremba, 1962), but randomization tests are still frequently encountered.

Here, methods will be presented for a more broadly based inferential process, treating d as an estimate of the parameter δ, one whose sampling distribution will depend on characteristics of the two distributions. These characteristics can be estimated from the sample, and inferences from d to δ can be made in a more generally useful way than simply testing identity of distributions. This involves estimating the variance of d from the sample. Then, whereas d has so far been proposed as applicable to the independent groups context, it is shown that it can be extended to repeated-measures designs. Finally, ways in which repeated-measure and independent-group ds can be adapted to more complex research designs are suggested.

WHY ORDINAL METHODS?

Robustness and Power

Three classes of motives for using ordinal methods were suggested in chapter 1 and at the outset of this chapter, and in this section arguments for and against them are are elaborated and discussed in the context of location comparisons. One class has to do with the statistical behavior of ordinal methods, and there are many studies of this question (Blair & Higgins, 1980a, 1980b, 1981, 1985; Bradley, 1968, 1978; Chernoff & Savage, 1958; Conover, 1980; Dixon, 1954; Fligner & Policello, 1981; Hettmansperger, 1984; Hodges & Lehman, 1956; Neave & Granger, 1968; O'Brien, 1988; Pearson & Please, 1975; Randles & Wolfe, 1979). The conclusions about the robustness and power of ordinal methods relative to normal-based ones seem to be well enough established to obviate the necessity of elaborate review. The general conclusions from studies such as those cited was that ordinal methods sacrifice a little power when circumstances are optimal for the normal-based ones, but often have greater power, sometimes substantially greater, when classical assumptions are violated. In addition, they are more robust in that their nominal alpha levels are more realistic than normal-based methods in a wide variety of circumstances. Thus, ordinal methods might well be regarded as the methods of choice on these grounds, unless the investigator expects that the classical assumptions are very likely to be true.

The studies on which these conclusions are based are, though numerous, largely characterized by a narrowness of design that limits the generality of the results. The variety of alternative conditions and distributions investigated cover only a small part of those that an investigator is likely to encounter in research. Feng and Cliff (1995), however, extended the designs to a wide variety of situations, examining not just alpha levels but power and c.i. coverage as well. They came to much more complex conclusions concerning the behavior of d relative to the t test. On balance, the results favor d, but there are circumstances under which t is superior. I will discuss this issue in more detail below.

There is a shortage of conceptual analysis of why the effects on power and size that occur do so. Such theorizing would aid the empirical investigator in evaluating whether his or her data is more appropriate for one type of analysis rather than another. A rationale for such effects will be suggested later in this chapter.

Researchers sometimes turn to computer-intensive methods when distributional assumptions are suspect. A procedure commonly used in support of mean comparisons is a randomization test in which the scores from different groups are pooled and then reassigned to groups a large number of times, with the mean difference or t ratio being tabulated each time. The original mean difference or t is then compared to the resulting distribution of mean differences. If it falls in the extreme α proportion of the distribution, this is taken as supporting the validity of a true mean difference at the α significance level. For example, LeVay (1991), whose data is reanalyzed subsequently, employed this method to support his conclusions.

Such methods are useful, yet they deal with only a minor part of the distributional assumption problem. They are equivalent to assuming that *both samples are coming from the same distribution*, and, as formulated here, the more important issue is that the differences between distributions other than their location difference will influence the validity of the probability statements we make about mean differences. In fact, the *t* test itself is known to be relatively robust to the form of the parent distributions, as long as both distributions are the same except in means.

Bootstrapping (Efron, 1982) is another alternative sometimes employed. Used with care, it can lead to improvement over just using the data itself, but the evidence (Westfall & Young, 1993; Wilcox, 1991) suggests that it is a less perfect remedy than its early promise suggested. It seems to go only part of the way that would be necessary to remove the influences of higher moments on the validity of our influences about means.

Scale Considerations

Another class of motives for ordinal analysis derives from the presumed scale properties of the data. This was the primary grounds for deciding on methods cited by Siegel (1958) in the original edition of his widely used book. The reasoning is that many variables in behavioral research have only ordinal justification. In the context of modern measurement theory (e.g., Krantz, Luce, Suppes, & Tversky, 1971), this judgment can hardly be challenged because, succinctly stated, interval-scale status requires the demonstration *on nontrivial empirical grounds* that nominally equal intervals at different points on the scale are equal. The argument that the majority of psychometrically defined variables do not meet this criterion has been made elsewhere (Cliff, 1989, 1991; Cliff & Donoghue, 1992; Chapter 1 here), so the details will not be repeated. The point is that an assertion that such variables cannot be subjected to arbitrary monotonic transformations without the loss of any externally validated information can rarely be refuted.

The use in behavioral research of physically defined dependent variables such as electrical resistance, time, and the like typically does not avoid the issue of ordinality. In a large proportion of cases, the form of a variable that is the one analyzed has no more justification than any of a number of systematic transformations of it, such as log, exponential, reciprocal, or power. The data from LeVay (1991), used later as an example, is an instance of this. When examined closely, such "physical" variables are often surrogates for some unobserved latent variable that is the one actually of concern. That is, an observed physical variable, such as skin conductance, is being used as an indicator of a psychological variable, such as anxiety or arousal. It seems unlikely that the relation between conductance and anxiety can be defended as a direct, linear one, although it is plausible to assert that it is monotonic. Response time does sometimes provide an exception to this principle. Townsend (1992) points out that the additivity that is displayed by time in some carefully designed experiments of sequential information processing supports the status of response time as an interval-scale variable. However, even time is often merely a surrogate for some unobserved variable such as processing difficulty, or at least its reciprocal, rate, can be argued as equally valid for the purposes of the experiment.

It is important to be clear what the issue is here. The issue is the invariance of substantive conclusions under legitimate transformation of the data. It has been argued for many years (Lord, 1953; Labovitz, 1967; Velleman & Wilkinson, 1993) that there is nothing that prevents us from analyzing numerical data, no matter what its scale status is. Lord pointed out that statistical inferences based on football jersey numbers, typically considered an example of a nominal scale because they merely identify the players, are just as valid as those based on any other set of numbers. Samples from a population of players will display mean differences that behave according to the properties of the population distribution. Inferences from such samples will behave just as any others. However, the mean difference will hold only as long as the current numbering convention convention is retained. When the numbering convention is changed, the mean difference will change. The substantive fact of the mean difference will not be invariant under transformation of the variable, and it is invariance of *conclusions* under transformation that has to be the concern of the investigator.

Thus, it is true that statistical inference, as such, is not affected by the scale status of a variable, and inferences that are drawn with one form of the variable, no matter how arbitrary it is, will hold as long as that form is unchanged. However, there is little to guarantee that such a conventional definition of numerical assignment would remain as stable in behavioral research as it has in football. More importantly, the relation that was observed is one between the convention as such and football position, rather than reflecting any natural tendencies for the two variables to go together, much less supporting any idea of a causal relationship. The issue with respect to possible scale transformation is *substantive* invariance of conclusions under transformation when they are based on what are really ordinal or nominal scales, not the statistical sampling behavior of such scales.

An equally salient argument is that the observed variable is different from the latent variable, and that it is the latter about which we are really concerned. It seems appropriate for me to be worried about whether the conclusions I am making, which are based on the manifest variable I am analyzing, will be valid for the latent variable that is my real concern, given that the latter is a probably nonlinear but plausibly monotonic transformation of it. In my view, the validity and generality of conclusions is the true crux of the scale-type issue as far as data analysis is concerned is: Will substantive conclusions based on one form of the variable hold for another, legitimate form of it? Conclusions based on ordinal methods remain unchanged under such monotonic transformation, whereas those based on parametric analysis do not, at least to some degree.

The argument has also been made (Abelson & Tukey, 1963) that standard statistics are relatively insensitive to all but the most grotesque transformations of the data because all such transformed variables will be highly correlated. To this, two types of counterarguments come to mind. The first is that since many conclusions from studies are based on whether some correlation or mean difference is significant or not (the fact that a significance-based research strategy has its own faults is beside the point), a rather modest change in a variable can have an important ("significant," so to say) effect because it is not so hard to change a variable enough to move a t or z ratio from 1.6 ("ns") to 2.1 ("$p < .05$"), or vice versa.

Also, strong effects of transformation on the t ratio for independent groups are in fact easy to demonstrate (Stuadte & Sheater, 1990). For example, given data on some variable from two groups, the overall highest score has to be from a member of one of the groups. The unpooled-variance version of the t ratio can *always* be made as close as we like to 1.00 in favor of that group, no matter what it was originally—positive or negative, high or low—by transforming the scale. The situation is even more interesting if the lowest score is from that same group because then the ratio can always be made −1.00 as well by transformation. If several scores from the same group are at the end of the distribution, the possible effects are larger. With the three highest scores coming from the same group, which has $n = 10$, then the t ratio can always be made 1.96, significant at .05, one-tailed, even with Welch's (1938) correction for degrees of freedom. More extreme t ratios can usually be derived via transformation of the scale, depending on the specific characteristics of the data, but these examples suggest that the possible effects of scale transformation are not necessarily to be dismissed. These effects can be generalized to an algorithm that transforms a scale to maximize or minimize Student's t, and similar effects on Pearson correlations are possible (Birkes & Dodge, 1993; Kimeldorf & Sampson, 1978).

Answering the Investigator's Question

At the outset, the rather unusual assertion was made that ordinal methods can provide more direct answers to the investigator's research questions than traditional methods can. The basis for this assertion is the experience that, when asked what question a study is supposed to answer, an investigator very often answers, "to see if people in this group (or in this condition) score higher than they do in that." If that response is pursued by the query, "Would you like to quantify the extent to which that is true?" the answer is often an enthusiastic yes.

It is true that traditional mean-comparison methods provide a tentative answer to the first part of the investigator's concern. If one mean is higher than another, then the majority of the scores on which that one is based will usually be higher than those defining the other one, but it is easy to construct two distributions where the opposite will be the case. For example, one distribution can have a lower mode than the other but have a long tail in the high direction whose extreme values make the order of the means opposite to the order for most scores.

It is quite difficult for mean-comparison methods to provide quantification of the sort which is needed to answer the research question in a quantified way. Using the means to provide the basis for such quantification is possible, as McGraw and Wong (1992), suggest, but that requires assumptions about equality of variances and about shapes of distributions, assumptions that most investigators would find difficult to support. An advantage of the d statistic is that not only does its sign indicate directly which group tends to have the higher scores, but its value provides a very direct and intuitive index of the extent to which that is the case. Furthermore, as will be seen, methods for assessing the statistical uncertainty underlying a sample d, such as its estimated standard error and, thus, a confidence interval for δ, are readily available. Doing anything similar with probabilities estimated from mean-based methods would be computationally complex and undoubtedly sensitive to the validity of the distributional assumptions that would be necessary for such a calculation.

Another advantage of δ in this regard is that it is a direct measure of effect size, and a distribution-free one, at that. One can speculate that one reason behavioral science has been slow to adopt the routine reporting of effect size is the extent to which the process requires a suspension of doubt about the distributional and measurement characteristics of one's data. An effect size of "two scale units" is hard to interpret when one knows the "scale units" are arbitrary, much less when the scale is arguably only ordinal. (It is true that there are exceptions. Conclusions such as, "the average client will spend 37 fewer days in therapy under this regimen than that" seems to be a perfectly valid measure of effect size.) Standardizing a mean difference by an assumed standard deviation is hardly better. (Which group's standard deviation will be used?) This removes the unit problem but not the one of ordinality; monotonic transformation will tend to change the value of a mean difference relative to the corresponding standard deviation. Furthermore, most mean differences can be expected to be accompanied by variance differences (O'Brien, 1988), so using one of the variances as the denominator can lead to misleading inferences about the true nature of the difference in the distributions. Dominance analysis can provide a more useful method than the usual one in another way. Many behavioral variables consist of a few ordered categories. Differences in response by two groups are often investigated via a $2 \times k$ contingency table ("chi-square") analysis that throws away the information that the categories are ordered, whereas a *d* analysis would make use of it. Thus, as long as the investigator's interest is really in the extent to which "people in this group score higher than people in that group," rather than actually being something quantifiable in terms of the original variables, the *d* statistic seems to offer advantages as an expression of effect size also.

Why the Scarcity of Ordinal Analyses?

Ordinal analyses enjoyed a flurry of popularity in the 1950s but have become relatively rare since then. If one accepts the preceding arguments, it is natural to wonder why this rarity has been the case. Possible answers to such a question provide much of the motivation for the present book. One such answer is that, as usually communicated by texts and computer package manuals, the nature of the available ordinal methods is typically presented too narrowly. Commonly omitted, for example, is the calculation of the descriptive statistic *d*; the widely available methods focus instead on the question of statistical significance of group differences. The inferential methods used with ordinal statistics are likewise narrow. They typically only test the hypothesis that two distributions are identical, whereas a sophisticated investigator is likely to be aware that group differences can be of a variety of kinds and that differences in spread, at least, may need to be taken into consideration.

Also, the ordinal methods have seemed to be applicable in only the simplest designs, whereas investigators often have more complex issues in mind. The general rubric provided by analysis of variance, on the other hand, allows an almost endless variety of designs, and the possibilities presented by the general linear model are even broader. A significant extension of the applicability of ordinal methods is possible, however. Ferguson (1965) provides some examples, and several others will be suggested here. Furthermore, it will again be argued that these ordinal analyses are likely to be closer to the investigator's true interest than are the corresponding analyses of variance.

A final influence has perhaps been the relative unavailability of computer programs to do any but the most unsophisticated of ordinal analyses. A beginning toward a remedy for this lack is likewise at hand in the form of simple programs written by the author and collaborators.

Conclusion

In this section, arguments have been presented in support of the assertion that ordinal methods for comparing location have advantages over traditional, normal-theory ones. The arguments are in three categories. One is the rather traditional one that ordinal methods are the more robust to distributional and equivariance assumptions, and are often the more powerful when such assumptions are not met. The second is that ordinally based conclusions will be invariant under monotonic transformation of the data, and that such monotonic transformation is often plausible as well as being likely to affect the valididty of conclusions based on traditional methods. Finally, it is argued that our research questions often translate more directly into analyses that are ordinally based than they do into ones of the traditional kind. Reasons why these motives have not been sufficient to ensure the wider application of ordinal methods were also suggested.

INFERENCES ABOUT δ

Given the potential problems with mean comparisons and the clear interpretative status of δ, it is an attractive alternative to mean differences. Inferences about δ can take two forms. One corresponds to the familiar Wilcoxon–Mann–Whitney (WMW) rank-sum test. There, it is assumed that the only issue is to test whether two samples come from identical distributions. It is, alternatively, a "randomization" test that tests the assumption that a single sample, here, of ranks, has been randomly divided into two groups. If identical distributions are assumed, the variance of d or U in the null case depends only on the group sizes: $\sigma_d^2 = (m + n + 1)/3mn$. The ratio d^2/σ_d^2 becomes a single-degree-of-freedom chi-square variate for large m and n, and tables are widely available for using U to test the null hypothesis in small samples. Alternatively, applying a correction for continuity that converts the numerator to $(|d| - 1/mn)^2$, parallel to what was done with t in a similar context, makes the chi-square approximation excellent as long as the smaller sample is at least 3 and the conventional .05 and .01 α levels are used. A very simple, but descriptively useful, point made earlier is that, if the WMW is used and the hypothesis is rejected, one can use d as an estimate of the distributions' separation by means of (5.3).

This kind of inference has limited applicability because it only allows a test of the hypothesis that the the two groups represent random samples from the same distribution. Rejection is taken as reflecting a difference in location of the two distributions. However, as noted, it could be that the two distributions differ in ways other than, or in addition to, location. For example, there may be a difference in spread or in the shape of the distributions. Such differences may invalidate inferences from the WMW test (Birnbaum, 1956).

It may be instructive to consider briefly the parametric model that underlies much statistical practice in simple cases. Suppose there is a treatment and a control group. We, under traditional schemes, assume that the effect of the treatment is a constant. Yet this seems contrary to common experience in which there are individual differences in treatment response. Subjects also display individual differences on a variable in the absence of treatment. After treatment, they differ from each other not only due to the factors that caused them to differ without treatment but also because of their differential response to treatment (O'Brien, 1988). Therefore, it is highly unlikely that the two distributions differ only in means or other measures of location. O'Brien (1988) makes this argument persuasively in the biomedical context, and it seems equally relevant in the behavioral one.

It seems similarly unreasonable to expect that intact groups would have distributions that differ only in means or some other measure of location. If distributions differ in location, they are also likely to differ in spread, also called scale, and in shape. The concern in making inferences is that differences of one kind—such as spread or shape—affect the validity of inferences about another—such as location. Thus, the substantive question is not so much to decide whether groups have identical distributions as opposed to having distributions that differ only in location as it is in estimating accurately what the nature of the differences are. Tests of d that are based on a null hypothesis of identical distributions are likely to be sensitive to differences in scale, just as the t test is. This means not only that we could be more—or less—likely than the stated α to reject the null hypothesis that $\delta = 0$ when it in fact is 0, or to have enhanced or reduced chances of rejecting the hypothesis when it is false, but we may even have an increased chance of mistaking the direction of δ. Thus, inferential methods for d that did not rely on assuming that the only way in which distributions differed was in location would be desirable.

At an early stage (e.g., Birnbaum, 1956; Zaremba, 1962) concern developed that the WMW was not robust to a kind of analogue of heterogeneity of variance. An extreme example is a "kill or cure" situation. Suppose the true state of affairs is that a treatment is equally likely to greatly enhance or greatly interfere with performance, and it is applied to a treatment group, which is to be compared to a control. In the extreme case, a random member of the treatment population has a 50–50 chance of being better than *any* control and an equal chance of being worse. The outcome of the study, as analyzed by WMW, would then depend only on how many of the treatment subjects are "improvers," and a WMW analysis will lead to misleading alpha levels. Suppose $n = m = 4$. Then the probability that all four treatment subjects happen by chance to be improvers, and therefore have the four highest scores among the eight subjects is actually $.5^4 = .0625$, whereas the WMW would give the probability that the four highest scores come from the treatment group as one out of "8 take 4" = 24/1680 = .0143. This observed outcome thus has a true probability, .0625, which is more than four times that given by the WMW. Thus, the WMW is not robust to differences in spread of distributions.

An approach that is generally more useful than assuming there can be only location differences, as in the WMW, is to treat δ as a parameter whose estimate is d, regardless of the nature of the two populations. Each population can have its own distribution, $F(x)$ and $G(x)$, say, respectively (cf. Hettmansperger, 1984), and nothing is said about their form; δ reflects the probability that a score from G is higher than one from F. Then d is an estimate of δ, and, like any other estimator, has a sampling distribution whose characteristics are used in making inferences about δ.

Discussions of the sampling properties of d are aided by the use of the dominance variables that represent the direction of differences between scores, identically to the case with tau. For any observation x_i from the first population paired with any x_h from the second, define

$$d_{ih} = \text{sign}(x_i - x_h). \tag{5.4}$$

That is, a score x_i from the first population is compared to one, x_h, from the second; $d_{ih} = 1$ if $x_i > x_h$; $d_{ih} = -1$ if $x_i < x_h$; and $d_{ih} = 0$ if $x_i = x_h$. A second definition of δ, equivalent to (5.1), is then as the expected value of d_{ih}:

$$\delta = E(d_{ih}). \tag{5.5}$$

The estimate d is similarly defined by comparing each x_i in the sample to each x_j to get the d_{ih}s and then averaging these d_{ih}s over the nm comparisons:

$$d = \frac{\sum\limits_{i}\sum\limits_{h} d_{ih}}{mn}. \tag{5.6}$$

Clearly, $E(d) = \delta$ by this reasoning as well as the earlier one.

Since d is a member of the family of average-like statistics called U statistics (Hettmansperger, 1984), its sampling distribution will tend toward normality as the sample size increases, and, in moderate-sized samples, normal-based inferences can be made if its variance can be estimated. To find σ_d^2 in the general case, rather than the special one given for the WMW, we need to define, for any score x_i in the first population, the proportion of the *other* distribution that it lies above, $G(x_i)$, and the proportion that lies above it, $[1 - G(x_i)]$. Then we let d_i stand for the difference: $d_i = G(x_i) - [1 - G(x_i)]$. (These d_i are related to the t_i used in deriving the sampling properties of t, and they will be seen to have a similar role here.) That is, for individual i from the first population, d_i is the proportion of scores in the second population that lie below it minus the proportion that lie above. [The definition (5.5) permits the same conclusions whether X is continuous or discrete, with tied values.] Similarly, in the second population, $d_h = [1 -$

$F(x_h)] - F(x_j)$. It can be seen that $\delta = E(d_i) = E(d_h)$. The effect of defining d_i and d_h is that x_i and x_h have been transformed to ranklike variates, but d_i and d_h depend only on what might be called the "crossranks," the ranks of the scores in one group relative to the scores in the other. The use of their sample counterparts, as will be shown, is therefore not the same as jointly ranking all the scores from both groups and doing a "t test" of the average ranks in the manner suggested by Conover and Iman (1981).

Several writers, of whom Birnbaum (1956) seems to have been the earliest (cf. Fligner & Policello, 1981; Hettmansperger, 1984; Mee, 1990; Siegel & Castellan, 1988; Zaremba, 1962), have noted that d is asymptotically normally distributed with a sampling variance that can be expressed as

$$\sigma_d^2 = \frac{(m-1)\sigma_{d_i}^2 + (n-1)\sigma_{d_h}^2 + \sigma_{dih}^2}{mn}, \tag{5.7}$$

where $\sigma_{d_i}^2$, the variance of the d_i, is $E(d_i - \delta)^2$, and similarly for $\sigma_{d_h}^2$; likewise, $\sigma_{dih}^2 = E(d_{ih} - \delta)^2$. If there are no ties, the latter is $1 - \delta^2$. In large samples, this variance will resemble the form of the variance of the difference between means, becoming approximiately $\sigma_{di}^2/n + \sigma_{d.h}^2/m$.

In samples, the d_i can be estimated straightforwardly as the proportion of the x_j that lie below x_i minus the proportion that lie above:

$$\hat{d}_i = \frac{\#(x_i > x_j) - \#(x_i < x_j)}{m}. \tag{5.8}$$

Clearly, $E(\hat{d}_i) = d_i$, and d_j can be estimated in a similar way. Asymptotically as the sample sizes increase, $\hat{d}_i = d_i$, so $\sigma_{d_i}^2$, $\sigma_{d_h}^2$, and δ could be estimated from the sample and substituted in (5.7) to give a consistent estimate of the variance of d. Thus, tests of the hypothesis that $\delta = 0$ can be made without assuming identical distributions, and confidence intervals for δ can be formed. Fligner and Policello (1981) report that this procedure behaves well in terms of power and size over a variety of conditions of population distributions in small samples with $n = 10$ and $m = 11$. Feng and Cliff (1995) have extended these results with similar, but modified, conclusions that are described below.

An alternative to substituting sample quantities directly in (5.7) and relying on asymptotic properties is to use its unbiased estimate. Using methods similar to those of Daniels and Kendall (1947; cf. Cliff & Charlin, 1991; Randles & Wolfe, 1979) and described in Chapter 3, it can be shown that

$$s_d^2 = \frac{m^2\Sigma(\hat{d}_i - d)^2 + n^2\Sigma(\hat{d}_h - d)^2 - \Sigma\Sigma(d_{ih} - d)^2}{mn(m-1)(n-1)} \tag{5.9}$$

is an unbiased estimate of σ_d^2. In practice, the negative sign on the last term allows the estimate to be occasionally negative, so an advisable modification is to use $(1 - d^2)/(mn - 1)$ as the minimum allowable value, similar to the case with tau. This substitution introduces a bias, but such adjustments usually increase the efficiency of an estimate, as well as eliminating impossible values. Also, a consistent estimate of σ_d^2, similar to that used for σ_t^2, will be suggested later. In large samples, the last numerator term becomes negligible compared to the others and could be ignored.

The mechanics of this formula can be illustrated with a small artifical example. (The example must be understood as simply providing an illustration. In real life, very little of a reliable nature can be learned from samples this small, no matter how the statistics come out.) Suppose there are two groups with $n = 4$ in A and $m = 5$ in B. The B scores are 1, 3, 4, 7, 8, and the A scores are 6, 7, 9, 10. The matrix of d_{ih} values is given in Table 5.1. Calculating $\sum\sum d_{ih}/nm = d$, we find $d = .65$. The $\hat{d}_{i\cdot}$ are given at the end of each row and the $\hat{d}_{\cdot h}$ at the bottom of each column.

One can define sample "variances" of the $\hat{d}_{i\cdot}$ and $\hat{d}_{\cdot h}$ as $s_{di\cdot}^2 = [\sum(\hat{d} - d)^2]/(n - 1)$ and $s_{d\cdot h}^2 = [\sum(\hat{d} - d)^2]/(m - 1)$, respectively, to get an idea of the sizes of $\sigma_{di\cdot}^2$ and $\sigma_{d\cdot h}^2$. Also, a sample variance of the d_{ih} can be defined as $[\sum\sum(d_{ih} - d)^2]/(n - 1)(m - 1)$. Using these definitions, we find from the table that $s_{di\cdot}^2 = .1467$; $s_{d\cdot h}^2$ is somewhat larger, .2375; s_{dih}^2 is considerably larger, .8792. An alternative version of (5.9) that uses these quantities directly is

$$s_d^2 = \frac{ms_{di\cdot}^2}{n(m - 1)} + \frac{ns_{d\cdot h}^2}{m(n - 1)} - \frac{s_{dih}^2}{nm}. \qquad (5.10)$$

Using this expression, we find that $s_d^2 = .0458 + .0633 - .0440 = .0652$, or the same answer can be found from (5.9) itself. Taking the square root gives .255, which would make an approximate .95 c.i. of .14 to 1.0, and $z = .650/.255 = 2.55$ ($p < .05$) if a hypothesis-testing procedure were used with such small samples. If the null hypothesis that the two samples come from identical

TABLE 5.1
Illustration of Independent Groups Dominance Analysis

A Scores	B Scores					
	1	3	4	7	8	$d_{i\cdot}$
6	1	1	1	−1	−1	.20
7	1	1	1	0	−1	.40
9	1	1	1	1	1	1.00
10	1	1	1	1	1	1.00
$d_{\cdot j}$	1.00	1.00	1.00	.25	0.0	.65

populations has any credibility, the WMW test can be calculated for comparison. This yields $z = (.65 - .05)/.408 = 1.47$ ($p > .05$).

Improved Inferential Procedures

The experience of Long and Cliff (in press) with respect to inferences about tau led to their introduction of the "consistent estimate" of the variance of t. It avoided the awkwardness of very small, even negative, estimates of σ_t^2 and gave, overall, improved confidence intervals. A similar modification can be made in estimating the variance of d. Individually, $s_{di.}^2$ and $s_{d.h}^2$ are unbiased estimates of $\sigma_{di.}^2$ and $\sigma_{d.h}^2$, respectively. We can define $\Sigma(d_{ih} - d)^2/(mn - 1)$ as $\hat{\sigma}_{dih}^2$, similar to what was done in the case of tau. Then these quantities are substituted directly for their counterparts in (5.7) to give the consistent estimate of σ_d^2:

$$\hat{\sigma}_d^2 = \frac{(m-1)s_{di.}^2 + (n-1)s_{d.h}^2 + \hat{\sigma}_{dih}^2}{nm}. \tag{5.11}$$

This obviates the necessity of using a minimum allowable variance, and it was found to improve the inferential performance of d (Feng and Cliff, 1995), which was already very good. In the little example previously given, it yields a higher value for the variance, .1008 instead of .0652. The values are more similar with reasonable sample sizes, and with low values of d this one can even be slightly smaller.

The experience of Feng and Cliff (1995) led to an additional modification of the procedure used to construct the c.i. They found that values of d near 1.0 were typically accompanied by small estimated variances, resulting in short c.i. that failed to contain δ somewhat too often, particularly in small samples. They therefore devised a modification of the c.i. so that it became asymmetric, longer on the side toward zero and shorter on the side toward ±1.0.

They found that, within a variety of population situations, σ_d^2 was approximately proportional to $1 - \delta^2$. Insofar as the sample d^2 is not equal to δ^2, s_d^2 will tend to overestimate σ_d^2 if it is smaller and underestimate if it is larger. If δ is really equal to a lower limit of the c.i., the variance of d will be larger than the current estimate, and contrariwise if it is equal to an upper limit. Feng and Cliff (1995) therefore suggested using the roots of the following equation as the limits for the c.i. rather than the usual, simple ones:

$$z_{\alpha/2}^2 = \frac{(d-\delta)^2}{[(1-\delta^2)/(1-d^2)]s_d^2}.$$

The resulting limits for the c.i. are

$$\frac{d - d^3 \pm z_{\alpha/2}\hat{\sigma}_d[(1 - d^2)^2 + z_{\alpha/2}{}^2\hat{\sigma}^2]^{1/2}}{1 - d^2 + z_{\alpha/2}{}^2\hat{\sigma}_d{}^2}. \qquad (5.12)$$

These asymmetric c.i. limits were found to give somewhat more accurate coverage in non-null cases with a slight loss of power because one limit of the c.i. is closer to zero than the simpler version. For example, in the small example, the c.i. using (5.12) is $-.16$ to $.94$ rather than the $.03$ to 1.00 that was found before. Note that 1.0 is no longer in the c.i. This is logical, because if δ is unity then d is always unity also. The asymmetry effects become smaller in larger samples and rapidly smaller with smaller values of d. The slight complication it introduces is mainly important when d is above $.6$ and at least one sample is as small as perhaps 10. It is, of course, simple to introduce it into a computer program.

d versus Analysis of Variance of Ranks

Basing inferences about location on d clearly has considerable resemblance to a t test or an analysis of variance (ANOVA) of the ranked scores. There are, however, differences that suggest that the d procedure is preferable. The first difference is interpretational: d has a clear interpretation under very general circumstances, whereas an average rank difference is more complex, at the least needing to be corrected for the group sizes. Although such an adjustment could be made fairly routine, specifics of how to do it might require some study and discussion, and some ambiguity might remain. On the other hand, no such adjustments are necessary for d.

More serious complications for average ranks exist on the inferential side. First, the sample rank of a given score has a rather complexly defined population counterpart that must consider the size of the other sample and the relative sizes of the two populations. The sample $\hat{d}_i$ has no such complications; the proportion of scores of the other group lying below a sampled x_i directly estimates the corresponding d_i. Moreover, if an investigator converts observed scores to ranks and does an ANOVA of the ranks (e.g., Iman, 1974), the numerator and denominator of F are completely dependent on each other. The reason for the dependence is very simple and arithmetical. The sum and sum of squared ranks in the total group are simple functions of $n + m$. This means that the ANOVA total sum of squares for ranks is fixed by $n + m$. Therefore, an increase in a between-groups sum of squares caused by increasing the separation of the sample mean ranks must be directly compensated by a decrease in the within-groups sum of squares. There is no more information in the F ratio than there is in the WMW U statistic itself.

Use of tabled values for the F ratio is invalidated because the assumption of independence of its numerator and denominator is completely violated. This fact is not recognized in a number of the sources that suggest this practice, and it calls into question the validity of inferences based on it. The relevant distribution for this particular ratio would be Fisher's distribution, as described by Kendall (1970) in the context of the coefficient of concordance.

These reasons should make it clear that averaging ranks and proceeding to apply standard methods has a dubious theoretical basis (Agresti & Pendergast, 1986). Its reasonable success empirically (e.g., Conover & Iman, 1981, 1982) is contradicted by Monte Carlo studies that examined a wider range of conditions (Blair, Sawilowsky, & Higgins, 1987; Sawilowsky, 1985; Sawilowsky, Blair, & Higgins, 1989). On the other hand, d and s_d^2 are not mutually dependent, although they do constrain each other, particularly in very small samples. That is, for given sample sizes, a certain value of d can be accompanied by any of a number of different values of s_d^2, although not any possible value. An effect that this has will be mentioned in a later discussion.

Dominance Diagrams

A useful visual aid to the d statistic is the dominance diagram, illustrated in Fig. 5.1. To construct it, the scores of one group, arranged in increasing magnitude, define the columns, and the scores of the other group, similarly arranged, define the rows. Then a + is entered if the row score is greater than the column score, a 0 is entered if they are tied, and a − is entered if the column score is greater than the row. The eye then readily perceives the relative frequency of + and −, the occurrence of 0s, and whether there

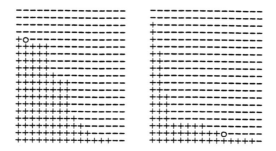

FIG. 5.1. Dominance diagrams for "homosexual" (rows) vs. "heterosexual" (columns) males. (A plus indicates row score higher than column, a minus indicates the reverse, and zero represents ties. The left diagram represents INAH-2 [area of hypothalamic nuclei] nucleus size [$d = -.266$] and the right represents INAH-3 nucleus [$d = -.595$]. Data are based on LeVay [1991].) From Cliff (1993a). Copyright © 1993 by the American Psychological Association. Reprinted with permission.

is wide variability in frequency of a given sign within rows or columns. The data on which the figures are based are from LeVay (1991). The left figure has $d = -.595$, and in the right $d = -.266$. More details on this application are given in the next section.

EXAMPLE

The data of LeVay (1991) will be used to illustrate application of the independent groups d methods to real data. LeVay measured the areas of two hypothalamic nuclei, INAH-2 and INAH-3, in two groups of cadavers. One group of 19 was presumed on the basis of other evidence to be from male homosexuals; the other group of 16 was from males presumed to be heterosexual. The values used in the present analysis were read from graphical frequency distributions presented by LeVay (his Fig. 2), so some minor inconsistencies with his data may have been introduced. The dominance diagrams from these data were presented as Fig. 5.1.

The quantitative results are summarized in Table 5.2, first using the unbiased estimate of σ_d^2 (5.9) and the symmetric c.i. For INAH-2, $d = -.266$ (i.e., "homosexual" INAH-2 tends to be smaller) but the s_d of .193 leads to a c.i. for δ of $-.65$ to $+.12$. The conclusions are that, although it is possible that a substantial majority ($\delta = -.65$) of homosexuals tend to have smaller INAH-2 nuclei than heterosexuals, a small difference in the reverse direction ($\delta = .12$) is also possible, so the observed d is not significant. Correspondingly, if we used the ratio d/s_d as a normal deviate, $z = -1.37$, which is not significant at .05, even one-tailed. When the asymmetric c.i. is constructed using the

TABLE 5.2
Dominance Analysis of INAH-2 and INAH-3 on
"Homosexual" and "Heterosexual" Hypothalamuses

	INAH-2	INAH-3
Inferences About δ		
d	$-.266$	$-.595$
s_d	.193	.163
c.i.	$-.654$ to .121	$-.921$ to $-.269$
z for d	1.37	-3.65
Components of s_d^2		
$s_{di.}^2$	.399	.229
s_{dj}^2	.262	.244
s_{dij}^2	.929	.644
Mean Comparisons		
t for means	-1.35	-3.45
df for t	33	33

From Cliff (1993a). Copyright © (1993) by the American Psychological Association. Reprinted with permission.

consistent estimate of σ_d, its limits are similar, $-.588$ to $.128$ with an almost-identical z ratio of 1.36.

On the other hand, the results show a quite clear-cut difference in INAH-3. The d of $-.595$ shows that the two sample distributions have little overlap. The unbiased estimate of s_d of $.163$ leads to a symmetric c.i. of $-.92$ to $-.27$ and a z ratio of -3.65. The asymmetric c.i. with consistent estimate of σ_d is $-.83$ to $-.20$, a bit lower than the other one, and the z ratio is very similar, 3.57.

In these data, the corresponding t_ws were very similar to the zs computed from ds, -1.35 for INAH-2 and -3.45 for INAH-3. However, we know that the d results will hold up under any transformation of the dependent variable.

To illustrate the magnitudes of the quantities that determine the estimated variance of d, the table includes s_i^2, s_h^2, and s_{dih}^2. The values of s_i^2 and s_h^2 here are somewhat higher than most we have encountered so far, but are not unusual. The value of s_{dih}^2, which without ties is $1 - d^2$, has so far been considerably larger than the other two, as it is here. It is possible for one of s_{di}^2 or $s_{d.h}^2$ to equal 1.0 in the case of extreme bimodality in that group, but the other variance must then be zero.

These analyses are felt to be useful for the three reasons set forth at the outset. The descriptive statistic $d = -.595$ is a useful quantification of the conclusion "cadavers of presumed homosexuals most often have smaller INAH-3 nuclei than presumed heterosexuals." As far as the second consideration, invariance over transformation, is concerned, one might contend that measured area is about as incontrovertible an example of a ratio scale as one would want. However, even here the monotonic transformation issue is relevant. If it is indeed true that the size of this nucleus is related to sexual object preference, then it seems more likely that it is the volume of the nucleus, not the area of a cross section, that is important. Or it could be that the number of neural connections, which would be perhaps some nonlinear but monotonic function of area, that is important. The results of the d analysis will be the same as they were here if any of these possible transformations of the size variable represent the true causative factor.

The third consideration, susceptibility to failure of distributional assumptions, may or may not be relevant here. One cannot be sure without knowing the population distributions. Samples this small can support nothing more than suspicions. However, LeVay's (1991) Figure 2 shows more than a hint of the long tails that can cause trouble for mean-based methods. LeVay was sensitive to the distributional issue and took the step of "confirming" his t-test results with a randomization test. However, I have argued here that randomization is an inadequate safeguard in this respect. While it does guard against non-normality, it does so only insofar as the distributions are identical. It does not guard against the possibility that the distributions differ in spread or shape. One can, then, presumably be more confident about the conclusions drawn from d than from t because of the former's presumably better sampling properties in the face of non-normality. We will see, however, that this, though likely, is far from certain.

ROBUSTNESS OF d

Monte Carlo Studies

Numerous studies, cited earlier, indicate that ordinal group comparisons are robust in the face of distributional differences other than location, but I remarked that those studies were not as wide in scope as would be ideal. Feng and Cliff (1995) attempted to remedy this deficiency by studying the behavior of d, and the t test, under a wide set of circumstances. Their results, although generally favorable to d, identified some situations where it can run into trouble and suggested some inferential modifications to use in certain circumstances, such as the asymmetric c.i. described above. These results also provided insight into why and when location inferences using either method might not be robust.

Feng and Cliff (1995) studied all three aspects of the inferential process, size in the null case, power in the non-null, and coverage in both, using pseudosamples from normal distributions that could differ in means, variances, or both. The pseudosamples had sizes of 10 or 30 and could be equal (10, 10 or 30, 30) or unequal (10, 30 or 30, 10). The two arrangements of unequal sample sizes are treated separately in most of the conditions studied because it can make a difference which size of sample goes with which variance, and, in the case of d, which sample had which mean. For comparison, the same properties of t, with Welch's correction for degrees of freedom (Welch, 1937), referred to in the sequel as t_w, were tabulated. Two thousand replications were generated in each condition. With this number, empirical size or coverage estimates that are .04 or .06 are significantly different from the nominal α of .05.

A special problem occurs when $d = 1.0$, parallel to the discussion of tau. This is that then $s_d^2 = 0$. Because d can be 1.0 when δ is not, it seems inappropriate to conclude that $\sigma_d^2 = 0$, leading to a point interval of $\delta = 1.0$, just because $d = 1.0$, so an adjusted c.i. similar to that described in Chapter 3 (3.10) was used here when $d = 1.0$ in addition to the asymmetric adjustment of the c.i., (5.12).

The empirical size of the two methods in the null, normal case, with the c.i. for d adjusted as described, was found to be close to .05 for both d and t_w, even when the ratio of variances was as high as 9:1, although the size for d was .063 in that case, this being the largest discrepancy from .05. The two methods were almost identical in power in nonnull normal data. Type II error probabilities averaged .01 higher with d than t_w when variances were homogeneous and .03 higher when they were heterogeneous.

Coverage probability also showed good performance for d, but there was some continued weakness when δ was high, in spite of the adjustments just described that reduced this effect. Overall, the coverage was very close to .95, but it could fall below this when δ is greater than .50 and one or both samples are as small as 10. Thus, the overall picture in the normal case is that d works well but t_w is slightly superior.

This line of research was extended by Feng and Cliff (1995) to non-normal distributions. Here, distributions could be skewed or not skewed so that comparisons of two groups could include one skewed and one not skewed, both skewed in the same way, or skewed in opposite directions, as well as cases where neither was skewed. The skewed distributions were lognormal, which means that they not only were skewed (skewness of 2.0) but leptokurtic (kurtosis about 5.0). This condition corresponds to data populations that, to the eye, are definitely asymmetrical but not radically so. This degree of non-normality is not uncommon in behavioral data (Micceri, 1989; Wilcox, 1991). Feng and Cliff (1995) included in their simulations variables that had a lower limit, as many behavioral variables like counts or times do, and both lower and upper limits, as test scores and other psychometric variables do.

Here, d behaved well also; if anything, it was better in these cases than in the normal data. It showed proper size in all the null cases studied, and coverage that was very close to .95 in the great majority of the 48 non-null conditions, although coverage was between .90 and .95 in a minority and below .90 in one. Thus, its behavior, though good, was not perfect.

On the other hand, t_w showed appreciable departures from a size of .05 in several null conditions, and coverage that was significantly below .95 in 39 out of 48 non-null conditions. Relative power of d and t_w showed a mixture of results, each being superior to the other in about the same number of conditions. However, many of those where t_w showed superior power corresponded to those combinations of sample size, relative variance, and relative skewness in which t_w had shown inflated Type I error probabilities in the null case. Thus, the power superiority of t_w in those cases is somewhat misleading.

Although this evidence comes down generally in favor of d over t_w in terms of inferential properties, the issue of which is superior turned out to be complex. Sometimes one showed up better, sometimes the other. Moreover, superiority in size under some null condition may go with inferiority in power or coverage in the corresponding non-null ones. These conclusions are different from what has previously been reported, which has shown rather uniform superiority of ordinal methods.

Several factors correlate with the complexity of Feng and Cliff's (1995) conclusions. One is that we included the assessment of coverage, whereas most previous research has focused on size and sometimes examined power but rarely has looked at coverage. Perhaps more importantly, we examined a wider variety of conditions. Different sample sizes, different spreads, and different skewnesses all interact to produce a complex pattern of effects on the behavior of location difference statistics.

In research on robustness, it seems particularly important to include conditions where sample sizes differ substantially. This has often not been the case in the past, or has been true only nominally, such as $n_1 = 10$ versus $n_2 = 11$ in Fligner and Policello (1981). The statistics d and t_w are both affected by distributional conditions, but the effects differ, depending on circumstances such as relative sample size. In the next section, a theoretical analysis by Cliff, Feng, and Long (1994) is proposed to explain these effects. It predicts effects of sample size, both relative and absolute, relative variance, relative skewness, and even kurtosis, and indicates that these factors interact. The principles on which the theory is based are simple, but the outcome shows that the effects can be complex.

Explanation for Behavior of Statistics

Cliff, Feng, and Long (1994) offer a general explanation of why and when location comparisons are robust and/or powerful. It is similar in conclusions to Cressie and Whitford (1986) but somewhat differently formulated. Cliff et al. point to (a) nonnormality of the statistic; (b) biased estimates of its standard error; (c) covariance between the statistic and the estimate of its standard error; (d) variability in estimated standard error that is greater than in the normal case. Factors (a) and (c) tend to go together because both the skewness of means and mean differences and the correlation between the statistic and its standard error depend on the skewness of the populations.

I will not introduce the formula on which their conclusions are based here because it is complex, and doing so would require the explanation of the notation used in it. What it shows is first the truism that an appropriate estimate of the standard error of the difference should be used. If, for example, the pooled version of the variance is used in a t test or the randomization-assuming variance is used for d, then the confidence interval simply will generally not have the appropriate width. It may tend to be either too wide or too narrow, depending on whether the larger or smaller group has the larger population variance.

The formula also shows effects of the higher moments. There is an effect for the skewness of the populations, but the way it operates depends on whether the skewnesses are equal and on the relative sample sizes; there can be no effect, or a large effect, depending on the interaction of relative sample size with the difference in skewnesses. Furthermore, the effects of skewness are different at the two ends of the confidence interval; if one end tends to be too short, the other tends to be correspondingly too long. This means that a two-tailed test may have more or less appropriate size, but a one-tailed test in the same context will have a size that is too large if it is done in one direction or too small if done in the other.

Kurtosis also has an effect. Normal-based methods will be too liberal with leptokurtic (long-tailed) populations but too conservative in platykurtic (short-tailed) ones. The former effect is potentially the more serious because kurtosis can hardly go below −1, but it can take on high positive values, values near 10 not being uncommon empirically. The way sample size operates with kurtosis is not as complex as it is with skewness, but there is still a differential effect. The kurtosis of the smaller group is the more influential.

The effects of both skewness and kurtosis diminish with sample size, the latter more rapidly. Even though the effect of kurtosis lessens more rapidly with sample size than does that of skewness, kurtosis tends to be numerically the larger of the two in non-normal populations, so its effect can remain non-negligible in surprisingly large samples. The overall conclusion is that non-normality can have appreciable effects on the inference process, but the way it operates can be complex. Thus different studies of robustness can have different conclusions.

However, a larger sample size is no cure for systematically misestimating the variance of the difference, whether one is using means in a t test or an ordinal comparison. Such misestimation causes one to be mistaken about the alpha level one is operating with, no matter what the sample size.

Application to Rank-Based Statistics

These principles apply to the d statistic, and other rank-based statistics, because they too are differences between means, but in a given set of data they will apply differently to d and to t because the two are based on distributions that have different properties. It may be thought that d, along with other statistics related to it such as WMW U, is "distribution free," but it is not. It is just based on distributions that are different from the original distributions of the variables.

The way in which this is true follows from the definition of δ. It is $\Pr(x_i > x_j) − \Pr(x_i < x_j)$ [that is, (5.1)], but this second part can also be stated as $\Pr(x_j > x_i)$. If x_i has a distribution $F(x_i)$ and x_j has a distribution $G(x_j)$, then the two original random variables can be transformed to new ones, $y_i = G(x_i)$ and $y_j = F(x_j)$. These are like percentile scores of the members of one population in the distributions for the *other* population. Each of these new scores has a distribution, $F'(y_i)$ and $G'(y_j)$, respectively, and these distributions will have their own properties. These properties are related to, but different, often radically different, from those of the original distribution because they depend on how each distribution falls relative to the other.

From this point of view, $\delta = E(y_i) - E(y_j)$ and d is a difference between sample means that estimates this population difference. As such, the moments of the distribution of d depend on the moments of the two new parent distributions, and so does the degree of nonindependence of d and s_d.[2] The d_i and d_j are direct functions of y_i and y_j, respectively: $d_i = 2y_i - 1$ and $d_j = 2y_j - 1$. The accuracy of inferences from d to δ will depend on whether these distributions of y_i and y_j are "nice" (Cliff et al., 1994) in almost exactly the same way that the characteristics of the original distributions affect inferences based on means. Usually, the characteristics of y_i and y_j are such that the inference process turns out to be well behaved, but there are circumstances where it is not. This is most likely to occur when δ is very high, above .8, and this can be explained by the fact that then the distributions of y_i and y_j are highly, and oppositely, skewed. Such a situation causes a problem, particularly for forming confidence intervals, because then not only is the distribution of d itself quite skewed, but d and s_d are highly correlated.

This conceptualization can also explain why d behaves well, even conservatively, in the null case. There the distributions of y_i and y_j are identical and rectangular, a circumstance that is optimal when d and s_d are both being estimated. However, it also provides a broader framework for the importance of using an appropriate estimate of the variance of d, the one recommended here, rather than the variance estimate that results from assuming randomization, as is done in the WMW itself. When the two distributions differ in spread, the estimate of the variance of d provided by the randomization assumption is simply wrong.

Thus we see that the issue of inferential robustness is a complex one. Ordinal statistics do not avoid it; they change its specifics. It seems to turn out that d behaves well more often than t_w does, but there are no guarantees that this will be true in a given set of data.

EXTENSIONS OF *d* ANALYSIS

Multiple Comparisons: Parameterwise or Familywise

When there are more than two groups, one faces some questions of inferential strategy. One is going to make inferences about more than one δ, and how best should this be done in a scientifically legitimate manner? Here, a useful distinction is between planned, or a priori, comparisons on the one hand and data-suggested, or a posteriori, ones on the other. There is a

---

[2]d is also influenced by the fact that the $\hat{d}_i$ only estimate the d_i, but this discrepancy is unimportant to the present considerations unless samples are very small.

related distinction about what the α probability of falsely rejecting a null hypothesis, or falsely stating that a parameter is in an interval, refers to.

One can be referring to α as the probability of rejecting H_0 about a single comparison or as the probability that a particular parameter is not in its c.i. This is called the comparisonwise or parameterwise α. The idea usually is that when multiple parameters are being estimated or hypotheses are being tested, based on theory or important practical issues, one should use parameterwise α levels. The reason is that one is looking at each research question separately, so each deserves its own test.

There are contrasting situations where one has no, or only weak, expectations. One is seeing whether there are any differences there. In that case, one should assume that it is possible that all the null hypotheses are true—for example, that all mean differences are zero or that all the regression coefficients in a multiple regression are zero. In such cases one should control the analysiswise α, making the probability α that one or more null hypotheses will be rejected when all are true.

The most important question to answer when there are multiple groups is therefore, "Why are there multiple groups?" The answer often is that there is a legitimate reason, that is, clear theoretical or practical grounds, for comparing many of the pairs of groups to each other. For example, one might have a treatment group and several control conditions and want to know whether the scores in the treatment group tend to be higher than those in *any* control group. Or one might have scores from inner city, rural, and suburban school children and want to know whether suburban differs from rural, rural from inner city, and suburban from inner city. Each comparison may have legitimate practical status.

In cases like these, it seems to me that we want to control parameterwise α, so the most appropriate procedure is to compute all the *d*s that are of interest and *assess their significance and establish their confidence intervals separately* rather than making any kind of multiple comparison adjustment.

When there are multiple groups, they can often be clustered into larger groups on a priori grounds. Then the comparisons can be made between these large clusters, reducing the number of comparisons. Also, multiple groups often are defined in terms of some natural order on a variable such as age, or stimulus intensity, or word list length. The research question can then often be formulated in terms of whether there is an ordinal relation between level on this ordinal grouping variable and the dependent variable. In that case, the research question may well be more directly tested through the tau correlation between level on the independent variable and X, and the methods of chapter 3 can be employed.

It is unfortunately the case that often editors and their consultants do not like this sort of thing. When one or more comparisons are significant, but perhaps not at such an extreme level as would stand up to a multiple-comparisons procedure, they may suspect that the rationale that led to testing a particular d on a priori grounds came after the result rather than preceding it. It is true that our imaginations as investigators are highly facile at explaining results, but it is not always the case that a rationale in the background section of a paper belongs as a rationalization in the discussion. Surely, the legitimacy of the comparison should depend on the force of the rationale rather than on an "assumed guilty [of second-guessing oneself] until proved innocent" bias on the part of editors. Procedures for controlling analysiswise alpha will be suggested next.

Controlling Analysiswise α

When there are several groups and there is a desire to control analysiswise (or "familywise") α in a d analysis, one can use a stepdown Bonferroni procedure. That is, if there are k groups, one compares the largest $z = d/s_d$ to the critical value that corresponds to α divided by $\frac{1}{2}k(k-1)$, the number of possible comparisons. If that leads to rejection, then the next largest can be tested at α divided by $\frac{1}{2}k(k-1) - 1$, and so on until no difference reaches the required level, whereupon testing stops. For confidence intervals, if one wants the probability to be $1 - \alpha$ that *all* the δs are in their defined intervals, one simply has to use z values that correspond to the α divided by $\frac{1}{2}k(k-1)$.

If there are more than three or four groups, these requirements become quite stringent. It would be preferable to use some procedure such as Tukey's or Dunnettes', but none is available at this time. They seem possible in principle, however. Neither is there any analogue to the omnibus test of the hypothesis that all the μs are equal, which is provided by the F test in a one-way ANOVA. Again, it seems possible in principle, but it has not been worked out.

Factorial Designs

Probably the most common situation in which there are multiple means for different groups is the factorial design. Clearly, the additive model that underlies the full analysis of a factorial experiment is not applicable when the data are ordinal. Often the data are ordinal. What can be done? On consideration, many of the questions that are answered in the typical factorial analysis can also be answered with a d analysis, and others, which have no direct counterpart in a d analysis, can often be reformulated so that they do.

In a factorial ANOVA, much of the interest often focuses on the main effects. In any beyond the most elementary treatment of factorial ANOVA it is pointed out that the main-effect sum of squares for factor A is equivalent to the between-groups sum of squares that would have been obtained if the groups simply had been combined across factor B. The same thing can be done with a d analysis, except now the groups are literally combined across the other factor before one or more ds comparing their locations are carried out.

Such an analysis has the disadvantage that effects due to factor B contribute to the within-groups variance, which is subtracted out in the typical factorial ANOVA. This can be circumvented in the d analysis by working with the average d with respect to levels of A, averaged across levels of B. We often interpret a main effect for A by saying, "Scores on X at A_1 tend to be higher than at A_2, whether or not B is at B_1 or at B_2." So why not do that directly? Compute d_1, comparing A_1 to A_2 at B_1, and d_2, comparing A_1 to A_2 at B_2, and average them. This average, call it d-bar, is the overall tendency for A_1s to score above A_2s, holding B constant, which is often what we are interested in.

Inferences from it are straightforward. Since d_1 and d_2 are based on independent data, $s_{d\text{-bar}}^2 = (s_{d1}^2 + s_{d2}^2)/4$, and this can be used in the usual ways with a z_α to test δ-bar $= 0$ or to form c.i. for it. It should be just about as powerful as the ANOVA test of main effect when circumstances are ideal for the latter, and offer the usual advantages when, as is often true, they are not, such as when the cells differ in variance as well as in means. Note one other advantage: No special treatment or decisions are necessary if the group sizes are unequal.

Clearly, the "main effect" for B can be evaluated in the same way. What about "interaction"? Many applications where the interaction is seemingly of interest can often be reformulated in some way that does not require looking at it, such as reorganizing the groups into a one-way design and examining one or more specific contrasts that capture the true nature of the research issue. When "interaction" really is of interest, the research question often sounds like "I want to see if the differences due to A are the same at all levels of B." This translates here into a null hypothesis, H_0: $\delta_1 = \delta_2$, and is readily tested by comparing d_1 to d_2. That difference has a sampling variance that can be estimated as $(s_{d1}^2 + s_{d2}^2)$, just like the sampling variance of any other pair of independently estimated quantities, so the hypothesis can be tested and the corresponding c.i. can be formed.

In ANOVA, testing interaction as the difference of the differences due to A is the same as doing it from the point of view of the other factor, B. That is not literally true in the present case. Generally the results from comparing ds for A across levels of B and those for B across levels of A should give the same results, yet it does not seem that they necessarily always would. Here, as in looking at main effects, one need not be concerned with whether the group sizes are equal.

It is not my purpose here to attempt to reformulate the full structure provided by ANOVA in terms of the d statistic, and indeed not all of that structure is susceptible to such reformulation. However, it may be that enough has been said to encourage the investigator to think about his or her real research questions in the expectation that many of them can be answered in this way. Some extensions to "repeated measures" are provided in the next chapter, and an alternative to analysis of covariance is suggested in the next section. Also, given the equivalence between discriminant analysis and multivariate ANOVA, the suggestion concerning the former that was given in the previous chapter on multiple regression is also relevant, and a simple alternative is suggested in the next section. This question is returned to in the next chapter as well.

An Alternative to Analysis of Covariance

With posttest and pretest scores from several groups, an alternative to investigating group differences by treating both scores in one mixed ANOVA is to treat the pretest as a covariate, using the posttest as the dependent variable. Although the investigator's interest here revolves around whether one group's scores lie generally above the other's, analysis of covariance in the typical application amounts to fitting separate regression lines in two groups, lines that can differ in intercepts or in both slopes and intercepts (Cliff, 1987).

The investigator typically wants to make a conclusion of the form, "the two groups differ systematically on the dependent variable, holding the control variable constant." Interpretations of such an analysis can be clear in the randomized-groups version of this design because then the populations are identical on the covariate by definition although even here conclusions may not be clear if the groups have differences in the slopes of the regression of Y on X. On the other hand, interpretations can be highly questionable when the groups are intrinsically different, such as being different age groups, different genders, and so on, because then the distributions on the covariate are not likely to be identical, and may be substantially different. In that case, the validity of conclusions about equality of regression parameters depends critically on the assumptions of linearity, homogeneity of conditional variance, and equality of slopes. The interpretational difficulties arise from the fact that, when the groups do not have the same distributions on X, one may be looking at different parts of the regression lines that describe the relation between X and Y in each group. In that case, when the different regression equations are fitted for different groups—this, after all, is what analysis of covariance does—one may just be looking at different parts of the same curvilinear regression line in the groups. Thus, any analysis of covariance with intact groups should be interpreted with considerable caution, and the interpretations should be supported by careful examination of the scatterplots.

Interpretational problems in ANCOVA are not solved by splitting the data into groups above and below the combined mean or median on the control variable (or into thirds or quarters on the same basis). With intact groups, such "control" of the covariate can mask considerable differences on the control variable because of the differences in the distributions. Thus, differences on the dependent variable may remain confounded by differences on the covariate (Maxwell & Delaney, 1993).

Several statisticians (Conover & Iman, 1982; Harwell & Serlin, 1988; Hettmansperger, 1984; Potthoff, 1974; Puri & Sen, 1969a, 1969b; Quade, 1967) have suggested various forms of what amounts to the ANCOVA of ranks as an alternative to ordinary ANCOVA. Several papers have examined the properties of such processes, using theoretical analysis or Monte Carlo studies (Agresti & Pendergast, 1986; Conover & Iman, 1982; Harwell & Serlin, 1988; Olejnik & Algina, 1984). In general, they have been found to behave quite well in terms of power and robustness.

These methods, then, provide an alternative to standard ANCOVA. However, they do so in a limited way, and they can be criticized on several conceptual grounds (Agresti & Pendergast, 1986; Sawilowsky, Blair, & Higgins, 1989). First, to an investigator who is concerned with anything beyond null-hypothesis testing—that is, one who has any interest in estimating parameters—it is not clear what the regression or ANCOVA parameters mean when the analysis is performed on ranks. In addition, there is often a failure to recognize the lack of independence of the mean squares that are compared in the various F ratios, similar to that noted already. Also, such methods have not dealt with what I feel to be the major inferential issue in many applications. This issue is that groups' distributions can differ in a number of characteristics, and differences in one characteristic (spread or shape) can mask or distort inferences about differences in another (location).

Analysis of covariance can be considered another case where the typical statistical analysis is not directly answering the question that the investigator would like to ask of the data. That question is often similar to "Do scores of one group generally lie above those of the other, even at fixed values of the covariate?" It is true that in ideal cases this is what ANCOVA does, but often our data depart substantially from these ideals.

It is possible to answer such a question fairly directly using dominance statistics by examining only that part of the data where the distributions on the covariate overlap. The procedure can only be sketched here, but essentially it turns the ANCOVA into a factorial design. The process begins by dividing those sections of the covariate within which the distributions overlap into several narrow categories, preferably containing a unique value of the covariate, but that may not be possible with most data. Then, a separate independent-groups d is computed within each category, along with the corresponding variances (5.9). The latter require that there be a least two members of each group within each category. The average of these ds represents the overall tendency for scores in one group to lie above scores in the other for constant values of the covariate. Since the ds within the subgroups are independent, confidence intervals and significance tests can be carried out by averaging the ds and their variances to arrive at a standard error for the average, as suggested in the factorial case, of which this is now really an example. A refinement would be to weight each group's d by the number of dominances in each (the product of the subgroup sizes), and the corresponding variances likewise. The procedure is thus an example of an inference about a weighted average of statistics:

$$\bar{d} = \Sigma w_g d_g / \Sigma w_g.$$

This can be done by using the general variance of a weighted average, which in this case is

$$\mathrm{var}(\bar{d}) = \Sigma w_g^2 s_{dg}^2 / (\Sigma w_g^2).$$

Such an analysis may result in a loss of efficiency compared to analysis of covariance when the latter is justified, due to the possible loss of cases, but it may be that an investigator will be more satisfied with the kind of analysis suggested here because of the much lower reliance on assumptions that may be questionable and the more direct answer to the research question. The procedure may be seen as essentially the same as the one suggested before for assessing main effects in a designed factorial experiment.

Multiple Dependent Variables

Sometimes one wants to compare two groups on more than one dependent variable: speed and error scores on a processing task, for example, or systolic and diastolic blood pressures or reading and arithmetic tests; or one could have one factor as a repeated measure and one that is a between-groups factor. Obviously, one could calculate separate ds on each variable and come to separate conclusions on each. Sometimes, though, it may be desirable to combine the information into an overall conclusion. One may hope to gain power this way, or one may want to control a familywise alpha, or one could simply want to test a main effect for groups in a mixed ANOVA. Traditionally, these analyses have been performed with a multivariate analysis of variance (MANOVA).

The d statistic can be used for this purpose as well, but with a caveat or two. The main one is that the direction of difference on the multiple dependent variables must be set in advance; MANOVA allows complete freedom in the weighting of the variables with a consequent penalty in the value of the test statistic. Suppose two groups are compared with ds reflecting dominances on diastolic and systolic blood pressure. An overall null hypothesis that the sum of the corresponding δs is zero can be tested quite straightforwardly in much the same way as the main effect of a variable was tested by averaging the ds at multiple levels of another factor. The difference here is that the ds are based on the same subjects and so will not be independent. This causes a little complication, but no problem.

We encountered exactly the same issue before in summing ts based on the same sample. The variance of $d_1 + d_2$ in the nonindependent case is just like that for any other sum:

$$\text{var}(d_1 + d_2) = \sigma_{d1}^2 + \sigma_{d2}^2 + 2\,\text{cov}(d_1,d_2). \tag{5.13}$$

The complication is that we need to estimate the covariance term, $\text{cov}(d_1,d_2)$. This is accomplished rather straightforwardly by generalizing the expression for the variance of d, (5.7):

$$\text{cov}(d_1,d_2) = \frac{(m-1)\text{cov}(d_{i.1},d_{i.2}) + (n-1)\text{cov}(d_{j1},d_{j2}) + \text{cov}(d_{ij1},d_{ij2})}{nm} \tag{5.14}$$

This formula parallels (5.7), except that the variances there have been replaced by covariances and there are additional subscripts, 1 and 2, referring to the data from X_1 and X_2, respectively. The quantities in this expression can be estimated by substituting sums of products of $\hat{d}$ for their sums of squares in (5.9) or, preferably, (5.11).

In this way, the dominances comparing two groups on diastolic and systolic blood pressure, or any other pair of dependent variables, can be combined. It may be obvious that the process can be generalized to any number of dependent variables:

$$\text{var}\left(\sum_u d_u\right) = \sum_u \text{var}(d_u) + \sum_u \sum_v \text{cov}(d_u,d_v). \tag{5.15}$$

Here, the subscripts u and v refer to dependent variables. The hypothesis that $\sum\delta_u = 0$ can be tested using $\sum d_u/[\text{var}(\sum d_u)]^{1/2}$ as a z test, and c. i. for $\sum\delta_u$ can be constructed in the corresponding way. Where several ds are being summed, the complications involved in constructing the asymmetric c.i. that were used for small-sample ds seem unlikely to be important.

The foregoing process is similar in spirit to the analogue of discriminant analysis that was suggested in Chapter 4. The difference here is that there are no empirically estimated weights, as there would be if ordinal multiple regression were used against a dichotomous dependent variable. This simplifies the inference process for the present procedure but risks a loss of efficiency.

The process of summing ds on several dependent variables will increase the power of the comparisons over using a single dependent variable in situations where the ds being summed are more or less equal. The reason is that the covariances between ds will be smaller, most of the time, than the variances. Thus, the numerator of the z ratio will increase more than the denominator as ds are summed. On the other hand, summing ds that are heterogeneous in size can lose power relative to testing the individual ds. It goes without saying that this process is only valid if the direction of the differences on all the variables is based on a priori considerations.

Again it can be seen that a dominance analysis can substitute for its mean-based counterpart. The substitution yields all the advantages that go with d and corresponds closely to the question that is usually being asked. There is a cost as well: We had to know the direction of the expected differences in advance rather than being allowed to choose weights that maximized d in some composite way. On the other hand, it may well be more satisfactory to say things like, "the average d between treated and untreated groups on this collection of outcome variables is . . . , and this average is different from zero at the . . . level," than it is to try to explain what the optimally weighted combination of outcome variables in a MANOVA means.

CONCLUSIONS

The d statistic has, then, two attractive aspects. First, it can serve as an important descriptive quantity in its own right, estimating δ, and, second, it can substitute for the independent groups t test in cases where the scale characteristics of the data or the distributional assumptions underlying the classical statistic are questionable. In either case, it has good inferential properties. Although ordinarily applied in simple two-group situations, its use can readily be extended to many of the more complex ones that occur in behavioral and biological science.

6

Extension of *d* to Correlated Data and Broader Applications

RATIONALE

The applications of the δ measure so far were to the independent-groups context. Also, the variance formulas presented there are well established in the literature, with the exception of the unbiased estimate formula (5.9) and the consistent estimate (5.11). The function of this chapter is to present an extension of *d* to repeated measures or data that is otherwise correlated, that is, *d* as an alternative to the paired observations *t* test, or simple repeated-measures ANOVA, and to suggest how this extension can be applied to many other designs that are traditionally analyzed by repeated-measures ANOVA.

Applications of paired-observations sort are quite common. Perhaps the most frequent is the pretest–treatment–posttest paradigm where the main interest lies in whether the posttest scores are generally higher than the pretest. "Treatment" can include the simple passage of time, as in a longitudinal study of development or aging, or the application can be to differences in paired subjects rather than directly repeated measures; this is exemplified by studies such as studies where subjects in different groups are individually matched, or where a twin or litter member is put in one condition and cotwin or littermate in the other, or one comparing husbands to their wives on some variable, and the interest is in the differences between the genders. In all these cases, there are two sets of scores, a member of one set is paired with a member of the other, and interest focuses on the extent to which members of one set are generally higher than the other.

The descriptive aspects of δ and d apply here just as they do in the independent-groups case. It is useful to estimate the probability that a randomly selected posttreatment score is higher than a randomly selected pretreatment score, the probability that children score higher at 8 years than they did at 6, the probability that male spouses score higher than female, that treated twins score higher than untreated, and so on.

There is a second, narrower question that can be quantified here also. This is reflected in the probability that a randomly chosen child changes in a particular direction, or that a treated rat scores higher than its untreated littermate, and so on. Some statistical inferences with regard to this question are readily made via the well-known sign test and its generalization, Friedman's test (Friedman, 1937), but users of such methodologies usually stop short of the descriptively useful step of estimating the probability of change. The two questions, the first reflecting movement of the group as a whole and the second referring to within-person change, are clearly not independent, but neither are they the same. Cliff (1991) illustrated the distinction between them.

A widely applied, rank-based inference procedure for the wider group-movement question is the Wilcoxon signed rank test (WSRT) (Wilcoxon, 1945). In paired-observation applications of it, the differences between scores in the first group or occasion and the matching scores in the second are ranked in absolute value, and then the signs of the differences are reattached. The ranks having one sign are then summed, and asymptotic statistics or tabled values can be used to test the hypothesis that the signs are randomly assigned to the ranks of the absolute differences with probability .5. This wording of the hypothesis may differ from some other ways that have been expressed, but it is an accurate translation of the probability model that underlies the test.

Originally proposed as a single-sample test of a hypothesis about the median (Wilcoxon, 1945), the WSRT has been used as a test of a null hypothesis of random changes (see Bradley, 1968; Blair & Higgins, 1985), but it would be more useful if there were a substantive interpretation of the rank-sum quantity, as there is for d in the WMW context. Also, since it is applied to *differences* on X, its result is not invariant under monotonic transformation of X because such a transformation will alter the order of the differences. Therefore, it is not really applicable to variables that can only be justified at the ordinal level. Its hypothesis-testing status is also not as general as one might like because random assignment of a sign to a rank of a difference can be false in a number of ways besides change in location; therefore, like other randomization tests, its sampling distribution could deviate from the null one for a variety of reasons, not just as because of the location difference, which is the primary interest. Thus, it is not necessarily robust to changes in other distributional characteristics.

My recommendation, therefore, is to use the d statistic instead of the WSRT. It was pointed out that d is useful descriptively here, so one would likely apply it inferentially as well, analogous to, but alternative to, the familiar t statistic for correlated means and its generalizations to repeated-measures ANOVA. The next section derives a sampling variance for d in the paired-observations case as a basis for doing that, and later I point out how its use can be extended to some analogues of repeated-measures analysis of variance.

VARIANCE OF *d* IN THE PAIRED CASE

The approach taken here follows previous work on Kendall's tau (Cliff & Charlin, 1991; Daniels & Kendall, 1947; Chapter 3 here) in deriving the variances of t, and that of d (Hettmansperger, 1984; Chapter 5 here) in that it is based on the dominance variables d_{ih}. For a population of paired X scores, δ can be used to measure the probability that a score from one occasion is higher than one from the other, or $\delta = E(d_{ih})$, just as in the independent-groups case. In a sample of n pairs of scores, $d = \sum\sum d_{ih}/n^2$ can be used to estimate δ. Here, though, there is a complication due to the fact that this definition combines information on within-pair changes with between-pair changes. It seems desirable to allow for the possibility that within-pair relations do not behave in the same way as those involving different units. That is, the probability that an individual changes in a certain direction may not be the same as the probability that a randomly chosen score from one occasion is larger than a random score from the second; it may be necessary to distinguish a δ_w, reflecting the probability that *individuals* change in a given direction, from δ:

$$\delta_w = E(d_{ii}), \tag{6.1}$$

whose sample estimate is $\sum d_{ii}/n$. This is the difference between proportion of individual subjects who change in one direction and the proportion who change in the other. It is

$$d_b = \frac{\displaystyle\sum\sum_{i \neq j} d_{ih}}{n(n-1)}, \tag{6.2}$$

which is a U statistic with expectation δ. This d_b is the proportion of scores on the second occasion that are higher than the scores by different people on the first, minus the reverse proportion. It measures the extent to which the overall distribution has moved, except for the self-comparisons. A d that was defined to include the d_{ii} has expectation $[\delta_w + (n - 1)\delta]/n$; in the presentation to follow, d_w and d_b are treated separately. For samples that are not too small and δ not too close to unity, d_b will be approximately normally distributed with mean δ and some variance $\sigma_{d_b}^2$, and d_w will also be approximately normal with mean δ_w and variance $\sigma_{d_w}^2$.

By taking the expectation of d_b^2, Cliff (1993a) showed in the manner of Cliff and Charlin (1992), Daniels and Kendall (1947), and Hettmansperger (1984) that[1]

$$\sigma_{d_b}^2 = \frac{\sigma_{d_{ih}}^2 + \mathrm{cov}(d_{ih},d_{hi}) + (n - 2)[\sigma_{d_i}^2 + \sigma_{d_j}^2 + 2\mathrm{cov}(d_i,d_j)]}{n(n - 1)}. \qquad (6.3)$$

In (6.3), d_i and d_j both have i as subscript (rather than i and h) because they refer to the same set of subjects. The covariance between terms with their symmetrically placed counterparts, $\mathrm{cov}(d_{ih},d_{hi})$, is treated separately because it is likely to have a different expectation than $\mathrm{cov}(d_i,d_j)$.

The positive sign on the last covariance term may seem out of place, relative to the negative sign on the covariance term in the paired t test, but the covariance is presumably negative, given the way d_{ih} has been defined because d_i represents, say, the proportion of pretest scores that are lower than i's posttest score, whereas d_j would reflect the proportion of posttest scores that are higher than i's pretest. Assuming that relatively high posttest scores tend to go with relatively high pretest scores, this covariance will be negative. With large n, the terms with double subscripts become negligible, and all that one need be concerned with is the variances of the d_i and the d_j, and their covariance in order to estimate $\sigma_{d_b}^2$. Then the sampling variance of d_b closely resembles the sampling variance of the difference between means with correlated data, $\sigma_1^2/n + \sigma_2^2/n - 2\sigma_{12}/n$. The difference is that in the present case the formulas involve the variances of the d_i and d_j and their covariance rather than the corresponding quantities based on the raw scores.

In the case of d_w, it is simple to show that

$$\sigma_{d_w}^2 = \sigma_{d_{ii}}^2/n, \qquad (6.4)$$

---

[1]At various points below, the terminology "var" is used to refer to the sampling variance of a quantity such as the sum or difference of two ds, and "cov" is used for the sampling covariance between two quantities, such as two ds or even between the differences between two pairs of ds. This avoids the use of σ with highly complex subscripts. Also, "Est" means "an unbiased estimate of."

in which $\sigma_{d_{ii}}^2 = E(d_{ii} - \delta_w)^2$; the latter is $1 - \delta_w^2$ if there are no self-ties, and, if so, $1 - \delta_w^2 = 4p(1 - p)$, where p is the probability of change in one direction.

An investigator may want to combine the information about within-subject change, d_w, with that about overall group movement, d_b, in coming to conclusions about change. Then inferences must take into account that the two statistics are not independent. It can be shown that their covariance is

$$\text{cov}(d_w, d_b) = [\text{cov}(d_{ii}, d_i) + \text{cov}(d_{in}, d_i)]/n. \tag{6.5}$$

One way to combine the information about δ and δ_w is to test the hypothesis that $\delta_w + \delta = 0$. Equations (6.3), (6.4), and (6.5) can be combined according to the rules about variances of sums to provide a variance for the sum of $d_w + d_b$:

$$\text{var}(d_w + d_b) = \sigma_{d_w}^2 + \sigma_{d_b}^2 + 2\,\text{cov}(d_b, d_w). \tag{6.6}$$

Unbiased Estimates

One can develop unbiased estimates analogous to (5.9) of the variances (6.3) and (6.4) and covariance (6.5) rather than simply substituting the sample quantities that parallel the terms of (6.6). Although the latter approach would lead to consistent estimates of $\sigma_{d^*}^2$, such a direct method can lead to appreciable bias in small samples because of the way the sample analogues of the separate terms in (6.3) contaminate each other in samples. However, defining $d_i^* = \hat{d}_i - d_b$, and other terms similarly, it can be shown that

$$s_{d_b}^2 = \frac{(n-1)^2(\Sigma d_i^{*2} + \Sigma d_i^{*2} + 2\Sigma d_i^* d_i^*) - \Sigma\Sigma d_{ih}^{*2} - \Sigma\Sigma d_{ih}^* d_{hi}^*}{n(n-1)(n-2)(n-3)} \tag{6.7}$$

is an unbiased estimate of $\sigma_{d_b}^2$. Then s_{d_b} can be used in the usual way to form c.i. for δ as $d - z_{\alpha/2}s_{d_b}$ to $d + z_{\alpha/2}s_{d_b}$ or test a hypothesis that $\delta = \delta_0$ by using $(d_b - \delta_0)/s_{d_b}$ as a standard normal deviate. The form of (6.7) is very similar to that of (5.9) and resembles the unbiased estimate of the variance of t.

Inferences about δ_w can be made in a similar way. It is relatively simple to derive the unbiased estimate of σ_w^2:

$$s_{d_w}^2 = \frac{\Sigma(d_{ii} - d_w)^2}{n-1}. \tag{6.8}$$

Then s_{d_w} can be used to form c.i. with or test hypotheses about δ_w in the same ways as is done using s_{d_b} with respect to δ.

Inferences about the sum $\delta + \delta_w$ need the covariance term (6.5). It can be shown by the methods used earlier that its unbiased estimate is

$$\text{Est}[\text{cov}(d_b, d_w)] = \frac{\sum_i [(\sum_h d_{ih} + \sum_h d_{hi}) d_{ii}] - 2n(n-1) d_b d_w}{n(n-1)(n-2)}. \qquad (6.9)$$

These unbiased estimates can be used to find confidence intervals for δ, δ_w and their sum, and this is done in the examples.

Simple programs[2] have been written to perform the calculations necessary for statistical inferences about δ in the paired as well as unpaired cases. To facilitate comparisons with traditional methods, they also calculate the corresponding paired t tests for the data.

EXAMPLES

Data

The analyses used to illustrate applications in the paired-data case come from McDowd and Oseas-Kreger (1991).[3] Twenty young and 20 elderly subjects performed a letter-reading task under a control condition and two conditions of interference, and response latency was measured. We focus here on within-group comparisons, returning later to an approach to between-groups questions about this data.

Although most research of this kind is performed by directly analyzing latency as a measure of *speed* of response, it can be argued that processing *rate* (i.e., the reciprocal of speed) is more appropriate. Alternatively, if the main interest is in the psychoneural aging process, one can speculate that the variable that defines aging is neither speed nor rate but some other, not directly observed, variable that is monotonically related to either. In addition, there can be concern about the distributional characteristics of the data. Finally, one can focus on the d statistics themselves and simply be interested in the probability that responses are faster under one condition than the other, both within and across subjects.

---

[2]Simple programs are available to perform the independent groups and matched-data d analyses that are described in this paper. They are available in Basic and FORTRAN. Persons desiring copies should send diskette and stamped, self-addressed floppy mailer to the address given earlier. Ms. Du Feng collaborated in writing these programs.

[3]The author wishes to thank Drs. Joan McDowd and Deborah Oseas-Kreger for making this data available.

Figure 6.1 shows three dominance diagrams for the young subjects. Similarly to the independent-groups case in Fig. 5.1, a + indicates that an interference time was greater than a control, and a − indicates the opposite. However, these matched-data diagrams differ in a couple of details from the ones shown for the independent-groups case. First, spacing is used to highlight the diagonal in order to facilitate display of the self-comparisons. Second, in order to show the self-comparisons clearly, the row and column orders of subjects are the same, rather than being independently ordered as is the case with independent groups where row and column orders are separate. This tends to make the diagrams look more ragged than in the independent case.

The first two diagrams compare the interference conditions to the control, and the third compares the interference conditions to each other. The first two diagrams show that the manipulations are very strong, but the raggedness suggests that the degree of the effect varies appreciably across subjects. The third diagram shows that there are inconsistent differences between the two interference conditions, but that the times tend to be higher for the second one.

Table 6.1 shows the *d* statistics and the inferential information about them. It can be seen that d_w is .75 in one comparison to the control and 1.00 in the other, the latter therefore having zero variance. The first d_b is .418 with a .95 c.i. of .189 to .648, and the second is .555 with c.i. of .318 to .792. Comparing the two interference conditions gives $d_w = .45$ and $d_b = .268$, the latter with c.i. of .063 to .474. Combining the data from d_w and d_b gives a highly significant result in the first two cases, and a significant one in the third.

For comparison, the classical *t* test of correlated means has also been computed in each case. These are very large in the first two cases, albeit

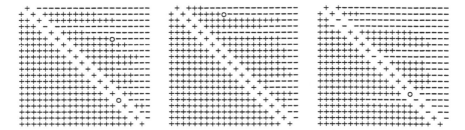

FIG. 6.1. Dominance diagrams for young subjects comparing control and interference conditions. (Subjects are ordered by row scores. A plus indicates interference higher than control, a minus indicates the reverse, and zero represents ties. Self-comparisons are in the diagonals. The left diagram compares first interference to control; the middle compares second interference to control; the right diagram compares the two interference conditions. Data are from McDowd and Oseas-Kreger [1991].) From Cliff (1993a). Copyright © (1993) by the American Psychological Association. Reprinted with permission.

TABLE 6.1
Dominance Analysis of Control and Interference Scores for Young Subjects

	Control vs. Inf-1	Control vs. Inf-2	Inf-1 vs. Inf-2
Inferences About δ_w			
d_w	.750	1.000	.450
s_{dw}	.143	0	.198
c.i.	.464,1.000	1.000,1.000	.054,.846
z	5.25	—	2.27
Inferences About δ			
d^*	.418	.555	.268
s_{d^*}	.115	.118	.103
c.i.	.189,.648	.318,.792	.063,.474
z	3.65	4.69	2.61
Components of $s_{d^*}{}^2$			
$s_{di.}{}^2$	.269	.218	.367
$s_{d.i}{}^2$	.364	.298	.353
$\text{cov}(d_{i.},d_{.i})$	−.192	−.125	−.258
$s_{dij}{}^2$	.822	.689	.928
$\text{cov}(d_{ih},d_{hi})$	−.338	−.198	−.493
Combined Inferences			
$d_w + d^*$	1.168	1.555	0.718
$\text{cov}(d_w,d^*)$	.0079	0	.0123
$s(d_w + d^*)$	.222	.118	.273
z	5.26	13.13	2.63
Mean Comparisons			
$m_1 - m_2$	.910	1.447	.538
s_{diff}	.679	.752	.671
$s(m_1 - m_2)$	.152	.168	.150
t	5.99	8.60	3.58
df	19	19	19

From Cliff (1993a). Copyright © (1993) by the American Psychological Association. Reprinted with permission.

somewhat smaller in actual value than the zs for the corresponding ds, and significant in the third, in fact larger than z-for-d was. The sample estimates of $\sigma_{di.}{}^2$, $\sigma_{d.i}{}^2$, $\sigma_{dih}{}^2$, and the two covariance terms are shown in order to give an idea of their size as well. The variances are about 0.1, and the covariances are substantial, reflecting high correlations between the $\hat{d}_{i.}$ and $\hat{d}_{.i}$, and the d_{ih} and d_{hi}. The latter covariance is noticeably larger than the former, as was anticipated in deriving (6.3).

Size, Power, and Coverage

Feng (1996) performed extensive simulations to evaluate the statistical behavior of the paired-observations d. She used several levels of effect size, sample size ($n = 10, 30, 100$), and degree of correlation between the two variables in a variety of distributional situations. The latter included skewed and normal distributions in all possible combinations: both skewed, one skewed, one skewed and one not, and skewed oppositely. She included cases where the variables were bounded at zero (chi-square distributions) and bounded at both ends (beta distributions). In all situations, the ordinary paired-data *t* test was included for comparative purposes.

With respect to Type I error rates in the null case, the main finding was that *d* was conservative in small samples with empirical size often around half the nominal .05 rate. Interestingly, the size of the *t* test differed significantly from .05 only once in the 18 distributions studied, being .039 in that one case.

With respect to power, d_b was generally intermediate in power to *t* and d_w, the latter being equivalent to the sign test. The power performance of d_b tended to decline relative to the other two with increasing correlation between the variables.

The coverage of d_b tended to be conservative, sometimes markedly so, particularly in small samples. On the other hand, the coverage based of *t* tended to be significantly—in both senses—below .95 with skewed distributions until samples reached 100 in size.

The results indicate that d_b behaved about as expected except that the procedure used by Feng (1996) led it to be conservative, therefore reducing power. She used the asymmetric c.i. (5.12), and it seems likely that this was the source of the conservatism. Therefore, the recommendation here will be to use the ordinary $d_b \pm z_{\alpha/2}\hat{\sigma}_d$ as the c.i. for δ in the paired data case.

EXTENSIONS OF PAIRED *d* ANALYSIS

Comparing *d*s in Different Groups

The methodology based on *d* has applicability beyond the simple case of paired observations in a single sample. An interesting case is the two-group repeated-measures design. Suppose two random samples are taken from a population and given different treatments, and a premeasure X is taken on both groups. The research hypothesis is that the treatments have differential effects on X, revealed by a postmeasure on the same variable. Such a hypothesis can be stated as, "posttest scores are more likely to be higher than pretest scores in the treatment group than in the control." In this rather common design, the typical analysis is the 2×2 mixed-design ANOVA, but there are several grounds for preferring an analysis based on *d*s to an ANOVA. First, the scale-type of X may not justify interval treatment, and this is very salient here due to the additive nature of the factorial ANOVA model. Second, there are often grounds to suspect heterogeneity of the variance–covariance matrix between the two groups, with consequent uncertainty about how to interpret a mean difference. Finally, if the typical, default analysis is used, the anticipated treatment difference effect is partly in the between-groups term, partly in the repeated measure, and partly in the interaction, so interpretation of results is complex, and power may be low. Finally, the specific research question seems more accurately translated into one that states that δs should be different in the two groups than it is into one that says μs should be different.

Using dominance methodology can yield results that more clearly reflect the study's intent as well as providing the other, more statistical advantages. The logic is particularly clear when the groups start out as samples from the same population. In that case, it is reasonable to ask whether the δs for the two groups are equal—that is, whether posttreatment scores are more likely to be higher than pretreatment in one group compared to the other. The analysis can take place as follows. There is a δ and a δ_w for each treatment group, which can be estimated from that sample. Likewise, the variance of each d can be estimated using (6.6) and (6.7). Since the treatment groups are independent, the variance of the difference of the two ds, whether two d_ws or two d_bs, call them d_c and d_e, is simply the sum of their two separate variances. That is,

$$(d_c - d_e) \pm z_{\alpha/2}(s_{d_c}^2 + s_{d_e}^2)^{1/2} \tag{6.10}$$

provides a $1 - \alpha$ confidence interval for the difference in the deltas. In (6.10), the ds and variances can refer either to the d_b or to the d_w or to their sums as long as consistency is followed in the formulas. Thus, tests of the hypotheses that deltas are equal and a confidence interval for the difference are readily available. This seems like a good alternative to the usual analysis.

This discussion assumed a randomized-groups design, and the logic of the analysis applies most clearly there. It is possible to apply the same analysis when the two groups are intact ones, such as old versus young subjects, provided proper care is taken in the interpretation. For example, in the McDowd and Oseas-Kreger (1991) data cited earlier, one could test the hypothesis that the δs for old and young subjects are equal. If the hypothesis were rejected, then the conclusion would be something like, "interference scores are more likely to be higher than control scores in old subjects than in young."

The McDowd and Oseas-Kreger (1991) data will be used in an illustration. The results concerning ds for old subjects are summarized in Table 6.2. The ds tend to be similar to those found for the young subjects, with the exception of the comparison of the two interference conditions, where the ds are larger for young subjects and significant, whereas they are not in the old.

The variances of the ds can be found from Tables 6.1 and 6.2 and combined into (6.7). Neither the d_ws, nor the d_bs, nor their sums is significantly

TABLE 6.2
Dominance Analysis of Control and
Interference Conditions for Elderly Subjects

	Control vs. Inf-1	Control vs. Inf-2	Inf-1 vs. Inf-2
Inferences About δ_w			
d_w	1.000	1.000	.100
s_{dw}	0	0	.228
c.i.	1.000,1.000	1.000,1.000	−.357,.557
z	−	−	.438
Inferences About δ			
d^*	.526	.521	.045
s_{d^*}	.116	.119	.042
c.i.	.294,.759	.283,.759	−.039,.129
z	4.53	4.38	1.07
Components of $s_{d^*}^2$			
$s_{di.}^2$	.177	.255	.439
$s_{d.i}^2$	.372	.298	.333
cov(d_i, $d_{.i}$)	−.146	−.143	−.366
s_{dij}^2	.723	.728	.990
cov(d_{ij},d_{ji})	−.224	−.229	−.797
Combined Inference			
$d_w + d^*$	1.526	1.521	.145
cov(d_w, d^*)	0	0	.009
$s(d_w + d^*)$	.116	.119	.268
z	13.13	12.80	0.54
Mean Comparisons			
$m_1 - m_2$	2.246	2.316	.070
s_{diff}	1.175	1.411	.665
$s(m_1 - m_2)$	.263	.315	.149
t	8.55	7.34	0.47
df	19	19	19

From Cliff (1993a). Copyright © (1993) by the American Psychological Association. Reprinted with permission.

different in old versus young subjects for any of the comparisons. The conclusions would be that the tendency for subjects to score higher in one condition than another did not significantly differ in old and young subjects.

In the case of the *d*s for I_1 versus I_2 the not unusual, but cognitively dissonant, finding of significance in one group, nonsignificance in the other, and lack of significant difference between the two occurs. Noting the degree to which the c.i. for the *d*s of old and young subjects overlap here helps to resolve the dissonance.

Multiple Conditions

One of the attractions of ANOVA is the way in which it permits the investigator to combine multiple groups or conditions into one analysis. Such simplicity is in part misleading because, once the composite analysis has been completed and some omnibus null hypothesis about an effect is rejected, there often remains the issue of where the differences lie. Some multiple-comparison procedure is then necessary to support inferences about those differences. It can even be argued that the omnibus test serves no purpose since the multiple-comparison procedures are necessary anyhow and could just as well be employed at the beginning. Furthermore, the combined analysis often hides heterogeneity of variances (and covariances, in the case of repeated measures) that make inferences about some comparisons seem firmer than they really are.

If there are several groups or conditions, there at present is no omnibus way of testing whether all the δs are zero, so a multiple-comparison procedure is necessary if analysiswise α is to be controlled. The only multiple-comparison procedure currently available is to perform stepdown Bonferroni tests, where for k pairs of means, the "most significant" d is tested at α/k. If the null hypothesis is rejected, then the next most significant is tested at $\alpha/(k-1)$, and so on until a nonsignificant comparison is reached, whereupon testing stops.

Such a procedure becomes notoriously conservative when there are more than a few groups, but such conservatism may be appropriate if there are no strong a priori expectations about where the differences are expected to lie. If there are such expectations, which can be justified to scientific peers, then it can well be more appropriate to take a parameterwise approach to testing, using then the nominal αs to test hypotheses about particular δs. This would seem to be the case in the McDowd and Oseas-Kreger (1991) study where there are well-established expectations that the conditions would differ, and good justification for interest in the values of the pairwise δs.

Multiple Repeated Measures Across Time

A research context that arises rather often is one in which scores are expected to increase, or decrease, systematically over time. Time can refer to calendar time, as in a longitudinal developmental study, or clock time, as in observing an autonomic response, or repetition time, as in a verbal recall study. Sometimes a specific mathematical model can be proposed for the relation between response and time, but often the research question is quantified in a looser way: "Does the magnitude of a subject's response tend to increase over time?" If the latter is the case, then an ordinal methodology may provide the most valid statistical answer for any of several reasons. First, it will be closer to the question asked than some approach that computes linear regressions or correlations with time since the question implies a monotonic, rather than a necessarily linear, relation with time. Second, any ordinal answer will be invariant to monotonic transformations of either the dependent variable or time itself. Thus, ordinal analyses seem attractive here as well as in other designs. Ferguson (1965) presents some suggestions of this kind, and alternatives to his analyses or extensions of them are possible. Some of these involve the use of tau.

The first suggestion here is that the τ_a of each subject's scores with the time variable be computed, giving a very direct index of the extent to which each subject's score has a monotonic relation with time. If a summary statistic is desired, then the τs can be averaged across subjects, and that statistic, supplemented by their median, standard deviation, quantiles, and any other descriptive information about the distribution of within-subject τs that seems desirable, will describe the extent to which subjects' scores have a monotonic relation with time.

Inferences about μ_t, the average subject's tau with time, can take one of two forms. In the first, the null hypothesis tested is that all possible orders on the dependent variable are equally likely to occur. That is, subjects' scores are independent of the time variable. If that hypothesis is true, then individual subjects' ts will be approximately normally distributed around zero with variance $(4k + 10)/9k(k - 1)$, where k is the number of occasions. The average t of n independently sampled subjects will have this variance divided by n, so m_t, the average t across subjects, divided by $[(4k + 10)/9kn(k - 1)]^{1/2}$, can be compared to z_α, the standard normal deviate corresponding to the intended alpha level. Ferguson (1965) also shows how to test this null hypothesis, but his analysis is based on the quantity S, which will be recalled from Chapter 2 as the raw disarray score. Basing the analysis on S rather than tau itself presumably reflects the earlier era's overriding concern with computational shortcuts and statistical significance to the exclusion of any of the descriptive aspects that seem to be more interesting.

A different inferential process is recommended here for such applications. It is usually the case with such analyses that subjects are considered to be more-or-less randomly selected, whereas the times are deliberately selected, not random at all. In that case, τ_i, the correlation of subject i's scores with time, may better be considered a characteristic of the subject, rather than something that is randomly sampled itself. Different subjects may have their own τ_is, so the sense in which τ_is are samples is that of sampling from a population of τs (each belonging to a population of subjects) rather than that of sampling from a population where all subjects' τs are zero. The issue then becomes, "what is the average τ_i with time for subjects in the population sampled?" including—but not restricted to—whether the average might be zero. Once τ_i is considered a score, then inferences about its mean can be carried out using the familiar single-sample t-test procedures that are used with any other score. That is, the sample mean τ is computed along with variance of these τs; the latter is converted to a standard error of the mean in the usual way to provide a confidence interval for μ_τ or test the hypothesis that it is zero.

Two other analyses often used here are Friedman's test (Friedman, 1937) and Kendall's W (Kendall, 1970). They are inferentially equivalent. In each, the scores of each subject would be ranked. Then the average rank for each time across subjects is calculated, along with the variance of these average ranks.

The procedure could take place as follows. Assuming n subjects have scores on k occasions and each subject's scores are separately ranked from low to high, let r_{ij} be the ranking of the jth ($j = 1, k$) score of the ith subject ($i = 1,n$), and let $r_j = \Sigma r_{ij}/n$, the average rank of the jth time; $r_{..}$ denotes the overall average rank, $(k + 1)/2$. Then $s_{r.}^2 = \Sigma(t_j - r_{..})^2/n$ represents the variance of the ranks. Its maximum value, denoting perfect agreement across subjects in the rankings, is $(k^2 - 1)/12$. Kendall's coefficient of concordance, W, is defined as

$$W = \frac{12s_r^2}{k^2 - 1}. \qquad (6.11)$$

Under the null hypothesis that each permutation of ranks is equally likely to occur, the variance of the average ranks has a known value. When k and n are small, the null hypothesis can be tested using special tables (Kendall, 1970). With larger datasets, the variance can be tested as a χ^2 variate with $k - 1$ df:

$$\chi^2 = n(k - 1)W = \frac{12ns_r^2}{k^2 - 1}. \qquad (6.12)$$

Then the hypothesis of equally likely permutations can be accepted or rejected according to whether the ratio exceeds χ_α^2.

The Friedman–Kendall procedures are omnibus tests in the sense that they are not shaped toward any particular relation between subjects' scores and time, whereas the corresponding procedure using taus that was suggested by Ferguson (1965), and restated here, is directly a test of correlation with time not just of nonrandom rankings. Our tau-based procedure is an ordinal analogue of using a linear contrast on means in a repeated-measures ANOVA.

Ranking procedures can be adapted to do this as well. Instead of summing the ranks, one can compute the r_S correlations between each subject's scores and time. Under the null hypothesis of scores being independent of time, these r_Ss each have, as we have seen in Chapter 3, a variance that here would be expressed as $1/(k - 1)$. The average of n subjects' r_Ss with time would have, under the independence null hypothesis, a mean of zero and a variance of $1/n(k - 1)$, so the sample's mean, m_{rS}, multiplied by $[n(k - 1)]^{1/2}$, can be used as a standard normal deviate to test this null hypothesis. In this way, a test of monotonic relation between score and time, within subjects, that is more direct than the Friedman–Kendall procedure, and probably more powerful, is possible.

An alternative, which does not assume that each of the r_Ss is independent, is possible here, just as was suggested using within-subject τs. If one prefers ρ_S to τ, one simply computes, for each subject, the ρ_S with time, and the mean of these, and the *empirical* variance of these ρ_Ss, and uses them in a one-sample t test of the hypothesis that $\mu_{\rho S} = 0$ or to find a confidence interval for it.

Alternatives Based on *d*

The d statistic can also be used when there are multiple repeated measures. The simplest analysis is simply to compute d and d_w between each pair of measurements, making inferences about the corresponding δs as if each were the only one being computed. This is justifiable in many contexts since there can be separate interest in each comparison. Fairly often, though, several, or all, of the δs are most validly viewed as constituting a family of parameters, and one would then want to control the Type I errors in a familywise fashion. The only way this seems possible is to fall back on Bonferroni methods, constructing confidence intervals for each parameter or testing a null hypothesis about each by using α/k to find the critical z values instead of α. This is likely to err on the side of conservatism even more than usual for such procedures since the various ds are most likely positively related. It seems possible in principle to develop a less conservative methodology here, but none seems to be available at this time.

The pairwise comparisons are perhaps the least interesting of the possible kinds of questions that can be investigated. Others can be investigated using sums, averages, or differences in ds, much as was discussed in the extensions of the independent-groups case at the end of Chapter 5, but some will be new here. For simplicity the discussion generally refers to d, rather than d_b or d_w, under the presumption that it applies to both, some additional comments being added about any special aspects pertaining to d_w. The ds have a pair of subscripts referring to the conditions or measures that led to that d; for example, d_{12} refers to condition 1 compared to 2, and so on.

We first consider cases with three repeated measures. Suppose they represent three ages in longitudinal data, leading to d_{12}, d_{23}, and d_{13} as the possible dominance statistics. The amount of overall trend can be represented by $d_{12} + d_{23}$. On the other hand, the question of whether trends are consistent, as opposed to leveling off or even reversing, would be reflected by $d_{12} - d_{23}$. The same reasoning can be applied when the various conditions reflect different levels of some ordered stimulus variable.

In a somewhat different way, suppose condition 1 is a control and conditions 2 and 3 represent different treatments or other manipulations, as in McDowd and Oseas-Kreager (1991). Then d_{12} and d_{13} show how different each treatment is from the control, but we might also wonder which is more different. This would be reflected by $d_{12} - d_{13}$. What about d_{23}? Does that not tell us about the comparison of conditions 2 and 3? It does, but it does so in a direct way, and indeed we would expect d_{23} to be large if $d_{12} - d_{23}$ were. However, the two questions being asked are slightly different. The $d_{12} - d_{13}$ difference is telling us whether "the tendency for scores in 2 to be higher than in 1 is the same as the tendency for scores in 3 to be higher than 1," whereas d_{23} itself is telling us whether scores in 2 tend to be higher than scores in 3. We would expect the answers to the two questions to be highly correlated, but they are not necessarily the same. Here, we are encountering a divergence between the properties of dominance analysis and the comparison means. When comparing means, it is necessarily true that $m_1 - m_3 = (m_1 - m_2) + (m_2 - m_3)$, because of the algebraic properties of means, but d_{23} is not generally equal to $d_{12} - d_{13}$. In my opinion, there are many contexts where the questions answered by the dominance coefficients, and by the differences between them, are more nearly the right questions.

Getting sums or averages or differences between ds is fine from a descriptive point of view, but what about inferences? Can we test hypotheses and form confidence intervals? The answer is yes we can, and the process is conceptually simple, but we need some additional statistics to do so.

The situation in inferences about sums and differences of nonindependent δs is the same as that encountered in Chapter 3 with respect to nonindependent ts. The variance of the sum or difference of ds depends on similar components:

$$\text{var}(d_u \pm d_v) = \text{var}(d_u) + \text{var}(d_v) \pm 2\,\text{cov}(d_u, d_v), \qquad (6.13)$$

where the u, v subscripts refer to pairs of occasions or treatments: 1,2; 1,3; 2,3; and so on. Since we have variances for the ds, (6.7) and (6.8), the only new statistic needed is the covariance terms. The same methods as before can be used to derive them; indeed, the covariances of ds are direct generalizations of their variances and can be estimated via a generalization of the unbiased estimates. Thus, we have the result that the covariance of two d_bs, d_{bu} and d_{bv}, is

$$\text{cov}(d_{bu}, d_{bv}) = \frac{1}{n(n-1)} \{ \text{cov}(d_{ihu} d_{ihv}) + \text{cov}(d_{ihu}, d_{hiv}) $$
$$+ (n-2)\text{cov}[(d_{.iu} + d_{.iu}), (d_{.iv} + d_{.iv})] \}. \qquad (6.14)$$

The unbiased estimate of this is

$$s_{d\text{bu}\cdot d\text{bv}} = \frac{(n-1)}{n(n-2)(n-3)}[\Sigma(d^*_{i.u} + d^*_{.iu})(d^*_{i.v} + d^*_{.iv})]$$
$$-\frac{\Sigma\Sigma d^*_{ihu}d^*_{ihv} + \Sigma\Sigma d^*_{ihu}d^*_{hiv}}{n(n-1)(n-2)(n-3)}. \tag{6.15}$$

It may be recalled that a subscripted d^* refers to the deviation of that quantity from the corresponding mean, which here is d_{bu} or d_{bv}. A sketch of the derivation of these formulas is given in the appendix at the end of the chapter.

Factorial Designs

These methods allow the application of d statistics to a variety of designs where factorial analysis of variance is traditional, similar to what was suggested in the independent-groups context in Chapter 5. The application of the methods can be illustrated with a hypothetical experiment in psycholinguistics. The research interest focuses on which of two grammatical constructions is processed more rapidly, but there is a secondary interest in the way processing is applied in sentences composed of common versus less common words. Thus, the stimulus materials are made up according to a 2×2 design: frequent ($f1$) versus less frequent ($f2$) words are presented in grammatical construction 1 ($g1$) or in construction 2 ($g2$). The dependent variable is the time it takes to process the sentences, measured in some appropriate way. All subjects are in all conditions, so this is an entirely within-subjects design.

There are several ds that can be calculated here, but, given the purpose of the research, the ones of main interest are $d(g1$ versus $g2$ at $f1)$ and $d(g1$ versus $g2$ at $f2)$. These refer to the dominance of $g1$ over $g2$ with common words and with less common ones, respectively. These ds correspond to the ANOVA *simple effects* of construction with the two kinds of words, and it is here where most of the interest would presumably lie. Inferences about the corresponding δs would be based on (6.7), (6.8), and (6.9).

In traditional ANOVA, interest would focus instead on the main effect of construction. A "main effect" reflects a mean difference between conditions that is averaged over an orthogonal dimension of the design. An analogue of the "main effect" of construction expressed in terms of ds is the average (or, equivalently, the sum) of the ds for construction at the two levels of word frequency. Inferences about that sum are made using the standard error derived via (6.13) from the two respective variances and the covariance estimated via (6.15). The ds reflecting frequency effects, and the "main effect" of frequency, can be calculated in exactly parallel ways.

A second research question might well be whether the construction effects are the same with common and less common words. This is the "interaction question" in ANOVA, but here would be evaluated by difference in the two ds that were summed to get the main effect analogue. Formula (6.13) again provides the standard error; the only difference is that now the sign attached to the covariance term is negative because we are looking at the difference rather than the sum.

The design can be extended in various ways, and there are corresponding dominance analyses that can be applied to provide answers to the research questions that the investigator has in mind. All that is necessary is that these be formulated clearly and the corresponding ds and their sums or differences calculated. Then the corresponding variances and covariances are identified and put into (6.13). The simplest applications are to $2 \times 2 \times 2$ . . . designs, but the presence of multiple levels on variables does not really require any new ideas. The ds reflecting a pair of levels on the A main effect can be calculated at multiple levels of B and averaged. Then (6.13) has to be elaborated in the same way presented in the tau context via (3.17). The differences between pairs of these ds (reflecting interaction) are handled in a similar way. Note, though, that interaction is always investigated by comparing just two levels on one factor. That is not necessarily an important disadvantage. Is it not generally true that it is more important to be able to say "these two ds are different," than it is to say "not all these ds are the same," which is the only conclusion from an omnibus test?

CONCLUSION

Thus it seems clear that dominance analysis can be applied in moderately complex within-subjects designs. The suggestion early in the chapter concerning the pretest-posttest between-groups design shows that d analysis can be applied to mixed designs as well, and that suggestion can be elaborated to more complex designs. All that is required is that the investigator decide what the research questions are and then identify which ds or sums or differences of ds apply. Their variances, and sometimes covariances, can be used to inferentially support the descriptive information provided by the ds. The questions answered by such an analysis are not exactly the same as those investigated by the linear models underlying ANOVA, but they may be at least as close to what the investigator has in mind in doing the research.

Chapters 5 and 6 have attempted to promote the use of an ordinal comparison measure, δ, and its estimate, d, as alternatives to comparing means or other measures of location. The reasons lie in several directions. The first is that δ corresponds more closely to the primary research question in a large proportion of instances. Related to this is the likelihood that, very often, two distributions will differ in several characteristics, not just in their means, so the interpretation of mean differences may have little generality. The δ measure, on the other hand, is a direct quantification of the statement, "A's tend to score higher than B's on this variable."

A second class of justification of δ is that it is invariant under monotonic transformation of variables. Although this has been dismissed as a concern in the past, either because it was argued that no transformation was contemplated or because transformation could have only a small effect on statistical conclusions, it was argued here that such scale-type concerns have a real basis. In the first instance, it was noted that there often exist alternative forms of a given dependent variable that are at least as defensible as it, and one should want the conclusions to be invariant under such changes of scale. Moreover, observed scores are often surrogates for latent variables that can well be monotonically rather than linearly related to them, and again one would want conclusions about the observed variable to be valid for the latent one. With respect to alleged insensitivity of statistics to transformation, examples were presented where monotonic transformation could have important effects. Thus, dealing with statistics that have invariance under monotonic transformation seems desirable.

Robustness with respect to distributional or equivariance assumptions is often cited as a positive characteristic of ordinal statistics. Here, the evidence tends to favor ordinal methods (Blair & Higgins, 1980a, 1980b, 1981, 1985; Chernoff & Savage, 1958; Dixon, 1954; Fligner & Policello, 1981; Hettmansperger, 1984; Hodges & Lehman, 1956; Neave & Granger, 1968; Pearson & Please, 1975; Randles & Wolfe, 1979), but we have seen (Feng & Cliff, 1995) that the situation is actually somewhat mixed in the case of the independent-groups *d*, although favoring it in most cases. The inferential superiority of the paired-data version of *d* over t_w is more marked, although here, too, there are instances where the latter has substantially more power.

Although most ordinal analyses are designed to test the null hypothesis that two distributions are identical, the alternative process recommended here is to make inferences about δ under a more general rubric in which the variance of *d* is estimated from the sample. This not only allows the testing of the hypothesis δ = 0 but also provides the basis for forming a confidence interval for it, or testing differences between δs, and so on. δ is a direct nonparametric measure of effect size, so its use facilitates the incorporation of effect sizes into group comparisons.

A main point of the chapter was to generalize δ and *d* to the repeated-measures case, thus providing an alternative to the *t* test for correlated data or to simple repeated-measures ANOVA. In additon, ways in which dominance analysis can be adapted to more complex research contexts were suggested.

In summary, it seems that ordinal data analysis has much to offer. It is powerful, robust to failure of classical assumptions, and does not require interval-level measurement. Such assumptions are often of very doubtful validity with our data. It also can answer research questions in a way that is more closely connected to them than is true of classical methods. Finally, it can be applied in a wider range of circumstances and research designs than is generally believed. It is hoped that the suggestions in Chapters 5 and 6 will broaden the application of ordinal methods as alternatives to mean-comparison procedures.

APPENDIX

By general principles, $\text{var}(u \pm v) = \text{var}(u) + \text{var}(v) \pm \text{cov}(u,v)$. This formula has been employed several times already, and here we use it as the basis for the variances of $d_{wc1} - d_{wc2}$, $d_{bc1} - d_{bc2}$, and $(d_{wc1} + d_{bc1}) - (d_{wc2} + d_{bc2})$, and the estimates of the terms can then be used in inferences about these differences. The variance of $d_{wc1} - d_{wc2}$ is

$$\text{var}(d_{wc1} - d_{wc2}) = \sigma_{dwc1}{}^2 + \sigma_{dwc2}{}^2 - 2\,\text{cov}(d_{wc1}, d_{wc2}). \qquad (6.16)$$

The variance estimate $s_{d_w}{}^2$ presented earlier as (6.8) is used in the first two terms, based on the comparison of control scores to first one and then the other experimental conditions. The covariance term in (6.16) is estimated by generalizing (6.8) to a covariance:

$$\text{Est}[\text{cov}(d_{wc1}, d_{wc2})] = \frac{\Sigma d_{ik1} d_{ik2} - n d_{wc1} d_{wc2}}{n(n-1)}. \qquad (6.17)$$

Substituting the estimates of the two variances obtained using (6.8) and the estimated covariance from (6.17) into (6.16) will give the estimated variance of the difference between d_{wc1} and d_{wc2}.

By the same reasoning,

$$\text{var}(d_{bc1} - d_{bc2}) = \sigma_{dbc1}{}^2 + \sigma_{dbc2}{}^2 - 2\,\text{cov}(d_{bc1}, d_{bc2}). \qquad (6.18)$$

In samples, $\sigma_{dbc1}{}^2$ and $\sigma_{dbc2}{}^2$ would be estimated using (6.7). That formula can be generalized to the covariance of two d_bs as

$$n(n-1)(n-2)(n-3)\text{cov}(d_{bc1}, d_{bc2})$$
$$= (n-1)^2(\Sigma d^*_{i.c1} d^*_{i.c2} + \Sigma d^*_{ic1} d^*_{.ic2} + \Sigma d^*_{i.c1} d^*_{.ic2}$$
$$+ \Sigma d^*_{i.c2} d^*_{.ic1}) - \Sigma\Sigma d^*_{ijc1} d^*_{ijc2} - \Sigma\Sigma d^*_{ijc1} d^*_{jic2}. \qquad (6.19)$$

[To reduce the number of terms in (6.19), we let starred ($*$) terms refer to the deviations from the respective d_b, as done earlier. For example, $d^*_{i.c1} = \hat{d}_{i.c1} - d_{bc1}$.]. Inferences based on the difference $d_{bc1} - d_{bc2}$ can be made by substituting the two values of (6.7) and the estimated covariance (6.19) into (6.18).

If the inferences about $\delta_{wc1} - \delta_{wc2}$ and $\delta_{c1} - \delta_{c2}$ are to be combined in the same way that inferences about δ_{wc1} and δ_{c1} or δ_{wc2} and δ_{c2} were, then the approach is the same as that used before, but the number of terms increases. The variance of $(d_{wc1} + d_{bc1}) - (d_{wc2} + d_{bc2})$ is

$$\text{var}(d_{wc1} + d_{bc1}) + \text{var}(d_{wc2} + d_{bc2}) - 2 \, \text{cov}[(d_{wc1} + d_{bc1}),(d_{wc2} + d_{bc2})]. \quad (6.20)$$

The two variance terms in (6.20) can be estimated by substituting the respective estimates using (6.7), (6.8), and (6.9) into the variance of sums formula (6.16). The covariance term in (6.20) expands to four parts:

$$\text{cov}(d_{wc1},d_{wc2}) + \text{cov}(d_{wc1},d_{bc2}) + \text{cov}(d_{bc1},d_{wc2}) + \text{cov}(d_{bc1}, d_{bc2}). \quad (6.21)$$

The first of these is estimated by (6.17) and the last by (6.19). The second and third can be estimated by generalizing (6.9) to a covariance:

$$\text{Est}[\text{cov}(d_{wca},d^*_{cb})] = \frac{\Sigma[n(\hat{d}_{i.cb} + \hat{d}_{.icb})d_{i.ca}] - 2n(n-1)d_{bcb}d_{wca}}{(n-1)^2(n-2)}, \quad (6.22)$$

where the subscripts a,b are equal first to 1,2 and then to 2,1.

This brief section indicated in general terms how the sampling variances and covariances of the sums and differences of ds, in various combinations, can be derived. The derivation of the formulas for the variances and covariances of ds themselves, and their unbiased estimates, involves a rather tedious process of taking expectations of squares and products of d_{ih}s having various combinations of same and different subscript values. The details of the process are used on similar problems in sources such as Daniels and Kendall (1947), Hettmansperger (1984), and Kendall (1970), and made use of in deriving the variance of t and its unbiased estimate in Chapter 3.

References

Abelson, R. W., & Tukey, J. (1963). Efficient utilization of non-numerical information in quantitative analysis: General theory and the case of simple order. *Annals of Mathematical Statistics, 34,* 1347–1369.

Agresti, A. (1984). *Analysis of ordinal categorical data.* New York: Wiley.

Agresti, A., & Pendergast, J. (1986). Comparing mean ranks for repeated measures data. *Communications in Statistics: Theory and Methods, 15,* 1417–1433.

Anderson, N. H. (1962). On the quantification of Miller's conflict theory. *Psychological Review, 69,* 400–414.

Anderson, N. H. (1981). *Foundations of information integration theory.* New York: Academic Press.

Birkes, D., & Dodge, Y. (1993). *Alternative methods of regression.* New York: Wiley.

Birnbaum, Z. W. (1956). On a use of the Mann-Whitney statistic. In J. Neyman (Ed.), *Proceedings of the Third Berkeley Symposium on Mathematical Statistics* (pp. 13–17). Berkeley and Los Angeles, CA: University of California Press.

Blair, R. C., & Higgins, J. J. (1980a). A comparison of the power of the *t* test and the Wilcoxon statistics when samples are drawn from a certain mixed normal distribution. *Evaluation Review, 4,* 645–656.

Blair, R. C., & Higgins, J. J. (1980b). A comparison of the power of the Wilcoxon's rank sum statistic to that of Student's *t* statistic under various non-normal distributions. *Journal of Educational Statistics, 5,* 309–355.

Blair, R. C., & Higgins, J. J. (1981). A note on the asymptotic relative efficiency of the Wilcoxon Rank-sum test relative to the independent means *t* test under mixtures of two normal populations. *British Journal of Mathematical and Statistical Psychology, 31,* 124–128.

Blair, R. C., & Higgins, J. J. (1985). Comparison of the power of the paired samples *t* test relative to that of Wilcoxon's signed-ranks tests under various population shapes. *Psychological Bulletin, 97,* 119–128.

Blair, R. C., Sawilowsky, S. S., & Higgins, J. J. (1987). Limitations of the rank transform in tests of interaction. *Communications in Statistics: Computations and Simulation, B16,* 1133–1145.

Bradley, J. V. (1968). *Distribution-free statistics*. Englewood Cliffs, NJ: Prentice-Hall.

Bradley, J. V. (1978). Robustness? *British Journal of Mathematical and Statistical Psychology, 31*, 144–152.

Browne, M. W. (1975). Predictive validity of a linear regression equation. *British Journal of Mathematical and Statistical Psychology, 28*, 79–87.

Campbell, D. T., & Fiske, D. W. (1959). Convergent and discriminant validation by the multitrait-multimethod matrix. *Psychological Bulletin, 56*, 81–105.

Caruso, J. C., & Cliff, N. (1995). *Empirical size, coverage, and power of confidence intervals for Spearman's rho*. Unpublished manuscript, University of Southern California.

Charlin, V. L. (1987). *Implementation and inferential issues of a multiple regression system with ordinal variables*. Unpublished doctoral dissertation, University of Southern California.

Chernoff, H., & Savage, I. R. (1958). Asymptotic normality and efficiency of certain nonparametric statistics. *Annals of Mathematical Statistics, 29*, 972–999.

Cliff, N. (1972). Consistencies among judgments of adjective combinations. In A. K. Romney, R. N. Shepard, & S. B. Nerlove (Eds.), *Multidimensional scaling: Theory and applications in the behavioral sciences* (Vol. II; pp. 163–182). New York: Seminar Press.

Cliff, N. (1983). Some cautions concerning the application of causal modeling. *Multivariate Behavioral Research, 18*, 115–126.

Cliff, N. (1987). *Analyzing multivariate data*. San Diego: Harcourt, Brace, Jovanovich.

Cliff, N. (1989a). Ordinal consistency and ordinal true scores. *Psychometrika, 54*, 75–91.

Cliff, N. (1989b). Strong inferences and weak data: Covariance structure analysis and its use. In J. A. Keats, R. Taft, R. A. Heath, & S. V. Lovibond (Eds.), *Mathematical and theoretical systems* (pp. 69–77). Amsterdam: Elsevier.

Cliff, N. (1991). Ordinal methods in the assessment of change. In L. M. Collins & J. L. Horn (Eds.), *Best methods for the analysis of change* (pp. 34–46). Washington, DC: American Psychological Association.

Cliff, N. (1992). Abstract measurement theory and the revolution that never happened. *Psychological Science, 3*, 186–190.

Cliff, N. (1993a). Dominance statistics: Ordinal analyses to answer ordinal questions. *Psychological Bulletin, 114*, 494–509.

Cliff, N. (1993b). What is and isn't measurement. In G. Keren & C. Lewis (Eds.), *A handbook for data analysis in the social and behavioral sciences: Methodological issues* (pp. 59–93). Hillsdale, NJ: Lawrence Erlbaum Associates.

Cliff, N. (1994). Predicting ordinal relations. *British Journal of Mathematical and Statistical Psychology, 47*, 127–150.

Cliff, N., & Charlin, V. C. (1991). Variances and covariances of Kendall's tau and their estimation. *Multivariate Behavioral Research, 26*, 693–707.

Cliff, N., & Donoghue, J. R. (1992). Ordinal test fidelity estimated by an item-sampling model. *Psychometrika, 57*, 217–236.

Cliff, N., Feng, D., & Long, J. D. (1995). *The influence of higher moments on confidence intervals for U statistics*. Unpublished manuscript, University of Southern California.

Cliff, N., McCormick, D. J., Zatkin, J. L., Cudeck, R. A., & Collins, L. M. (1986). BINCLUS: Nonhierarchical clustering of binary data. *Multivariate Behavioral Research, 21*, 201–227.

Cohen, J., & Cohen, P. (1975). *Applied multiple regression/correlation analysis for the behavioral sciences*. Hillsdale, NJ: Lawrence Erlbaum Associates.

Conover, W. J. (1980). *Practical nonparametric statistics* (2nd ed.). New York: Wiley.

Conover, W. J., & Iman, R. L. (1981). Rank transformations as a bridge between parametric and nonprametric statistics. *The American Statistician, 35*, 124–129.

Conover, W. J., & Iman, R. L. (1982). Analysis of covariance using the rank transformation. *Biometrics, 38*, 715–724.

Cressie, N. A. C., & Whitford, H. J. (1986). How to use the two sample *t*-test. *Biometric Journal, 28*, 131–148.

Daniels, H. E., & Kendall, M. G. (1947). The significance of rank correlation where parental correlation exists. *Biometrika, 34,* 197–208.

David, F. N., & Mallows, C. L. (1961). The variance of Spearman's rho in normal samples. *Biometrika, 48,* 19–28.

Davison, M. L., & Sharma, A. R. (1988). Parametric statistics and levels of measurement. *Psychological Bulletin, 104,* 137–144.

Dixon, W. J. (1954). Power under normality of several nonparametric tests. *Annals of Mathematical Statistics, 25,* 610–614.

Donoghue, J. R., & Cliff, N. (1991). A Monte Carlo evaluation of ordinal true score theory. *Applied Psychological Measurement, 15,* 335–351.

Efron, B. (1982). *The jackknife, the bootstrap, and other resampling methods.* Philadelphia: Society for for Industrial and Applied Mathematics.

Efron, B. (1987). Better bootstrap confidence intervals. *Journal of the American Statistical Association, 82,* 171–185.

Entwisle, B., Hermalin, A. I., & Mason, W. M. (1985). *Sociometric determinants of fertility in developing nations* (Tech. Rep. 17). Washington, DC: Committee on Population and Demography.

Feng, D. (1996). *Power, size, and coverage of the paired-data d statistic.* Unpublished doctoral dissertation, University of Southern California.

Feng, D., & Cliff, N. (1995). *Comparisons of power and size of d and t statistics under normal and nonnormal assumptions.* Unpublished manuscript, University of Southern California.

Ferguson, G. A. (1965). *Nonparametric trend analysis.* Montreal: McGill University Press.

Fieller, E. C., & Pearson, E. S. (1961). Tests for rank correlation coefficients. II. *Biometrika, 48,* 29–40.

Fligner, M. A., & Policello, G. E., II. (1981). Robust rank procedures for the Behrens–Fisher problem. *Journal of the American Statistical Association, 76,* 162–168.

Freeman, L. C. (1986). Order-based statistics and monotonicity: A family of order-based measures of association. *Journal of Mathematical Sociology, 12,* 49–69.

Friedman, M. (1937). The use of ranks to avoid the assumption of normality in the analysis of variance. *Journal of the American Statistical Association, 32,* 675–701.

Gonzalez, R., & Nelson, T. O. (1996). Measuring ordinal association in situations that contain tied scores. *Psychological Bulletin, 119,* 159–165.

Goodman, L. A., & Kruskal, W. H. (1954). Measures of association for cross-classification. *Journal of the American Statistical Association, 49,* 732–804.

Goodman, L. A., & Kruskal, W. H. (1959). Measures of association for cross-classification. II. Further discussion and references. *Journal of the American Statistical Association, 54,* 123–163.

Gulliksen, H. (1946). paired comparisons and the logic of measurement. *Psychological Review, 53,* 199–213.

Guttman, L. (1971). Measurement as structural theory. *Psychometrika, 36,* 329–347.

Harwell, M. R., & Serlin, R. C. (1988). An empirical study of a proposed test of nonoparametric analysis of covariance. *Psychological Bulletin, 104,* 268–281.

Hawkes, R. J. (1971). The multivariate analysis of ordinal measures. *American Journal of Sociology, 76,* 908–926.

Hays, W. L. (1963). *Statistics for psychologists* (1st ed.). New York: Harcourt.

Hettmansperger, T. P. (1984). *Statistical inference based on ranks.* New York: Wiley.

Hodges, J. C., & Lehmann, E. L. (1956). The efficiency of some nonparametric competitors of the *t* test. *Annals of Mathematical Statistics, 27,* 324–355.

Hodges, J. L., Jr., & Lehmann, E. L. (1960). Comparison of the normal scores and Wilcoxon tests. *Proceedings of the Fourth Berkeley Symposium: Vol. 1* (pp. 307–317).

Iman, R. L. (1974). A power study of a rank transform for the two-way classification when interaction may be present. *Canadian Journal of Statistics, 2,* 227–229.

Kaiser, H. F. (1960). Directional statistical decisions. *Psychological Review, 67,* 160–167.

Kendall, M. G. (1970). *Rank correlation methods* (3rd ed.). New York: Hafner.

Kendall, M. G., & Gibbons, J. D. (1991). *Rank correlation methods.* New York: Oxford University Press.

Kendall, M. G., & Stuart, A. (1958). *The advanced theory of statistics: Vol. 1. Distribution theory.* New York: Hafner.

Kim, J. (1975). Multivariate analysis of ordinal variables. *American Journal of Sociology, 81,* 261–298.

Kimeldorf, G., & Sampson, A. R. (1978). Monotone dependence. *Annals of Statistics, 6,* 895–903.

Kraemer, H. C. (1974). The non-null distribution of the Spearman rank correlation coefficient. *Journal of the American Statistical Association, 69,* 114–117.

Kraemer, H. C. (1975). On estimation and hypothesis testing problems for correlation coefficients. *Psychometrika, 40,* 473–485.

Krantz, D. H., Luce, R. D., Suppes, P., & Tversky, A. (1971). *Foundations of measurement: Vol. I.* New York: Academic Press.

Labovitz, S. (1967). Some observations on measurement and statistics. *Social Forces, 46,* 151–160.

LeVay, S. (1991). A difference in hypothalamic structure between heterosexual and homosexual men. *Science, 253,* 1034–1037.

Long, J. D., & Cliff, N. (in press). Confidence intervals for Kendall's tau. *British Journal of Mathematical and Statistical Psychology.*

Long, J. D., & Cliff, N. (1995). *The performance of Pearson's r as a function of correlation, sample size, and non-normality.* Unpublished manuscript, University of Southern California.

Lord, F. M. (1953). On the statistical treatment of football numbers. *American Psychologist, 8,* 750–751.

Luce, R. D., Krantz, D. H., Suppes, P., & Tversky, A. (1990). *Foundations of measurement: Vol. III.* New York: Academic Press.

Luce, R. D., & Tukey, J. W. (1964). Simultaneous conjoint measurement: A new type of fundamental measurement. *Journal of Mathematical Psychology, 1,* 1–27.

Lyerly, S. B. (1952). The average Spearman rank correlation coefficient. *Psychometrika, 17,* 421–428.

Mann, H. B., & Whitney, D. R. (1947). On a test of whether one of two random variables is stochastically larger than the other. *Annals of Mathematical Statistics, 18,* 50–60.

Maxwell, S. E., & Delaney, H. D. (1993). Bivariate median splits and spurious statistical significance. *Psychological Bulletin, 113,* 181–190.

McCullagh, P. (1980). Regression models for ordinal data. *Journal of the Royal Statistical Society, B, 42,* 109–142.

McDowd, J. M., & Oseas-Kreger, D. M. (1991). Aging, inhibitory processes, and negative priming. *Journal of Gerontology: Psychological Sciences, 46,* 340–345.

McGraw, K. O., & Wong, S. P. (1992). A common language effect size statistic. *Psychological Bulletin, 111,* 361–365.

Mee, R. W. (1990). Confidence intervals for probabilities and tolerance regions based on a generalization of the Mann–Whitney statistic. *Journal of the American Statistical Association, 85,* 793–800.

Micceri, T. (1989). The unicorn, the normal curve, and other improbable creatures. *Psychological Bulletin, 105,* 156–166.

Michell, J. (1990). *An introduction to the logic of psychological measurement.* Hillsdale, NJ: Lawrence Erlbaum Associates.

Muthen, B. (1984). A general structural equation model with dichotomous, ordered categorical, and continuous latent variable indicators. *Psychometrika, 49,* 115–132.

Narens, L. (1981). On the scales of measurement. *Journal of Mathematical Psychology, 24,* 249–275.

Neave, H. R., & Granger, C. W. J. (1968). A Monte Carlo study comparing various two-sample tests for differences in mean. *Technometrics, 10,* 509–522.

O'Brien, P. C. (1988). Comparing two samples: Extensions of the *t*, rank-sum, and log-rank tests. *Journal of the American Statistical Association, 83,* 52–61.

Olejnik, S. F., & Algina, J. (1984). Parametric ANCOVA and the rank transformation ANCOVA when the data are conditionally non-normal. *Journal of Educational Statistics, 9,* 129–150.

Olkin, I., & Finn, J. D. (1995). Correlations redux. *Psychological Bulletin, 118,* 155–164.

Pearson, E. S., & Please, N. W. (1975). Relations between the shape of the population distribution and the robustness of four simple test statistics. *Biometrika, 63,* 223–241.

Potthoff, R. F. (1974). A nonparametric test of whether two simple regression lines are parallel. *Annals of Statistics, 2,* 295–310.

Puri, M. L., & Sen, P. K. (1969a). Analysis of variance based on general rank scores. *Annals of Mathematical Statistics, 40,* 610–618.

Puri, M. L., & Sen, P. K. (1969b). A class of rank order tests for a general linear hypothesis. *Annals of Mathematical Statistics, 40,* 1325–1343.

Quade, D. (1967). Rank analysis of covariance. *Journal of the American Statistical Association, 62,* 1187–1200.

Ramsay, J. O. (1978). Confidence regions for multidimensional scaling analysis. *Psychometrika, 43,* 145–160.

Ramsay, J. O. (1982). Some statistical approaches to multidimensional scaling data. *Journal of the Royal Statistical Society (A). 145,* 285–312.

Ramsey, P. (1980). Exact Type I error rates for robustness of Student's test with unequal variances. *Journal of Educational Statistics, 5,* 337–349.

Ramsey, P. H. (1989). Critical values for the Spearman rank correlation. *Journal of Educational Statistics, 14,* 245–253.

Randles, R. H., & Wolfe, D. A. (1979). *Introduction to the theory of nonparametric statistics.* New York: Wiley.

Reynolds, T. J., & Suttrick, K. H. (1986). Assessing the correspondence of a vector to a symmetric matrix. *Psychometrika, 51,* 101–112.

SAS Institute. (1987). *The MATRIX procedure: Language and applications.* Cary, NC: SAS Institute.

Sawilowsky, S. S. (1985). *Robust and power analysis of the 2 × 2 × 2 ANOVA, rank transformation, normal scores and expected normal scores transformation tests.* Unpublished doctoral dissertation, University of South Florida, Tampa, FL.

Sawilowsky, S. S. (1990). Nonparametric tests of interaction in experimental design. *Review of Educational Research, 60,* 91–126.

Sawilowsky, S. S., & Blair, R. C. (1992). A more realistic look at the robustness and Type II Error properties of the *t* test to departures from population normality. *Psychological Bulletin, 111,* 352–360.

Sawilowsky, S. S., Blair, R. C., & Higgins, J. J. (1989). An investigation of Type I error and power properties of the rank transform procedures in factorial ANOVA. *Journal of Educational Statistics, 14,* 255–267.

Shepard, R. N. (1962). The analysis of proximities: Multidimensional scaling with an unknown distance function. I, II. *Psychometrika, 27,* 125–140, 219–246.

Siegel, S. (1958). *Nonparametric statistics.* New York: McGraw-Hill.

Siegel, S., & Castellan, J. (1988). *Nonparametric statistics for the behavioral sciences* (2nd ed.). New York: McGraw-Hill.

Smith, R. B. (1972). Neighborhood context and college plans: An ordinal path analysis. *Social Forces, 51,* 199–217.

Smith, R. B. (1974). Continuities in ordinal path analysis. *Social Forces, 53,* 200–229.

Somers, R. H. (1968). An approach to the multivariate analysis of ordinal data. *American Sociological Review,* 971–977.

Somers, R. H. (1974). Analysis of partial rank correlation measures based on the product-moment model: Part One. *Social Forces, 53,* 229–246.

Stallings, M. C. (1993). *Testing behavioral genetic hypotheses concerning familial resemblance for social attitudes using Kendall's tau.* Unpublished doctoral dissertation, University of Southern California.

Stevens, S. S. (1951). Mathematics, measurement, and psychophysics. In S. S. Stevens (Ed.), *Handbook of experimental psychology* (pp. 1–49). New York: Wiley.

Stuadte, R. G., & Sheater, S. J. (1990). *Robust estimation and testing*. New York: Wiley.

Stuart, A. (1953). The estimation and comparison of strengths of association in contingency tables. *Biometrika, 40*, 105–112.

Suppes, P., Krantz, D. H., Luce, R. D., & Tversky, A. (1989). *Foundations of measurement: Vol. II.* (Vol. II). New York: Academic Press.

Takane, Y. (1981). Multidimensional successive categories scaling: A maximum likelihood method. *Psychometrika 46*, 9–28.

Takane, Y. (1982). Maximum likelihood additivity analysis. *Psychometrika, 47*, 225–241.

Takane, Y., Young, F. W., & de Leeuw, J. (1977). Nonmetric individual differences multidimensional scaling: An alternating least squares method with optimal scaling features. *Psychometrika, 42*, 7–67.

Takayanagi, S., & Cliff, N. (1993). The fuzziness index for examining human statistical decision-making. *Proceedings of the 1993 IEEE*, 1150–1155.

Teeuwen, J. H. N. (1989). Application of methods for ordinal data in contingency tables. In M. G. H. Jansen & W. H. van Schuur (Eds.), *The many faces of multivariate analysis: Proceedings of the SMABS-88 Conference* (Vol. I; pp. 153–165). Groningen, Netherlands: RION. Institut voor Onderwijsondezoek, Rijkuniversiteit Groningen.

Terza, J. V. (1984). Estimating linear models with ordinal qualitative regressions. *Journal of Econometrics, 34*, 275–291.

Townsend, J. T. (1992). On the proper scales for reaction time. In H.-G. Geissler, S. W. Link, & J. T. Townsend (Eds.), *Cognition, information processing, and psychophysics* (pp. 105–120). Hillsdale, NJ: Lawrence Erlbaum Associates.

Velleman, P. F., & Wilkinson, L. (1993). Nominal, ordinal, interval, and ratio typologies are misleading. *American Statistician, 47*, 65–72.

Welch, B. L. (1938). The significance of the difference between two means when the population variances are unequal. *Biometrika, 29*, 350–362.

Westfall, P. H., & Young, S. S. (1993). *Resampling-based multiple testing*. New York: Wiley.

Wilcox, R. W.(1990). Comparing the means of independent groups. *Biometrical Journal, 32*, 771–780.

Wilcox, R. W. (1991). Bootstrap inferences about correlation and variances of paired data. *British Journal of Mathematical and Statistical Psychology, 44*, 379–382.

Wilcox, R. W. (1992). Why can methods for comparing means have realtively low power, and what can you do to correct the problem? *Current Directions in Psychological Science, 1*, 101–105.

Wilcox, R. W. (1996). *Statistics for the social sciences*. New York: Academic Press.

Wilcoxon, F. (1945). Individual comparisons by ranking methods. *Biometrics, 1*, 80–83.

Wilson, T. P. (1971). Critique of ordinal variables. *Social Forces, 49*, 432–444.

Wilson, T. P. (1974). On interpreting ordinal analogies to multiple regression and path analysis. *Social Forces, 53*, 196–199.

Winship, C., & Mare, R. D. (1984). Regression models with ordinal variables. *American Sociological Review, 49*, 512–525.

Wong, G. W., & Mason, W. M. (1985). The hierarchical logistic model for multivariate analysis. *Journal of the American Statistical Association, 80*, 513–524.

Young, F. W. (1972). A model for polynonial conjoint analysis algorithms. In R. N. Shepard, A. K. Romney, & S. Nerlove (Eds.), *Multidimensional scaling* (Vol. 1; pp. 69–104). New York: Seminar Press.

Young, F. W. (1984). Scaling. *Annual Review of Psychology, 35*, 55–81.

Young, F. W., de Leeuw, J., & Takane, Y. (1976). Regression with qualitative and quantitative variables: An alternating least-squares method with optimal scaling features. *Psychometrika, 41*, 505–529.

Young, F. W., & Hamer, R. M. (1987). Multidimensional scaling: History, theory, and applications. Hillsdale, NJ: Lawrence Erlbaum Associates.

Yu, M. C., & Dunn, O. J. (1982). Robust tests for the equality of two correlation coefficients. *Educational and Psychological Measurement, 42*, 987–1004.

Yule, G. U. (1900). On the association of attributes in statistics. *Transactions of the Philosophical Society, London, Series A.* 257–319.

Zaremba, S. K. (1962). A generalization of Wilcoxon's test. *Monatshefte fur Mathematik, 66*, 359–370.

APPENDIX I.A

TABLE A.1
Cumulative Normal Distribution Function

z	0.00	0.01	0.02	0.03	0.04	0.05	0.06	0.07	0.08	0.09
0.0	0.5000	0.5040	0.5080	0.5120	0.5160	0.5199	0.5239	0.5279	0.5319	0.5359
0.1	0.5398	0.5438	0.5478	0.5517	0.5557	0.5596	0.5636	0.5675	0.5714	0.5753
0.2	0.5793	0.5832	0.5871	0.5910	0.5948	0.5987	0.6026	0.6064	0.6103	0.6141
0.3	0.6179	0.6217	0.6255	0.6293	0.6331	0.6368	0.6406	0.6443	0.6480	0.6517
0.4	0.6554	0.6591	0.6628	0.6664	0.6700	0.6736	0.6772	0.6808	0.6844	0.6879
0.5	0.6915	0.6950	0.6985	0.7019	0.7054	0.7088	0.7123	0.7157	0.7190	0.7224
0.6	0.7257	0.7291	0.7324	'0.7357	0.7389	0.7422	0.7454	0.7486	0.7517	0.7549
0.7	0.7580	0.7611	0.7642	0.7673	0.7704	0.7734	0.7764	0.7794	0.7823	0.7852
0.8	0.7881	0.7910	0.7939	0.7967	0.7995	0.8023	0.8051	0.8078	0.8106	0.8133
0.9	0.8159	0.8186	0.8212	0.8238	0.8264	0.8289	0.8315	0.8340	0.8365	0.8389
1.0	0.8413	0.8438	0.8461	0.8485	0.8508	0.8531	0.8554	0.8577	0.8599	0.8621
1.1	0.8643	0.8665	0.8686	0.8708	0.8729	0.8749	0.8770	0.8790	0.8810	0.8830
1.2	0.8849	0.8869	0.8888	0.8907	0.8925	0.8944	0.8962	0.8980	0.8997	0.9015
1.3	0.9032	0.9049	0.9066	0.9082	0.9099	0.9115	0.9131	0.9147	0.9162	0.9177
1.4	0.9192	0.9207	0.9222	0.9236	0.9251	0.9265	0.9279	0.9292	0.9306	0.9319
1.5	0.9332	0.9345	0.9357	0.9370	0.9382	0.9394	0.9406	0.9418	0.9429	0.9441
1.6	0.9452	0.9463	0.9474	0.9484	0.9495	0.9505	0.9515	0.9525	0.9535	0.9545
1.7	0.9554	0.9564	0.9573	0.9582	0.9591	0.9599	0.9608	0.9616	0.9625	0.9633
1.8	0.9641	0.9649	0.9656	0.9664	0.9671	0.9678	0.9686	0.9693	0.9699	0.9706
1.9	0.9713	0.9719	0.9726	0.9732	0.9738	0.9744	0.9750	0.9756	0.9761	0.9767
2.0	0.9772	0.9778	0.9783	0.9788	0.9793	0.9798	0.9803	0.9808	0.9812	0.9817
2.1	0.9821	0.9826	0.9830	0.9834	0.9838	0.9842	0.9846	0.9850	0.9854	0.9857
2.2	0.9861	0.9864	0.9868	0.9871	0.9875	0.9878	0.9881	0.9884	0.9887	0.9890
2.3	0.9893	0.9896	0.9898	0.9901	0.9904	0.9906	0.9909	0.9911	0.9913	0.9916
2.4	0.9918	0.9920	0.9922	0.9925	0.9927	0.9929	0.9931	0.9932	0.9934	0.9936
2.5	0.9938	0.9940	0.9941	0.9943	0.9945	0.9946	0.9948	0.9949	0.9951	0.9952
2.6	0.9953	0.9955	0.9956	0.9957	0.9959	0.9960	0.9961	0.9962	0.9963	0.9964
2.7	0.9965	0.9966	0.9967	0.9968	0.9969	0.9970	0.9971	0.9972	0.9973	0.9974
2.8	0.9974	0.9975	0.9976	0.9977	0.9977	0.9978	0.9979	0.9979	0.9980	0.9981
2.9	0.9981	0.9982	0.9982	0.9983	0.9984	0.9984	0.9985	0.9985	0.9986	0.9986
3.0	0.9987	0.9987	0.9987	0.9988	0.9988	0.9989	0.9989	0.9989	0.9990	0.9990
3.1	0.9990	0.9991	0.9991	0.9991	0.9992	0.9992	0.9992	0.9992	0.9993	0.9993
3.2	0.9993	0.9993	0.9994	0.9994	0.9994	0.9994	0.9994	0.9995	0.9995	0.9995
3.3	0.9995	0.9995	0.9995	0.9996	0.9996	0.9996	0.9996	0.9996	0.9996	0.9997
3.4	0.9997	0.9997	0.9997	0.9997	0.9997	0.9997	0.9997	0.9997	0.9997	0.9998

z_α	1.282	1.645	1.960	2.326	2.576	3.090	3.291	3.891	4.417
$1 - \alpha = \Phi(z_\alpha)$	0.90	0.95	0.975	0.99	0.995	0.999	0.9995	0.99995	0.999995
2α	0.20	0.10	0.05	0.02	0.01	0.002	0.001	0.0001	0.00001

Reproduced by permission from A. M. Mood, *Introduction to the Theory of Statistics*, McGraw-Hill Book Company, New York, 1950.

APPENDIX I.B

TABLE A.2
Exact Critical Values of r_S for $n \leq 18$ and
Edgeworth Approximations for $19 \leq n \leq 37$

				Quantiles					
	.75	.90	.95	.975	.99	.995	.9975	.999	.9995
				Directional alpha levels					
	.25	.10	.05	.025	.01	.005	.0025	.001	.0005
				Nondirectional alpha levels					
N	.50	.20	.10	.05	.02	.01	.005	.002	.001
3	1.000								
4	0.600	1.000	1.000						
5	0.500	0.800	0.900	1.000	1.000				
6	0.371	0.657	0.829	0.886	0.943	1.000	1.000		
7	0.321	0.571	0.714	0.786	0.893	0.929	0.964	1.000	1.000
8	0.310	0.524	0.643	0.738	0.833	0.881	0.905	0.952	0.976
9	0.267	0.483	0.600	0.700	0.783	0.833	0.867	0.917	0.933
10	0.248	0.455	0.564	0.648	0.745	0.794	0.830	0.879	0.903
11	0.236	0.427	0.536	0.618	0.709	0.755	0.800	0.845	0.873
12	0.217	0.406	0.503	0.587	0.678	0.727	0.769	0.818	0.846
13	0.209	0.385	0.484	0.560	0.648	0.703	0.747	0.791	0.824
14	0.200	0.367	0.464	0.538	0.626	0.679	0.723	0.771	0.802
15	0.189	0.354	0.446	0.521	0.604	0.654	0.700	0.750	0.779
16	0.182	0.341	0.429	0.503	0.582	0.635	0.679	0.729	0.762
17	0.176	0.328	0.414	0.488	0.566	0.618	0.659	0.711	0.743
18	0.170	0.317	0.401	0.472	0.550	0.600	0.643	0.692	0.725
19	0.165	0.309	0.391	0.460	0.535	0.584	0.628	0.675	0.709
20	0.161	0.299	0.380	0.447	0.522	0.570	0.612	0.662	0.693
21	0.156	0.292	0.370	0.436	0.509	0.556	0.599	0.647	0.678
22	0.152	0.284	0.361	0.425	0.497	0.544	0.586	0.633	0.665
23	0.148	0.278	0.353	0.416	0.486	0.532	0.573	0.621	0.652
24	0.144	0.271	0.344	0.407	0.476	0.521	0.562	0.609	0.640
25	0.142	0.265	0.337	0.398	0.466	0.511	0.551	0.597	0.628
26	0.138	0.259	0.331	0.390	0.457	0.501	0.541	0.586	0.618
27	0.136	0.255	0.324	0.383	0.449	0.492	0.531	0.576	0.607
28	0.133	0.250	0.318	0.375	0.441	0.483	0.522	0.567	0.597
29	0.130	0.245	0.312	0.368	0.433	0.475	0.513	0.558	0.588
30	0.128	0.240	0.306	0.362	0.425	0.467	0.504	0.549	0.579
31	0.125	0.236	0.301	0.356	0.419	0.459	0.496	0.540	0.570
32	0.124	0.232	0.296	0.350	0.412	0.452	0.489	0.532	0.562
33	0.121	0.229	0.291	0.345	0.405	0.446	0.482	0.525	0.554
34	0.119	0.225	0.287	0.340	0.400	0.439	0.475	0.517	0.546
35	0.118	0.222	0.283	0.335	0.394	0.433	0.468	0.510	0.539
36	0.116	0.219	0.279	0.330	0.388	0.427	0.462	0.503	0.532
37	0.114	0.215	0.275	0.325	0.383	0.421	0.456	0.497	0.525

For $n > 37$ the normal approximation is adequate, being slightly conservative at small α levels.
Reproduced by permission from P. H. Ramsey (1989), Critical values for the Spearman rank correlation. *Journal of Educational Statistics, 14,* 245–253.

Author Index

187

Subject Index